Sam and Debbie Wood provide fresh daily reflections, bringing inspiration and encouragement for couples on the intimate journey of "two becoming one." Sharing moments that are personal, instructional, and sacred from their own marriage and experience, they add authenticity to the numerous transformational insights contained in this work. Readers will discover precious gems from Scripture, generating conversations that will deepen their love for God and one another, thus aligning with the biblical picture of Christian marriage.

—W. R. CUTRER MD, director of the Gheens Center for Marriage and Family; professor, The Southern Baptist Theological Seminary; author, *The Church Leader's Handbook: a Guide to Counseling Families and Individuals in Crisis*

Marriage is a precious gift, created in the heart and mind of God. Contained within these daily treasures are personal and practical insights, grounded in the authors' deep and abiding faith in Christ. They will help grow your love and commitment to one another and expand your understanding of God's love for you and your family. *Time for Three: God, My Spouse, and Me* is an enduring reminder that "a cord of three is not easily broken" (Ecclesiastes 4:12).

—SANDRA C. GRAY, president, Asbury University

For decades, Sam and Debbie Wood have passionately encouraged husbands and wives to embrace a God-honoring, biblical vision for marriage. Now their devotional, *Time for Three*, extends their helpful ministry to yet more couples. In reading this book, you will be challenged and encouraged.

—ROBERT L. PLUMMER PHD, professor of New Testament interpretation,
The Southern Baptist Theological Seminary

I highly endorse Sam and Debbie Wood's devotional for the biblically-based and practical help it offers every couple—to grow spiritually, emotionally, and physically in marriage.

—DR. PAUL MARTIN, marriage counselor; former professor at Tennessee Temple University

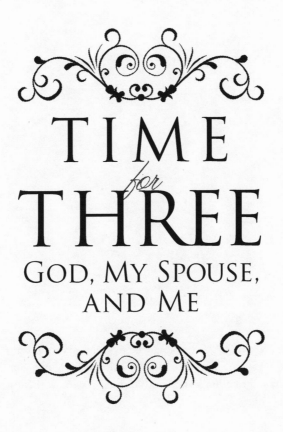

TIME
for
THREE
GOD, MY SPOUSE, AND ME

SAM & DEBBIE WOOD

Deep River BOOKS

Time for Three: God, My Spouse, and Me
© 2013 Sam and Debbie Wood
www.FamilyFortress.org
www.PreparingForPartnership.org

All Scripture quoted is from The Holy Bible, King James Version. Public domain.

Published by
Deep River Books
Sisters, Oregon
www.deepriverbooks.com

This book is published in association with The Benchmark Group, Nashville, TN,
benchmarkgroup1@aol.com.

ISBN-13: 9781937756994
ISBN-10: 1937756998

Library of Congress: 2013949505

Printed in the USA
Design by Robin Black, Inspirio Design

This book is dedicated to our children.
We love you very much!

Joshua & Erin Wood
Adam & Amanda Wood
Daniel Wood & future wife
Philip Wood & future wife

INTRODUCTION

A couple visiting from a local church knocked on the door of our basement apartment. We had only been married a few months and were new to the neighborhood, so we were eager to make friends. Little did we realize that when we opened our door to them, they would be the catalysts to open our relationship to a fascinating growth spurt. When the visitors discovered we were already attending a church of a different denomination, they immediately presented compelling arguments for beliefs that differed from ours. We basically knew how our church stood on the matters, but were unable to support our position with Scripture. We promised to consider the issues they had discussed with us, and then we said goodbye. Although our paths never crossed again, we were motivated to set aside our preconceived ideas and thoroughly investigate the Bible. We purchased books that covered both doctrinal positions. We would read a portion of the books together, then look up and discuss, in context, each Scripture referenced. Every day we prayed that the Lord would reveal Truth. When God individually stirs the heart of a believer, he or she is warmed and strengthened, but when husband and wife experience this together, it seems like the Spirit of God wraps around them and their bond is intensified. This pursuit drew us closer to the Lord and each other. We found ourselves looking forward to our special time when the three of us could connect. We determined it would become a lifelong habit.

Taking time to consider aspects of our Creator and His principles results in an incredible, spiritual bond where transparency and confidence in our relationships flourish. After twenty-five years of training couples to live according to the Word of God, we can proclaim that this practice solidifies marriages. Many spouses, however, fail to implement this practice in their marriage—many times because they don't know where to start. *Time for Three* daily directs a husband and wife to specific Scriptures and provides insights that apply the passage to life and marriage.

We recommend that you as a couple carve out a specific time for daily devotions. View this as a time of worship in which the two of you marvel at the character of God revealed in His Word each day. Pray that both of you will sense His presence and that your hearts will be receptive. Read the Scriptures for that day out loud. As one of you reads the devotion to the other, allow time to acknowledge how the Bible backs the principles that are presented. Discuss how the points relate to your marriage, how you should respond, and how you can use them to encourage hurting couples the Lord brings into your lives. Conclude your devotion time each day thanking God for one another, and the truths that were conveyed through His Word.

We challenge you to make this practice a habit for life. Consistency will add stability and connection to your relationship. We pray that the time you spend as a couple together with God, focused on His Word, will deeply impact your marriage as it has done for us.

GOD'S TIMING

Read Ecclesiastes 3:1–8, Romans 8:28, and Ephesians 5:15–16

*N*ew Year's Eve ushered in many colorful times and mixed emotions. Right after midnight, I prayed and talked with one of my sons about college and his future. Our conversation was intense and thought provoking. Early in the morning, Debbie, the dogs, and I took a leisurely walk to the bluff line. We talked, prayed, kissed, and enjoyed special moments as husband and wife. Later in the morning, I invested several hours with another son constructing a book shelf. We built a memory for the future. After lunch, Debbie and I attended the funeral of a friend. Since we knew he was a Christian, it involved both mourning and joy. Next, we gathered around the television to watch our favorite college football team win their bowl game. We celebrated a time of victory! In just twenty-four hours, we experienced a huge variety of events.

Life runs on a great time clock, and God is the master timekeeper. Every moment has a God-ordained purpose (Eccl. 3:1–8). As His children, we must trust Him when we cannot figure out what is happening (Rom. 8:28). When we take matters into our own hands, we step out of God's timing in our life. Just as timing in a car keeps the motor running correctly and timing in space keeps the planets in their proper orbits, God's timing regulates our lives. When we are filled with and submissive to His Spirit, we stay in time and allow Him to perform His will in and through us. This year presents another timeline of 365 days, 8,760 hours, or 525,600 minutes. God warns us to be cautious. He exhorts us to make the best use of our time by striving to understand and apply His principles (Eph. 5:15–17). If we get in time and stay in time with Him, this year will be directed by His wisdom!

TIME FOR THREE

Read Matthew 18:18–20 and Psalm 62:8

Sam recently preached a challenging message concerning God's purposes for marriage. At the end, he encouraged couples to pray together about issues the Lord had brought to their attention. Since Sam had explained prayer is a vital part of spiritual oneness, many couples responded by coming to the altar to pray together. As I prayed God would grant a special blessing of His presence, I noticed varied behavior. While some of the couples had their heads together or on each other's shoulders, whispering earnestly in conversation with the Lord, others were kneeling side by side, facing straight ahead in complete silence. Even though God hears the unspoken prayers of an individual believer, I was grieved because I realized these silent couples could not be agreeing together or seeking Him as one because they could not hear one another's thoughts.

In the context of Matthew 18:18-20, where preceding verses talk about exercising church discipline, Jesus promises those who are witnesses that if they gather in His name to carry out His purposes, He will be in their midst (v. 20). Matthew Henry states, "Every believer has the presence of Christ with him; but the promise here refers to the meetings where two or three are gathered in His name, not only for discipline, but for religious worship, or any act of Christian communion."[1] The original language has the connotation that the presence of the Son of God invades and fills the empty space around those who agree in prayer. What an opportunity to actually experience divine power in a marriage! The silent couples I observed were neglecting the chance to unite in prayer.

Psalm 62:8 describes prayer as pouring out your heart before God. I know of nothing that more tightly joins my heart with anyone, especially my husband, than pouring out our hearts together in complete dependence upon the Lord. Agreeing together with God in prayer joins the three of us as one.

BUBBLES FOR YOUR BRIDE

Read Ephesians 5:25–33

A relaxing bath promotes peaceful rest. An invigorating shower energizes. A husband can refresh his wife in similar ways. Ephesians 5:25–33 challenges husbands to follow the example of Christ and His bride, the church. He sacrificially loved His bride and gave Himself for her (v. 25). His goal is to present His bride to Himself in glory, beauty, and holiness (v. 27). Part of this process involves refreshing and cleansing.

Verse 26 explains the cleansing. A husband shares with his wife the specific message God has shown him from the Word. This sharing assures the wife that her husband is listening to the Lord. She relaxes and trusts him to follow God's leading. Often, tension and difficulty related to submission stem from the fact that a wife is voluntarily making herself vulnerable to her husband's mistakes. This anxiety is relieved when she experiences his willingness to listen to the Lord. The couple delights together in the personal attention from God, the Father. This act of trusting and delighting in the Lord demonstrates what it means to rest in God. It is refreshing.

Receiving fresh understanding about the character or purposes of God is also energizing. Enthusiasm rises when the insight is shared with another person, especially one's spouse. Consider someone watching a ball game. When a player catches an amazing, unexpected spiraling pass, the viewer generates excitement when he or she proclaims the surprising details of the play and declares how unbelievable it is. Other fans add their exclamations, and the whole crowd is fired up! Likewise, when a husband shares the joy that has been revealed to him in his study of God's Word, his wife is energized.

As a husband bathes and showers his bride with the words God has used to specifically enlighten him, they both experience restful, energizing refreshment. The result is a spiritual bond of oneness. Prepare a spiritual bubble bath for your bride by opening the Word of God and expressing your awe of its personal message.

TANGLED IN SEAWEED

Read Jonah 1:3, 8, and 2:1–10

Sometimes when I am emotionally spent – and I view the people around me as unreasonable, irresponsible, and undeserving of my attention – I board a boat and sail away in the sea of activity. I hide in the hull of my agenda, and ignore the storming consequences. The question eventually surfaces, just like it did for Jonah (1:8); what is the cause of all my turmoil?

When the storm rages wildly enough, I admit I am fleeing from the Lord and take the dive into the cold sea of confession (2:3). My life and attitude announce my guilt, and God uses the swirling, uncontrollable depths to reveal truth. His perspective billows over me, wave after wave. The flood of God's water uncovers broken shells of self-effort. Dead, stinking fish of various shapes and colors – resentment and selfishness – float over my head. Weeds of pride wrap around my throat and choke me as I drown in helplessness. In the prison at the dark bottom of the fish's belly, my soul faints (vv. 6 –7). I am powerless to swim out, but then I remember the Lord. I cry out with nothing to rely on but His all-sufficient mercy. He reminds me that clinging to my idols, my perspectives, and my rights causes me to forfeit His mercy (Jonah 2:8) and leaves me miserable. He wraps me in seaweed, and the entanglement forces me to recognize my need. When I confess my sin and cry out for help, God releases me onto the shore of His purpose (v. 10). I am freed to love my spouse and family, and cherish them as His precious gifts.

SCRATCHED RECORDS

Read 2 Corinthians 10:4–6

As a small boy, I watched my older brothers gently and meticulously set the arm of their record changer onto their precious vinyl. Each record had what seemed to be a never-ending groove. The needle, which detected the sound from the groove, followed the slot tirelessly until it concluded on the last song. If my brothers weren't careful, they could scratch the record and damage the groove where the needle traveled. When that happened, the needle got stuck and played the same segment of a song over and over again.

Similarly, when we repeatedly heed the deceptive but convincing arguments of Satan – you deserve revenge, there is no hope for you, lying this one time won't hurt, nobody cares –we develop a stronghold or a mental habit pattern of reaction. This is nothing more than a scratch that causes us to veer off the track of truth and obedience. Something as simple as an exasperating event can nudge the needle of our minds into the scratch or stronghold. We react with the predetermined mindset that has been etched into our thinking, such as defensiveness, selfishness, despair, anger, drunkenness, gluttony, or others. Once our minds are engraved with a stronghold, we automatically play the same reactionary tune over and over, justifying and deepening the rut.

A scratched record can never be restored, but in today's verses, God instructs us to repair the scratches in our thinking. He urges us to be aware of the spiritual battles taking place in our minds, and to cast down imaginations, arguments, and opinions that exalt themselves against the knowledge of God. Every thought must be examined in light of His Word. Any thinking that does not align with truth should be eliminated—taken to Christ for cleansing. Are there scratches in your mind that cause you to habitually react in an ungodly way to your mate? It is vital that we ask the Lord to help us recognize wrong thought patterns, and replace them with truth and obedience.

SHINE LIKE AN ANGEL

Read Acts 7:54–60

*W*hat an irritating day! Almost every month for the past year, we've received a bill from a certain company with the same incorrect monthly charge. We've filled out several documents and I've talked to dozens of representatives who promised to correct the problem. Today I tried yet again to get it fixed: pushing phone buttons, listening to lists and lists of menu instructions, then pushing more buttons. I was instructed to hold until finally, I heard a human voice. I explained my problem and asked to speak to someone in billing. The employee was sure she could handle the situation, and I answered all the questions I've answered every other month. Over the last year, I have spent hours trying to resolve this simple matter. I was FRUSTRATED over the waste of my time and the incompetence of the "system." I know my irritation was apparent in my voice.

I was still annoyed after the phone call was finished. My attitude spilled over into other areas of my life, affecting loved ones who had nothing to do with the problem. The peace of God was not ruling my heart.

In Acts 7:54 – 60, Stephen experienced a pretty high stress day, too. He was proclaiming the truth, but no one believed him. The unbelievers not only accused him, but they also set up false witnesses. These people did much more than waste his time; they gnashed their teeth (v. 54) and prepared to stone him. How devastating! But Stephen was not irritated. His disposition was angelic. He intently gazed into heaven and marveled at the glory of God. He spoke truth and showed concern for the people who opposed and threatened him.

My faithful Father reminded me that if I focus on His glory and the steadfast love of His son, if I worship in the midst of aggravating circumstances, I will not steam with frustration. Rather like Stephen, I will shine like an angel to my spouse and family as they observe my life.

LISTENING THE LOVE IN

Read Psalm 139:1–3 and 116:1–2

A few years ago, two people very dear to me voiced opposing expectations. Fulfilling their hopes was directly linked to how each of them perceived my love and respect. Either way, I faced rejection. Someone would be disappointed.With my Bible in my lap, I anguished before the Lord. I described every angle of my perspective. The faithful Spirit of God enlightened me through a fresh understanding of Psalm 139:1–2. God reminded me that He understands my thoughts from afar and He empathizes with me. I was flooded with loving gratitude and a sense of acceptance. My dilemma did not change, but just knowing that someone understood strengthened me to face the challenge.

Psalm 116:1–2 further explains the bond that develops because God listens. He doesn't just acknowledge my words, but He perceives my emotions. I have His undivided, caring attention because He inclines or bends toward me. My automatic response is to depend upon Him and trust Him as long as I live.

This same principle can apply in my marriage. If I intently and empathetically listen to my spouse … if I offer my undivided attention and concern … my mate will feel accepted and be stirred to bond with me in loyal, grateful love.

CRUSHED

Read Colossians 3:13 and Luke 23:32–34

*I*nsults and unfounded cutting remarks from acquaintances arouse hurt, irritation, and anger. Likewise, unexpected criticism from a spouse often yields an irritated, defensive response. If justifications fail to influence the offending spouse to withdraw or soften the accusations, a sense of hopeless, crushing rejection can result.

The opinions of an acquaintance are often not significant, but the approval and acceptance of a spouse are linked with a fierce need to please because of the divinely-joined, one-flesh relationship between husband and wife (Matthew 19:4–6). Spouses grow accustomed to the security and comfort of emotional oneness. Their relationship should be a refuge where inmost fears, dreams, ideas, and cares can be exposed without fear of rejection. When the protective bubble bursts, emotions of betrayal and despair generate such deep anguish that forgiveness seems impossible.

Colossians 3:13 challenges believers to forgive as Jesus does. He was crushed by those He deeply loved, but He released the hurt by declaring to the Father that His loved ones did not know what they were doing (Luke 23:34). When the wounds of accusation are overwhelming, you can reason that your loved one does not comprehend the piercing nature of the experience. You can replace defensive thinking with the acknowledgment that your spouse just does not understand. The door then opens for forgiveness.

FULL

Read Ephesians 3:14–21 and 5:18

Before Paul addresses the relationships of husbands and wives in Ephesians 5:21–31, he urges Christians in Ephesians 5:18 to be filled with the Spirit of God. Fulfilling our roles as husband or wife stretches us beyond responsibilities and routine living. They require the power of God. Sheer will, determination, and desire alone do not produce satisfying relationships, nor do they ensure a filling of the Spirit. Although the necessity of being filled is undeniable, the reality of it can seem elusive or mystical.

In Ephesians 3:14–21, Paul powerfully prays that Christians will be filled with all the fullness of God. He calls upon God as Father of all to grant by grace—that is by His goodness–a strengthening in the inner person so that our understanding will be expanded to grasp the vastness of the love of Christ (Eph. 3:16, 18). Paul asks that Christ would root and ground believers in His love (Eph. 3:17). These verses declare such an emphasis on our need to be firmly established and founded on God's love! Paul prays that this comprehension advance beyond head knowledge to experience, so Christians will be filled with all the fullness of God (Eph. 3:19). Being filled with the Spirit, an essential element of married life, is directly linked to an individual's personal understanding of the immensity of God's love. The more completely a spouse grasps how deeply the Father loves him or her, the more powerfully he or she will live as a Spirit-filled spouse. If you desire to love and serve your family, daily meditate on the magnitude of God's love. Consider His passion, His sacrifice, His patience, and His steadfastness. Embrace the security that His acceptance provides. Unashamedly express your gratitude. Your family will reap the benefits.

FLOODING

Read Philippians 1:9–11 and Ephesians 3:20–21

or days, water has showered from the heavens. The rain has been steady, soaking the ground until it is soggy. At times lightning and tremendous thunders accompany a heavy drenching. The creeks swell, not by their own determination and effort, but from sheer necessity. The banks cannot contain the evidence of what is within. The water seeps and creeps, covering grass, dead leaves, and tree trunks, giving the appearance of a pond and then a lake. The surrounding terrain changes in response to the overflow.

Likewise, understanding the immensity and completeness of the Father's love can flood us to the point that every decision and action is a result of our enlightenment. Perfect compassion and commitment filters each response (Phil. 1:9–11). Christ living within a spouse overflows in abundant power, eliciting results beyond his or her wildest dreams or most vivid imaginations. When a husband or wife is overwhelmed by Christ's love and concern, they cease performing their marriage duties through self effort. The power of God resident within them floods their life and thinking with joy and peace. The most menial tasks and responsibilities flow out of the refreshing of God rather than the mechanical routine of duty. This joy and peace cannot be worked up through self effort, nor can it be contained within the banks of our hearts. It springs from the well of Christ's overflowing goodness. To Him be the Glory!

THE LONELY NUMBER

Read Genesis 2:18–23

I love mission trips. The diversity in culture is fascinating, and the presence of God seems to be more prevalent. I am inspired by the hope that sparks in the eyes of the local people when they start to understand the gospel. They are passionate and eager to learn. Every moment is packed with expectation, and I could not be busier. But there is an incredible void. I miss my wife. I am incomplete without her.

God impressed on the first man that he, too, was incomplete. Every male cat—the mighty lion, the bright and steady tiger, the powerful jaguar—all proudly paraded their graceful female companions before Adam. The male giraffes, zebras, and stallions each lovingly nudged their mares to strut across his path to receive their descriptive names. The female orangutans and chimpanzees reeled and clapped as their males swung on the vines. A clumsy black bear wiped a paw of honey across his mate's mouth, then licked against her lips. The distinctive identity of each couple added to the inspiration of the name chosen. Each partner uniquely and specifically belonged to the other. God had already taught Adam that all of creation was good. Now in His unfathomable wisdom, He instructs him by word and vivid living examples that "one is a lonely number." Man had provision, purpose, and peace, but in all that perfection there was a void. He was missing connection, relationship, a sense of belonging. The all-wise Creator had skillfully prepared man's heart to receive His next gift. When Adam saw Eve, he knew without a doubt that she belonged to him (v. 23). God taught Adam that creation was now very good. Adam understood. He was no longer alone; he was complete. He could love in the way that Dr. Jay Adams teaches, "Love in marriage focuses upon giving one's spouse the companionship that he or she needs to eliminate loneliness."[2] Seize the moment. Fill a void. Connect with your spouse today.

A ROCK OF HELP

Read Genesis 2:18 and I Samuel 7:1–12

Have you ever been in a desperate situation and needed help? Several weeks ago, two of my sons and I were moving a cumbersome and heavy desk into the basement. As we maneuvered through the door, the desk tilted sideways and forced me to support most of the load. I shouted to my older son, "Come over here quick; I'm not sure how long I can hold it!" He immediately responded and lightened the load. What a relief to share the burden!

In Genesis 2:18, God reveals that Adam needs help because it is not good for a man to be alone. Adam needs someone to share the load, to be a helper. Translated from Hebrew, helper is the word "ezer," one who enables or empowers.

I Samuel 7:12 gives insight into the same word. Samuel had led the stubborn children of Israel to repent before God (1 Sam. 7:3–6). When the Philistines launch a vicious attack, the Israelites desperately turn back to the Lord and He grants them a dramatic victory. Samuel places a stone as a memorial and names it Ebenezer, meaning the Lord is our rock of help. The Israelites acknowledged God as the reason for their victory. He had not just helped them a little, He had fully enabled and empowered them to stand against their enemies. In the same way, God positions a wife as a rock of help for her husband! He intends that she be a dependable source of strength that inspires him to fulfill God's purposes for their family. A husband should gratefully recognize the strengths that his wife brings to the relationship. Her perspectives, talents, and abilities are vital in completing him. In what specific ways can the two of you team together to "share the load" in the battles your family faces?

PRECIOUS

Read Genesis 1:26–27 and 2 Corinthians 3:17–18

God blessed us with four precious boys! I say precious because they are ours, made in our likeness, and we have a unique bond with them. We are aware of details about their personalities – strengths, weaknesses, likes, dislikes, struggles, and victories – that are not known to others. We have a vested interest in the boys' well-being. They trust that whether they come to us with needs or aspirations, we will respond in their best interest.

Both man and woman are created in the image of God (Gen. 1:26–27). He is our Father and we are made in His likeness. We are the only part of creation given this distinction! We are precious to God. Just what does this mean? Because we are created in His image, we have the unique capacity to know and have communion with Him. What a privilege! We can commune with Jesus, Creator of the universe (Col. 1:13–17). In the garden, as sinless image bearers of God, both the man and woman had the ability to reflect the glory of God. This makes us the most cherished part of God's creation, the pinnacle of it. Although sin marred and distorted the image, it is still there. Through redemption in Jesus Christ, we can be reconciled to our Father and the process of restoring the divine image begins (2 Cor. 3:17–18). As a Christian husband and wife, we must continually remember how precious our mate is. When we look at our spouse, we are looking at a reflector of God, a valued image bearer. We have the opportunity to either enhance or degrade the glory of God he or she bears. If we continually see each other this way, we will be careful what we say, how we act and react. Make it a habit to acknowledge Christ-like characteristics in your spouse, and tell them how you see the Father using unique aspects of their personality to reflect His image.

REST

Read Genesis 2:1–3, Isaiah 58:13–14, and Hebrews 4:9–10

After a long day's work, isn't it nice to come home, sit in your favorite chair, and rest? After six days of creating, the Bible says that God rested. Was God tired? Was He weary? According to Isaiah 40:28, God does not faint or grow weary. The word "rested" in Genesis 2:2 simply means that He ceased from His creative activity. He surveyed His creation, declared that it was very good, and then stopped creating. He paused to reflect on His world and to delight in it. All of creation, including man, was now glorying in God, abiding in His rest and delighting in what He had done. There were no restrictions on Adam and Eve concerning the Sabbath. The restriction would come only after man sinned and the law was given. Adam and Eve found complete pleasure in the creation and the Creator. This was the divinely-designed purpose of Sabbath rest – to delight and be so in awe of Jehovah God that all else faded in relevance (Isa. 58:13–14). The result was no striving, no fretting, just pure delight.

This sweet rest still remains for us today. Hebrews 4:9–10 explains there is a rest for the people of God who cease from their attempts to earn His acceptance and look instead to the work He accomplished through the cross of Christ. When a husband and wife rest in God, they cease worrying, fretting, and seeking revenge for unfair treatment. They are so focused on who He is and what He has done that they automatically depend upon and trust Him to meet every need. They confidently release their problems to Him, and are freed to respond to life with grateful hearts. Look to God, and worship your way to true rest today.

CULTIVATING THE GARDEN

Read Genesis 2:7–15

After creating man, God placed him in the garden and assigned him two specific tasks—to cultivate/work the garden and keep/protect it. These two aspects defined not only the duties man was to perform in the garden, but also pictured his responsibilities as a husband. The word husband, as a verb, means to take care of or provide for. Cultivating a garden normally requires toil and sweat, but for Adam the original task did not involve grueling work. His was a labor of love … enjoyable and pleasant. In the same way, God gave man the task of taking care of and providing for his wife. The work would be enjoyable as long as the man rested in the Lord. When sin entered the picture, the curse brought weeds and thorns. Cultivating the garden would now require true labor and sweat.

Being a husband who provides for his wife involves effort. As a husband, I deeply desire to keep our home and family functional. For example, when a pipe is clogged, whether I tackle it myself or hire a plumber, I make sure the problem is resolved. When my wife coughs for several days, I insist that she see a doctor. I train my sons to respect their mother. This is how I cultivate my garden. I find that the work can be sweet when I am resting in the Lord as Adam originally did, allowing God to direct and lead me as I minister to my family physically, emotionally, and spiritually. When I strive in my own way, instead of yoking with God, I will not rest and my wife and family will suffer (Matt 11:28–30). Weeds of distraction and resentment will begin to overtake the beautiful garden God has given me to nurture. When I become aware that the labor in my garden is becoming tedious or stressful rather than motivated by love, I know it is time to consult the Master Gardener.

KEEPING THE GARDEN

Read Genesis 2:7–15 and 3:6

Have you ever been asked to protect something or someone? How you guard the item or person will depend largely on the value you place on what you are protecting. God gave Adam the task of keeping a very valuable piece of real estate, the Garden of Eden, safe and productive for a very special person who was dwelling there. The word "keep" means to guard or protect. Just what was he to guard against? Wasn't he living in Paradise, free from sin, with a perfect helper? When God instructed Adam to guard the garden and his wife, He implied the presence of an enemy! This enemy was none other than Satan, who because of his rebellion against God, had been cast from heaven to earth (Isa. 14:12). Similarly, in order for a husband to keep his "garden," he must identify the real enemy. He must realize it is not his wife or his children, but the devil! To effectively protect his home, a husband must understand the enemy's devices and schemes. Satan is still subtle and crafty. He will employ the same destructive strategies to corrupt our homes that he used in the garden: the lust of the flesh, the lust of the eyes and the pride of life (Gen. 3:6, 1 John 2:16). As a husband, it is my responsibility to monitor what enters my home – whether through TV, guests, or attitudes. I must guard against anything that promotes or excuses greed, sassiness, pride, resentfulness, or selfishness. I pray God will grant me discernment and vigilance to block these subtle mind-sets before they infiltrate our family in any way. A husband who is "keeping his garden" will take responsibility to protect his home against the devices of the enemy!

FALLING FOR THE LIE

Read Genesis 3:1–6 and James 1:14–17

While Adam and Eve are living in paradise, all of their thoughts are focused on the wonder of God and His creation. They are experiencing perfect peace and perpetual pleasure when Satan interrupts and shifts Eve's attention away from God and His provision to the restriction (Genesis 3:1). Once he changes her mind-set, the serpent can suggest a lie and then back it with logical reasoning (4). Since Eve is no longer considering the goodness and greatness of God, Satan can twist God's purpose of setting the restriction for her protection to appear that He desires to suppress her (5). Then, like a child, Satan taunts Eve with the thought, "God knows something you don't know." The chant rings in her ears and compels her to discover the secret. Her drive intensifies as her perspective shifts to self and the opportunity for personal gain and benefits. Self-centered reasoning demands that Eve choose the fruit.

Satan employs the same tactics in our marriages today. He shifts our focus from the character and love of God to financial restrictions or to responsibilities that control our time. He makes us feel limited by the demands of our mate. Our drive to improve our current situation compels us to consider options. Like Eve, we weigh the benefits of each from our perspective and logically choose, but from a "human" viewpoint. The choices available are often temptations insuring that we get what we want vs. accepting what God gives (James 1:14). When we concentrate on the restrictions and how life is affecting us, we, like Eve, unsuspectingly fall for Satan's lies and deals (James 1:15). Self-centered reasoning will demand that we choose what appears to benefit us. Beware of a shift in focus that might cause you to taste ostensibly beneficial, but forbidden fruit (James 1:16).

SOUR MILK

Read Genesis 3:1–6 and James 1:14–17

dam and Eve are living in a Paradise of perfect love, rest, and pleasure. They know only good — the goodness of God and the blessings of His creation. The serpent offers Eve the chance of a lifetime; now, she can know evil, too. What a deal!! How could she even consider an offer like that? By accepting this proposal, she is implying, "I feel great. Help me to be miserable." No one would voluntarily want to disrupt personal peace with the opportunity to experience evil, or would we?

A couple of months ago, Sam and I were ministering at a marriage retreat. We were seated with the group eating breakfast when a woman exclaimed, "Yuck, my milk is sour!" She passed her carton to the person next to her and encouraged her to smell it. One by one, each person at the table took a whiff, agreed that it was not only sour, but disgusting. Who would voluntarily want to interrupt the delicious blessing of a tasty breakfast with the torture of a sickening odor? Like Eve, most of the people at our table wanted to expand their understanding and experiences to include misery.

We follow this pattern of thinking each time we choose defensiveness rather than peacemaking, when our thoughts dwell on the faults of our spouses instead of their strengths, or when we dig to uncover every detail of gossip rather than defend the character of those involved. Like Eve, as Christians shift their thought patterns away from the character and goodness of God, they are lured into wrong choices and fall into a trap of pain and destruction (James 1:14-16). Avoid the trap by focusing on the good gifts that the Father has given (17).

A FAITHFUL MESSENGER

Read Proverbs 25:13, 10:26, and 26:6

There's something magical about a snowy day. As snowflakes steadily float to the ground, everything that was once dim or dirty becomes fresh and pure. Just observing the white blanket makes one feel clean. The temperature outside drops enough to warrant a fire in the fireplace, and I love how everyone tends to congregate around the hearth. We can drink hot chocolate, read a book, and enjoy being together. As I write these words, I can see the snow on the ground outside and it brings refreshment to my soul!

Solomon describes a faithful messenger as a person who brings refreshment to the one who sent him just as the cold water from the snow of a nearby mountain spring refreshes a weary worker during a hot day (25:13). He contrasts this soothing picture by stating that an unfaithful messenger is like having vinegar in your mouth and smoke in your eyes (10:26). Just as smoke burns your eyes and vinegar has a bitter taste, so is a servant who breaks the trust of his master by bringing a distorted report. A spouse becomes an unfaithful messenger when he or she communicates something different to others than what was originally said by their mate. This can happen when our mate asks us to share a specific message with someone and we decide to either minimize or embellish it, changing the original content. When the spouse who sent the message hears how it has been distorted, the experience is as irritating as a mouth of vinegar and smoke-filled eyes. Trust has been broken by an unfaithful messenger who happens to be their spouse. At this point, the relationship can only be healed through repentance and forgiveness. The husband or wife who is faithful to deliver an accurate message enhances the relationship like a carpet of clean, pure snow that refreshes the dusty ground. The marriage is covered with a beautiful layer of trust.

CELEBRATE

Read Ecclesiastes 9:9–10

Solomon, described in the Bible as the wisest man who ever lived, encourages husbands and wives to "live joyfully" together. God intends that marriage be a continual celebration. He goes on to say we are to celebrate our marriages, not just once in a while or sometimes, but all the days of our life! God never intended the husband and wife relationship to be dull, listless, or dreary, where we just endure each other. Rather, marriage is to be romantic, exciting, and fulfilling each and every day.

Can you remember the first time you saw your husband or wife ... when your eyes met and your heart began to beat a little faster? Think back to the first time you went out with each other. You could hardly wait. Each moment together was a thrill and full of excitement. When you left one another, all you could think about was the next time you would be together. Then came marriage. Someone once said that the greatest hindrance to romance is marriage. What happened? Many couples claim that reality sets in. "He or she didn't turn out to be what I expected. I didn't know he was a slob! I didn't know she couldn't cook!" If we are not careful, over time we establish a mental list of conditions our mate must fulfill to keep us happy. God never intended for us to live this way. We are not to live with a list of selfish expectations, but our marriages are to be continually filled with the grace of God. Solomon devotes the entire book of Ecclesiastes to warning readers to avoid vanities—consuming thoughts centered on personal worth and satisfaction. Vanities distract us from what really matters and interrupt the celebration. Today's verses declare that what will matter at the end of our life is the joy we shared with our mates. Are there any vanities stealing joy from your marriage?

CONTROLLING THE ERUPTIONS

Read Genesis 4:7, 3:16, and Romans 5:20, 6:13–14

A few weeks after an excavating company had finished paving the road in front of our house, I walked along the new surface and noticed something strange. In one section of the road, tiny volcano-type mounds had erupted through the asphalt. Each day as I walked, I curiously investigated the cause until I finally discovered a blade of grass shooting through one of the mini-volcanoes. I pondered the impossibility of grass being powerful enough to push through two inches of pavement, but the evidence proved me wrong. Because of the intense desire of this grass to live, it broke through the heavy covering and stuck its head out for all to see. A tiny blade was ruling and dominating the pavement.

In Genesis 4:7, God warns Cain that if he does well, he will be accepted. However, if he doesn't do what is right, sin desires and waits to rule over him! Like Cain's sin, pride and self-centeredness want to burst through and dominate our lives. Similarly, in the curse to woman in Genesis 3:16, the word "desire" represents an overwhelming urgency to control her husband. A wife's intense desire to rule her husband can result in the sins of rebellion or manipulation that erupt within a marriage and overrule submissive cooperation.

These sins are like the blades of grass—seemingly insignificant, but powerfully assertive. God tells Cain that he must not let sin rule him, but rather he must master it! Paul teaches that if Christians are yielded to God, sin will not dominate them (Rom. 6:13–14). To deal with our mini-volcanoes, we had the excavation company return and squirt herbicide into each mound, killing the grass and controlling the problem. Pursuing intimacy with God will apply the power of His righteousness to the seemingly insignificant weeds within us. It's amazing that He not only instructs us to master the weeds, but also provides just what we need for the task (Gen. 4:7, Rom. 6:13–14).

SHIPWRECKED

Read I Timothy 1:18–20

*W*e chartered a small fishing boat and headed off the Florida coast into deep water. We hoped to see the boys snag some game fish. As soon as we puttered out of the inlet, strong waves began to rock the small craft. They increased in intensity and size, and splashed over the side of the boat. Soon we were forced to tightly grip the railing. I started entertaining visions of the boat capsizing! To my relief, the captain decided the sea was too rough, and steered the boat back to the dock.

Paul challenges Timothy to use strategy and resources that would equip him well for the storms and struggles of life. He pictures life as a battleship mission. The ship will be proficiently equipped with two oars to guide him through turbulent waters, but he will need to tenaciously hold on to them. The first oar is called "faith," and the second "good conscience."Without these two oars, Timothy would end up shipwrecked in the ocean of life!

According to Hebrews 11:6, without faith it is not possible to please God. Faith is so vital that without it, we will lose the battle and our mission will fail. Faith comes from hearing the Word of God (Rom. 10:17). The oar of faith is rooted in intense study and meditation of the Word. The more one studies, the tighter the grip on the oar of faith becomes. Holding faith and a good conscience is similar to the teamwork involved in using a pair of oars. Where faith comes from learning the Word, a good conscience results from responding to every life matter as the Word instructs. The Bible warns that our consciences can be seared (1 Tim. 4:1); that is, our spiritual nerves become dull and indifferent, and we no longer respond to God. Spiritual shipwreck is the result! Spouses who passionately study the Word, and let it direct their every thought and action, successfully navigate stormy waters. Hold tight to the oars.

THE "IF ONLYS"

Read 2 Kings 4:8–13

A prominent woman from Shunem had high regard for Elisha because she knew he was an anointed servant of God, a holy man. She occasionally fed him meals, but desired to do more for him. She suggested to her husband that they furnish a spare room where the prophet could rest and receive nourishment. Being grateful for the woman's hospitality, Elisha instructed his servant, Gehazi, to ask her what he could do as a token of his appreciation. Her answer was profound. She simply replied that she was satisfied to dwell among her own people. She was content, and needed nothing!

Contentment is a missing element in most homes today. The result is a search for happiness in all the wrong places. The typical thought becomes, "if only." If only I had a better job; if only I had a bigger house or better car; if only my mate was this way or that way. In Hebrews 13:5, God calls us to be content with what we have because He promises to never leave or forsake us. It is worth noting that this command comes after God declares in the previous verse that marriage should be honored by all, and the marriage bed should not be defiled. We do not have to look for happiness in our marriages or families "out there" somewhere. It can be found every moment in the realization that we have a sovereign and good God. Happiness is not found in things but in the person, God the Son. As we become content in Jesus Christ, we can become satisfied in our marriages and homes. We can get rid of the "if only's."

WITHOUT A WORD

Read 1 Peter 3:1–8

hen a husband denies himself for the benefit of his family – protecting and providing for them physically, emotionally, and spiritually — and when he exhibits dependence upon and surrender to the Lord, a wife is normally compelled by gratitude and respect to submit to his leadership. Submission is nonetheless still difficult because a wife is voluntarily choosing to be vulnerable to the mistakes of an imperfect human being. The challenges and risks greatly increase when her husband is not yielding to the Word of God. The consequences of his disobedience will affect her, just as the disobedience of man brought suffering to Christ. Even the godliest men on earth will, at times, struggle with their sin nature, just like godly wives will struggle with submission. 1 Peter 3 offers hope and incentive to every wife. No matter the spiritual condition of her husband, he may be influenced and won to God's way as he observes his wife's godly behavior.

When women want to convince their husbands to change, they naturally attempt to shift the men to their perspective by using elaborate explanations, emotional stories, convincing arguments, subtle hints, and nagging reminders. Although an effective helper should – without pressure, resistance, or repetition – lovingly express her perspective, the Bible says her husband will be influenced more by her attitude than her words. A godly attitude expresses itself as the fruit of the Spirit: love, joy, goodness, gentleness, patience, kindness, faithfulness, peace, and self-control (Gal. 5:22). When a wife displays the fruit of the Spirit and expresses respect for her husband in the routine matters of life, 1 Peter 3 says he may be won to this godly lifestyle without her even speaking a word.

MAJESTY

Read Titus 2:1–8

In today's passage, Paul instructs Timothy to urge believers to exercise sound doctrine; that is, to choose right behavior, for the right reasons, in their everyday lives. He addresses the older men, the leaders of the families, to be temperate and serious. Paul uses the word "likewise" to include the older women, younger women, and younger men in these instructions as well. At first, he seems to imply that believers should maintain a somber, serious expression, but he is emphasizing the need to be serious because godly attitudes and actions do not come naturally. Believers need to purposefully consider the principles that he is teaching, or they will overlook them in their routine of life.

Titus 2:3 challenges women to be reverent. To be reverent means to so esteem the majesty of God that one not only lives in a continual attitude of worship, but inspires others to do the same. When we lived in North Carolina, I had several friends who were mentored by a lady named Gladys. They each told me that no matter why they called her, no matter their challenge or question, they always hung up the phone amazed at the greatness of God. Gladys lived her daily routine so full of enthusiasm, joy, and confidence in the person of God that she inspired others to live accordingly. As Paul warned, this does not come naturally (vv.1-2). This aspect of Gladys' character was developed and engrained as she seriously and consistently studied the character of God. What a difference believers can make in the lives of family and friends as they grow knowledgeable concerning the majesty—the greatness and goodness—of God Almighty!

PARASITES

Read 1 Corinthians 8:1 and 13:1–7

I detected tapeworms in one of our English mastiff dogs today! The evidence was barely noticeable, but if not treated, the effects could be deadly. A tapeworm possesses both reproductive sexual cells and is able to reproduce itself thousands of times. A tapeworm produces more eggs in one segment of its body than all the people alive in the world today. In humans, this parasite can grow up to sixty feet long, continually dividing and multiplying. It is a horrible parasite that lives and feeds off its host, not realizing that by draining the life of the host, it will eventually eliminate its own. If you think this sounds nasty, ugly, and despicable, it certainly is! In fact, without de-worming, the dog would die.

Some marriage relationships are parasitical. One partner continually feeds off the other, slowly sucking the life out of his or her spouse until one day the marriage is emotionally empty. This is the opposite of God's description of love. He says that love builds up (1 Cor. 8:1)." Love strengthens. Love enriches another's life. When you genuinely love your spouse, your main concern is not what you are receiving from the relationship, but what you can give! This sounds like Reba McEntire's song, "Love Isn't Love (Til You Give It Away)."

This mind-set doesn't come naturally. Jesus explains that to live, we must first die (Matt. 10:38-39). Giving your life in the marriage relationship requires the death of self! You must deny your own flesh (interests, rights, desires) in order to allow the resurrected life of Jesus Christ to flow through you to your mate (Phil. 2:4). A parasitical spouse seeks benefits for self, but an edifying husband or wife sets concerns for self aside in order to seek opportunities to bless.

ANGER

Read Ephesians 4:26–31 and 6:4

Be angry, but at the same time, don't sin? That's a bit confusing! Just what does Paul mean? The instruction to be angry without sin is in the present imperative verb tense, which means Paul is commanding a continuous action. He is describing an incessant righteous indignation against sin and sinful things. He warns that this righteous anger may develop into sin if not checked. The word "wrath" or "anger" at the end of the verse is a different Greek word that describes anger that is mingled with irritation, exasperation, and bitterness. This kind of anger is forbidden in Ephesians 6:4 where Paul instructs the father not to provoke his child to wrath, and in verse 31 of chapter 4 where God tells believers to get rid of wrath. Paul instructs us to continually have righteous indignation against sin and sinful things, but not to let this righteous anger turn to sinful attitudes in our hearts. If anger advances to wrath where we lose the peace of God and become irritated and exasperated, we must confess it and get it back in check before the sun goes down!

In marriage, it is tempting to nurture righteous indignation by feeding it with a little irritation and resentment until it grows into frustrated anger toward your spouse not only over sin, but petty issues as well. God tells us to keep short accounts with each other and resolve the conflict before going to bed. I can remember instances in the past in which I became exasperated with Debbie. Instead of resolving the issue, I would give her the silent treatment. In fact I walked around the house looking for her, so that when I found her, I could ignore her! My behavior built walls of separation between us. I would waste time brooding when I could have been smooching. Heed God's warning to control anger before it becomes sinful (4:31). Life is too short and too valuable to waste fretting over petty issues.

BUGS

Read Ephesians 4:26–27 and Proverbs 4:23

*I*n the area of Tennessee where we live, there has been an epidemic of pine beetles, which have infested thousands of acres of pine forest. Once these beetles attack a tree, the tree will rot and eventually fall down if the problem is not treated in a timely manner. The devastation resembles that of a forest fire, miles and miles of fallen, dried up pine trees. As a result of this infiltration, millions of dollars are being spent to clear thousands of acres of trees in the surrounding counties.

God warns that the devil is just like those pesky pine beetles. He will seize any opportunity to infiltrate and take hold (Eph 4:27). He scouts for an unguarded heart the way beetles hone in on pine. The Greek verb tenses in God's warning are so urgent that they actually indicate He is demanding that we stop allowing this opportunity. We give opportunity for the devil to infest our lives whenever we yield to his devices and treachery. The previous verse (v. 26) mentions that we are not to let the sun go down on our wrath. When we do, we allow the devil opportunity to destroy the relationship we have with our spouse, child, or brother and sister in Christ. Proverbs 4:23 instructs us to guard our hearts diligently. The devil is looking for the child of God who has his or her guard down. The beginning stages of wrath—unchecked irritation, resentment, and bottled up frustration—are his favorite entry points. God demands that we stop leaving these entry points unguarded because the devastation is extremely damaging. Pine beetles devour forests, but the devil devours lives (1 Pet. 5:8). Apply the insecticide of self-examination. Are you harboring resentment? Are you nourishing irritations? Protect your forest of marriage. Stop allowing the opportunity for infestation.

GOLDEN DELICIOUS APPLES

Read Ephesians 4:29, Mark 7:21–23,
Proverbs 4:23, 25:11, and Philippians 4:8

*H*ave you ever bitten into a rotten apple? The immediate impulse is to spit it out. Would you feel loved by your spouse if he or she offered you a rotten apple? I would feel poisoned and betrayed. When we demean our spouse or use sarcasm, we may skillfully prove our point, but our words will leave the listener with a taste as offensive as rotten apples. The Bible tells us that the words that proceed from our mouth originate in our heart (Mark 7:21, Proverbs 4:23). When corrupt, rotten words roll off our tongue, we should immediately check the condition of our heart. What are we thinking that would make us spew rotten apples from our mouth toward our spouse?

While God warns against corrupt communication that destroys a person's spirit, He encourages speech that builds up and ministers grace. Ministering grace refers to imparting spiritual blessings and benefits, expressing positive thoughts that are appropriate to the occasion. Because communication proceeds from our heart, grace-filled words will require meditating and concentrating on gospel truths to inspire our innermost beings. This is the pattern of communication found in Paul's letters. He always began by reminding himself how blessed he was to possess a relationship to Christ. He would review specifics of heavenly blessings that thrilled him, and then he would direct his thoughts to admirable characteristics of his readers. This would lead to a prayer of thanks. His words were obviously heartfelt. The readers were edified and their relationship to Paul was strengthened. The apples of his communication were crunchy and juicy, delicious slices served on a tray of polished silver (Prov. 25:11). What have you been you serving to your spouse? How can you adjust your thought life so you will have fresh, golden apples to offer your mate?

BE SENSITIVE

Read Ephesians 4:30 and 1 John 1:9

When we become children of God, we immediately receive His sweet Spirit. The Holy Spirit within comforts and empowers, but also convicts us. I can remember a time when we were building our house several years ago and I became very frustrated. My older two sons were helping me do some framing, and I became impatient and spoke harshly to them. As soon as the words rolled out of my mouth, the Holy Spirit made me aware of my harsh, critical attitude. At that point, I had a choice to make—ignore and grieve the Spirit, or listen to what God was saying to me and repent. That day I chose to repent! I went to my sons and admitted that my harshness was unnecessary. I asked them to forgive me for sinning against them with my words. That time, I chose to listen to God's voice and obey Him. God will not force us to make the right choice, but will urge us by His Spirit to do so.

When we grieve and ignore God, our insensitivity affects everyone around us. Disregarding the gentle prompting of the Spirit destroys fellowship with God and with the one who is touched by our sin. For example, it's not easy to admit to my wife that I am wrong when I act ungodly toward her, but the consequences of not doing so damage our relationship. My wife and four sons need to know I am humble and sensitive enough to the Spirit that I can admit my sin. God is quick to forgive (1 John 1:9). Your mate and children will be, too, when you approach them with a humble, broken heart and ask for forgiveness. Always be sensitive to the Spirit's prompting in your life.

DRIP, DRIP!

Read Proverbs 27:15–16

The faucet in our kitchen provides fresh water for cooking, drinking, and cleaning. We know that without it, our kitchen would be much less efficient, but it constantly DRIPS, DRIPS, DRIPS. The continuous "plink" annoys everyone who tries to concentrate, not just there, but in every room on that floor of our home. The sound amplifies when a droplet hits water that has collected in a bowl or a metal pan. Our creativity abounds as we attempt to stifle the sound. We send the kids to jerk the spout around so nothing is directly beneath the spout. We squeeze our frustrations against the handle with all our might. We float a dish cloth in the water to muffle the noise. We jump out of bed and slam the bedroom door as a barrier between the irritation and our peace. Until we replace the faucet's faulty parts, it is impossible to hide from the nuisance.

Proverbs 27 pictures life with a contentious, nagging woman as the same irritating drip. She may serve her family efficiently and purposefully. Her intent may be to improve the quality of their lives by steering them to her perspective, but like the drip, she forces them to attempt to stifle her presence. Scripture explains this is in vain. It is as impossible to hide from this woman as it is to hide from the wind or to hold oil in your hand because she focuses so intently on her agenda. She is blind to the aggravation she creates.

The annoying drip of our faucet will cease when we hire a plumber to replace the defective pieces with new ones. The contentious drip from a wife or mother comes to a halt as she reconsiders the way she is viewing a situation. Nagging and complaining are normally rusty attempts to regulate what's happening. Viewing situations from the perspective of the Master Plumber, Jesus Christ, stops the drip and allows Him to control the flow of life.

DIVINE JOINING

Read Matthew 19:1–6 and Ephesians 5:32

*I*s it lawful for a man to divorce his wife for any cause? The Pharisees, desiring to discredit and destroy the public ministry of Jesus, asked Him this question. This was not a quick blurt out of their mouths, but rather a well thought out and planned attack against Him. Divorce had become commonplace with the Jews, so common that men would divorce their wives for any and every cause. In fact, there was a rabbinical debate going on between two leaders named Shammai and Hillel. Shammai believed divorce was never permitted and Hillel believed you could divorce your wife for any cause (she burned the toast, or her hair looked bad). They hoped Jesus' answer to the much debated question would cause the Jews to reject Him!

When He replies, Jesus reminds them of the first marriage in Genesis chapter two. As He rhetorically questions whether they know the Creator's instructions to the first married couple, Jesus exposes the Pharisees as misrepresenting the intent of God's Word. Their goal is not to glorify Him, but to get as close to sinning as possible. Instead of asking about specific grounds for divorce, they should be inquiring how marriage could be what God intended. Jesus reminds them that when a man and woman are joined together, they are no longer two but one. This is not just a casual getting together that man can decide to separate. The joining of a man and woman into a one-flesh relationship is a divine act of God Himself! This is a miracle, a great mystery (Eph. 5:32).

As husband and wife, we must continually remind ourselves that marriage is not a humanly contrived institution. It does not and cannot operate with human reasoning. Our minds must be subject to the divine will of God. We must embrace His perspective of marriage; we are no longer two but one.

FEBRUARY 2

LOVE AT FIRST SIGHT

Read Genesis 24:50–67

A woman's deepest longing is normally security—to be loved in a way that fulfills her physical and emotional needs. In Ephesians 5, God repeatedly emphasizes that husbands should love their wives. Isaac's relationship with Rebekah pictures the importance and benefits of conveying this love.

Before Isaac even meets his wife, he determines to shower love on her. He wants her to understand that he commits to be a generous husband, so he and his father supply their servant with expensive, thoughtful presents for Rebekah and her family (v. 53). The gifts not only offer evidence that Isaac has adequate income to properly provide for her, but they also signify that he will cherish her as a valuable treasure.

While Isaac is praying and seeking strength from the Lord, he sees Rebekah for the first time, veiled and at a distance. The servant explains the amazing details of how God had provided Rebekah to be Isaac's wife (v. 66). He knows nothing else about his bride, but verse 67 implies that he realizes she is a special, cherished gift when he gently opens his home and his life to her. This realization compels Isaac to immediately love and unconditionally accept his new wife. He not only meets Rebekah's deepest longings through his display of affection, but this love becomes God's answer to his own yearning for comfort. Isaac was experiencing a void in his life brought about by the death of his mother. In the Garden of Eden, God had declared it was not good for man to be alone (Gen 2:18). The divine plan to eliminate loneliness is to fill man's void with a wife whom he can love and cherish. God perfectly satisfies the husband's longings for comfort and companionship as the wife responds to his striving to fulfill her desire to be cared for and treasured.

LOVE AT FIRST SIGHT DEEPENS

Read 1 Peter 3:7–8 and Genesis 25:21

Peter 3:7 instructs husbands to live with their wives in an understanding way; that is to spend time with them, getting to know their hearts, their cares, and their concerns. God challenges men to understand their wives and to respond to them by honoring and respecting their thoughts and feelings. Failing to relate to his wife in this way will hinder a husband's prayers. The instruction continues in verse 8 by reminding both husbands and wives to be of one mind—to strive to understand each other's perspective and humbly have compassion for one another.

Isaac provides an example of this affectionate empathy. In Genesis 25:21, he is concerned about Rebekah's barrenness. He entreats the Lord, not from his point of view that he needs a child to carry on the family name or to work in the family business, but he pleads with the Lord for his wife. His concern is for her depression, her desire, and her longing to be a mother. He has lived with her, listening to the inner struggles and desires of her heart. He is moved to passionately pray on her behalf. Genesis 25:21 concludes when the Lord answers Isaac's prayers. He is able to effectively intercede because he lovingly empathizes with his wife by seeking to understand her perspective.

Has anyone ever poured out his or her heart to the Lord on your behalf? What a moving experience! What comfort floods your being! What a bond of gratitude that results! This type of empathy becomes an integral part of oneness as a husband and wife compassionately pray for each other. What concerns do you see in your spouse's life that you could lift to the Lord?

LOVE AT FIRST SIGHT CONTINUES

Read Genesis 25:26–27, 26:6–9, and Ecclesiastes 9:9

Isaac was sixty years old when Esau and Jacob were born (Gen. 25:26). By the time they were grown men (Gen. 25:27), he and Rebecca had been married more than thirty years. When Abimelech glanced out the window and noticed Isaac sporting with Rebekah (Gen 26:8), he witnessed playful affection between spouses who had been together a long time. Even though the stress of life was so great that Isaac succumbed to the pressure and wrongfully deceived the king, his love for Rebekah continued. They set the stress aside and enjoyed being with each other. He caressed her as a loving husband, and their tender, strong bond was evident to an outsider.

In Ecclesiastes 9:9, Solomon is an old man. He recognizes the mistake he made when he failed to concentrate on his first wife. Instead of finding joy with her every day of his life, he pursued other women and pleasures. Now he looks back on his busy, empty life and wisely urges men to live joyfully with their wives all the days of their lives. He instructs that even though life brings adversities and futility, men should strive to enjoy their wives. This is God's plan. When a couple is first married, the newness of the relationship keeps their focus intent on the pleasures of companionship. As time passes, the demands of life tend to distract the couple from having fun with each other.

Are the pressures of life distracting you? Have you forgotten to relax and have fun? Plan a date or a vacation. Concentrate on each other. Laugh again. Enjoy the wife of your youth.

INHERIT A BLESSING

Read 1 Peter 3:9

When I was in engineering school, the professors taught that for every action, there is an equal, yet opposite reaction. This is a law of science, but as I observe many married couples, it seems to also be a law of relationships. Their behavior reminds me of my dogs. A tiny, wimpy stray will approach our yard barking. My 175-pound mastiff will immediately bark loudly and deeply enough to shake the window in the house next door. The crazy little stray will squeak a bark right back in his face. The cycle continues until I chase the small dog away. If husbands and wives are not careful, we, like dogs, develop the habit of automatically responding to our mate in the same way he or she acts toward us. Of course, if the action is Christ-like, then a Christ-like response is more likely. All too often, however, we return evil for evil or accusation for accusation. How do we break this cycle of retaliation? In 1 Peter 3:9, God instructs us that when our mate insults or accuses us, we are to respond with a blessing. If I speak with a harsh voice or render an unkind comment to my wife, and she answers with loving concern or kind words, her response immediately causes me to reconsider what I just said to her. It causes me to reflect, and allows God to work in my heart. If I am responsive to the Holy Spirit, then I will probably respond back to her with a "blessing" rather than another "curse." The retaliation cycle is broken. Think about how you react to harsh words. Instead of replying with accusations or defensiveness, respond by offering a compliment. This will soften your spouse's heart and provide an incentive for him or her to bless you … so you can inherit a blessing.

LET YOUR LOVE SHOW

Read John 13:34–35

An eight-year-old boy explained to his mother, "When I'm in a restaurant, I can tell the people who are in love. They stare into each other's eyes and their food gets cold. The other people care more about their food."

In the Middle Ages, young men and women drew names from a bowl to see who their valentines would be. They would wear these names on their sleeves for one week. To wear your heart on your sleeve now means it is easy for other people to know how you are feeling.[3] Would the eight-year old boy recognize your love for your spouse? Does the heart you wear on your sleeve announce that you are affectionate and committed to your mate, or does it reveal cold indifference?

We continually observe married couples. Some hold hands, sit closely together, whisper secrets, and exchange gentle kisses on the cheek. Others seem to fear contracting some dreaded disease from each other. They look straight ahead with expressionless faces. They are careful not to touch one another. Both extremes wear their hearts on their sleeves.

Jesus taught His disciples that they should wear His heart on their sleeves. A disciple is one who spends time with his leader, learning his ways. For three years, Jesus had conveyed love and concern for His disciples. Daily in their presence, He had demonstrated love for others. He had taught numerous lessons on God's love. In today's passage, He instructs His followers to implement these lessons personally by demonstrating love to each other (v. 34). Jesus tells His disciples that the love they have for one another will be evident to outside observers (v. 35). Likewise, the love of Christ will be evident in your marriage when you spend time with Jesus because His character and His way of thinking will be instilled in your heart. You will begin to view your spouse as He does. You will begin to express sweet affection. You will be more interested in what's happening in your mate's life than in what you are eating. Let your love show.

THE COST OF LOVE

Read Ephesians 5:2 and 24–27

I recently went to the gas station, and was once again shocked at the tremendous increase in fuel prices. I left thinking to myself, "The cost of living is skyrocketing." Later that same day, I heard a radio announcer report that over one billion dollars is spent on greeting cards, and another billion on candy purchases, for sweethearts on Valentine's Day. I thought to myself, "The cost of loving is going up, too!"

Just how much does true love cost? Ephesians 5:2 challenges us to walk in love in the same way that Christ did. The price of His love was His life, sacrificed to God for our sins. Just as Christ gave His life for His bride, a husband should give his life for his wife (Eph. 5:25). Giving his life, however, involves much more than being willing to die physically. A husband is to follow Christ's example through denial of self for the good of his wife (v. 27). To give his life is to devote his time, his money, and his ambitions to ensure that his bride flourishes not only in her relationship with him but also with Christ. If necessary, he should sacrifice TV time in order to lead devotions, pray, or communicate with his wife. He should be willing to occasionally sacrifice sleep to help with a crying baby. A wife manifests this same self-sacrificing love through submission to her husband (v. 24). She should be willing to adjust her spending to fit his income, to adjust her schedule to be helpful to him, and to allow him the final decision after both of their perspectives have been considered. The cost of love for both the husband and wife is the death of self, for the good of the one loved!

Candy, roses, and cards may temporarily serve to express affection, but the true cost of love in marriage is daily self-denial. Dying to self allows the grace of God to flow through you, and demonstrate His perfect, lasting love to your mate.

KISS THE GIRL

Read Song of Solomon 1:1–2

*T*housands of love songs have been written throughout time. If people were asked to name a favorite, their answers would be many and varied. In 1 Kings 4:32, Scripture tells us Solomon wrote 1,005 songs. Of those, God declares that the Song of Solomon is the song of all songs! This most beautiful and significant love song is nestled in the middle of the Holy Scripture. It includes fifteen reflections (little songs) of Solomon and his Shulamite bride. It is an elegant ballad that offers glimpses into their courtship, wedding day, and marriage. Through these artfully written reflections, much insight can be acquired that is both theological and practical as it relates to relationships before and after the wedding.

The first stanza begins on the wedding day as the Shulamite bride passionately proclaims her desire to kiss her future husband. She anticipates their union and reveals a strong physical attraction for her groom. She expectantly proclaims that his love is better than wine! The Hebrew word for "love" refers to sexual love or intimacy, while the word "wine" represents a joyful banquet or feast. To the bride, her groom's kisses represent a feast of celebration where she savors the luscious taste of his lips. Frequent kissing expresses pleasure and desire that should naturally increase in intensity. The love between a husband and wife should be passionate—each one drawn to the other, feasting in love. God gives sexual intimacy to a married couple as a precious gift. Pause now, and kiss the girl!

PURIFIED CHARACTER

Read Song of Solomon 1:1–3

everal years ago I put my trust in a person only to find out this individual had used me and committed fraud. I was deeply hurt, and since that time have had no respect for his character. As a result, I am no longer drawn to be with him, but rather am repelled away from him. Respect is important in any relationship, and God uses the Shulamite bride to emphasize how vital it is to marriage.

The bride exclaims her delight in the kisses of her husband (v. 2). Then, she gives us insight into why she is so passionately attracted to him. She explains that she is not only drawn to him because he smells wonderful like expensive perfume, but his name is just as precious as the good smelling ointment. The ointment referred to comes from carefully selected flowers and spices that have been refined through a press. When the mixture comes out, it has been purified. The sound of the husband's name attracts her because of his purified character. John Luther states, "Good character is more to be praised than outstanding talent. Most talents are, to some extent, a gift. Good character, by contrast, is not given to us. We have to build it piece by piece, thought by thought, choice by choice, which requires great courage and determination."[4] Ecclesiastes 7:1 states that a good name is better that precious ointment. Trust is the bridge to every relationship. A solid, lasting relationship requires purified character in which to trust.

Husband, is your wife passionately attracted to you? Her passion is linked more to your inner character than your outer physique. Can your spouse trust you to keep your word, avoid deception, and always tell the truth?

DRAW ME

Read Song of Solomon 1:1–4

Although politically incorrect for our culture, God's plan is that every wife looks to her husband for leadership in their marriage. In today's reading, the bride has just acknowledged that she admires Solomon's character (v. 3), and she expresses her desire for him to "draw" her. Evidently, the admirable traits she alludes to include leadership qualities because the word "draw" means to be in front, to guide, or to take the lead. This leader is not a dominating, dictatorial man who treats her as a brainless slave. No one is attracted to a person who considers others as inferior. Rather, a woman is drawn to a man who cherishes the unique abilities, insights, and talents God has entrusted to her. A wise husband values his wife's abilities as blessings that will complement his God-given purpose. He respects her opinion.

Occasionally, a husband may feel threatened by a wife because she is more capable in a certain area, such as handling finances. God's intention, however, is that he gratefully acknowledges her strengths and lovingly directs their use for the overall good of the family. Marriage is teamwork, with the coach (husband) utilizing each player's (his wife's and children's) distinctive talents to bring his team to victory. A coach invests in the development of his players and welcomes their respectful input. When a coach leads his team in this manner, they appreciate him and are loyal to his position of leadership. But that doesn't mean leadership is easy! The husband must prayerfully study his wife, understand her, love her, encourage her, and exercise discernment as he leads.

Because the Shulamite bride had previously pondered the character of her man, she could voice her confidence and willingness to follow his lead (v. 4). Trusting God's plan for the family, while meditating on her husband's integrity and leadership, prepares a wife to respond with an attitude of loyal devotion.

PAVE THE WAY

Read Song of Solomon 1:2–16

The Song of Solomon provides insight into God's plan for initiating physical intimacy, as the newlywed couple exchanges sincere compliments. The conversation begins hours before the couple enters the bedroom (v. 16), and covers the span of time during the wedding feast. The bride expresses her desire for the groom (vv. 2–4), but implies insecurity concerning her looks (vv. 5–6) and her ability to adjust to the new lifestyle (vv. 7–8). The groom affirms his admiration for her by comparing her to the strong and beautiful, but rare horses used to pull Pharaoh's chariots (v. 9). No one in the kingdom owns exquisite, Egyptian horses except Solomon. These horses are his prized possessions. Through the comparison, he emphasizes he is proud to claim his wife and her rare qualities as his very own.

The groom continues to admire the bride's natural beauty and express approval of her stunning attire. He reassures her with promises of expensive gifts (vv. 10–12). The once insecure bride confidently indicates her desire to please by offering alluring descriptions of her fragrance floating across the table to her husband (v. 13). She compares her new husband to the bundle of spices she wears around her neck at night, the spices responsible for the pleasing aromas he is experiencing. The comparison implies that he brings out the best in her, arousing a pleasant disposition that becomes apparent to those around her. She describes him as a refreshing cluster of flowers in the midst of the desert (v. 14).

The compliments continue to intensify and become more intimate as the couple moves into the bridal chamber (vv. 15–16, 2:1–6). Dr. Ed Wheat describes a wife's perspective, "As long as she feels encircled and surrounded by his love, she can give herself completely to him."[5] Exchanging sincere, loving compliments paves the way for intimacy.

THE MOST IMPORTANT ROOM

Read Song of Solomon 1:5–17

What a dramatic change unfolds when King Solomon ushers his new bride from her familiar surroundings in the country to his elegant palace in the city. When the bride refers to the tents of Kedar, vineyards and flocks with shepherds, she illustrates her rural perspective and hints at twinges of homesickness (vv. 5–7).

Solomon proves his sensitivity to her insecurities as the couple exchange compliments during the wedding feast (vv. 8–16). His thoughtfulness in attempting to ease her homesickness is apparent when the new bride approves the bridal chamber. Solomon has constructed their bedroom of cedar and fir, materials chosen to remind his bride of her homeland. Traditionally, Jewish husbands would spend the year prior to their wedding day preparing a bridal chamber that expressed a commitment to delight in and provide for their new wife. Ancient Easterners covered the walls of the bedroom with silk and fine linens. They burned incense and dusted the sheets with scented powder and spices. The bedroom was a haven, a refuge that expressed their unique oneness.

During the hectic years of raising toddlers, our bedroom unintentionally depreciated to serving as a hiding place for unfolded laundry and stacks of paperwork. My goal was to keep the living room presentable for company. When extra funds allowed, we accessorized the area that would be noticed by visitors. Then one day, Sam explained that our relationship was more important than impressing guests. He urged me to purchase bedroom paint and decor that were inviting to me personally. I bought candles and romantic oil lamps. I found a new place to stash unfinished work. Our bedroom "graduated," and became the most important room in our home.

THE LITTLE FOXES

Read Song of Solomon 2:10–15

Solomon and his Shulamite bride-to-be are strolling through the spring countryside on a romantic walk. He encourages her to open up and talk (v. 4). The bride-to-be, wanting to be transparent, suggests they catch the little foxes that spoil the tender grapes on the vine. The tender grapes refer to the delicate fruit of their budding relationship. She had worked in the vineyards when she was growing up, and knew that although little foxes might seem insignificant, they could steal into the vineyard, dig holes, loosen dirt around the roots, and hinder healthy growth. She was aware of vine keepers' families diligently watching for the little creatures. They would even sleep outside to protect the vines.

When a friend of mine planted her first garden, she determined it would be a beautiful sight of weed-free perfection. She was careful to daily hoe around each bean plant. Not one weed grew, but not one bean plant prospered because the roots were continually nudged. The Shulamite wife knows that little foxes, like varied opinions or backgrounds, are potential, annoying sources of disturbance that can irritate a marriage. Today's verses emphasize the wisdom of discussing differences of perspective in a non-confrontational environment, before the pressure and urgency of a conflict demands it. The couple described in Song of Solomon strolling through the countryside enjoys a perfect, relaxing setting to promote transparency and deepen their level of communication. A husband and wife are more rational and open to understanding differences before the heat of conflict sets in. Are there potential foxes in your relationship that you should "catch" and discuss?

SAINT VALENTINE

Read 1 Corinthians 13:1–13

*P*aul reminded the ambitious, success-oriented Corinthians that life is pointless without God's love. Without love, a person eventually loses incentive to communicate (v. 1). Without love, vast knowledge is meaningless (v. 2). Sacrifice or achievements seem empty unless they are motivated by love (v. 3). Out of love for their families, husbands daily climb out of bed to earn wages. Because of love for their families, wives continually prepare meals that quickly disappear. Love has always generated incentive for living and performing.

Emperor Claudius II of Rome forced his country to wage many bloody and unpopular campaigns. In AD 269, when he was having a difficult time convincing soldiers to join the military, he assumed the men did not want to leave their wives and families, so he canceled all engagements and marriages. St. Valentine was a priest who determined to live according to God's principles, no matter what Claudius decreed. St. Valentine aided Christian martyrs and secretly married couples. As a result, Claudius had St. Valentine imprisoned. He was condemned to be beaten to death with clubs and have his head cut off. The young people of the town wanted the priest to know they believed in love, so they threw flowers and notes up to his jail window. The daughter of the prison guard would visit the beloved priest in his cell. She lifted his spirits as they sat and talked for hours at a time. She agreed with St. Valentine that sacrificing your body in a war for your country was in vain without love. On February 14, the day St. Valentine was martyred, he left the jailer's daughter a farewell note thanking her for her friendship and loyalty. He signed it, "Love from your Valentine." At the end of the fifth century, Pope Gelasius set aside February 14 to honor St. Valentine as the patron saint of lovers. Thus, the custom of sending poems, flowers, or simple gifts began.

Thank God that He has granted you a love for your valentine that generates the incentive for a more fulfilling life.

MORE THAN LEFTOVERS

Read 1 Peter 3:1 and Ephesians 5:25–33

The Greek word for submission (subjection) is "hypotasso," meaning to arrange under a leader. It implies cooperation characterized by voluntary allegiance or loyalty, flowing from the helper to the leader. The helper adapts to and supports the purpose of the leader. This devotion also includes an attachment that elicits compelling motives to serve.

Peter reminds wives to submit to their "own" husbands. According to God's plan, a woman's loyalty, devotion, and helpfulness to her husband and his purposes rank above her commitment to a job, boss, school, church, children, or anything else. Given the myriad of responsibilities that family, outside jobs, or activities demand, a wife can unintentionally find her energy and creativity drained, leaving nothing but leftovers for her husband. Being devoted implies that before a wife attends to other needs, she first nourishes and cares for her husband. This dedication extends beyond routine chores, to lifting his spirits and conveying that he is special to her.

I read about a wife who, on the way to the grocery store, stopped by her husband's car and filled the front seat with balloons. Instead of being fatigued by the drudgery of the shopping chore, she was energized as she let her husband know he was special to her. Her gesture was not "leftovers," but rather a unique expression that singled out her "own" husband as being specifically significant in her life. She was celebrating their relationship. Oh, that God would fill my mind with creative, loving ways to reach out to my spouse!

AS IN CIVIL GOVERNMENT

Read 1 Peter 2:13–16 and 3:1

Because of the tendency to view life from our own perspective and because of the desire to control any given situation, submission presents difficulties. The principle of submission requires a wife to voluntarily make herself vulnerable to the mistakes of another person, her husband. God indicates that He understands this challenge by using the word "likewise" in 1 Peter 3:1. He directs us to consider the previous examples of submission noted in chapter 2.

The first occurs in 1 Peter 2:13–15, where Peter urges all Christians to submit to civil government. God ordains government for the protection and welfare of the people. Citizens are to obey the law of the land so order will be maintained. Verse 15 explains that such cooperation will silence ignorant charges and ill-informed criticisms asserted by the foolish public. Whenever individuals honor and convey respect to government, whether by obeying traffic laws, exercising the right to vote, or honestly paying taxes, order prevails.

Some wives resist submission claiming that it implies they are less capable or not as intelligent, but the illustration of civil government eliminates that argument because it applies to all citizens. When a brain surgeon or a pastor or a high school student exceeds the speed limit, each one submits to the law enforcement officer who issues the tickets. Citizens submit to the law out of respect.

The civil government example in 1 Peter 2 also illustrates how God's design of submission promotes rather that quenches freedom. Verse 16 challenges citizens to enjoy their freedom and employ it to serve God. In a similar manner, "likewise," a wife's submission to her husband is offered in obedience to God. Just as submission to government promotes order in the land, submission to husbands encourages harmony in the home. Voluntary allegiance and loyalty exhibited toward a husband does not indicate inferiority, but rather a devoted willingness to cooperate. In God's design, wives are free to exercise creativity and productivity as they submit to their husbands, ultimately serving Him in all they do.

ON THE JOB, IN THE HOME

Read 1 Peter 2:18–20 and 3:1

The "likewise" in 1 Peter 3:1 refers to previous Scriptures that clarify the issue of submission. Servants are to respectfully submit to their masters (v. 18). This example compares today with a worker cooperating with a supervisor. Good employees strive to efficiently fulfill the requests of supervision. When a dentist requests the scraping instrument, the dental assistant does not override the decision and pass a brush. A filing clerk may suggest a new filing system, but continues to follow current office policy until management approves the new process. Likewise, a wife strives to please her husband and adapt to a home environment that meets his particular needs and desires. Just as a wise supervisor values helpful suggestions from employees, a wise, secure husband enjoys and encourages the creativity and wisdom of his wife.

When Peter instructs servants to submit to their masters, he specifically includes not only masters worthy of honor, but also those who are unreasonable. To exercise patience when a supervisor demonstrates just judgment is expected and logical, but God commends and approves an employee who responds patiently when a supervisor acts harshly. Verse 19 explains that the Christian employee responds out of respect for God. At times, wives must respond to the character of God rather than to the unfairness of a tired or grouchy husband. God commends this type of godly patience in wives.

Businesses thrive when employees feel valued and when they believe in the mission of the organization. When supervisors communicate encouragement and gratitude, production increases. When employees share in the profits, efficiency rises. Homes operate on the same principles. Expressions of respect and thanks from a husband encourage voluntary allegiance and loyalty from a wife. Submission becomes a desire rather than a duty.

AS CHRIST

Read 1 Peter 2:21–23, 3:1, Philippians 2:6–8, and Romans 8:28

"Likewise" in 1 Peter 3:1 refers to previous Scriptures that clarify the issue of submission. Jesus Christ is our ultimate example (v. 21). Christ resided in heaven where He was recognized and worshipped as King of Kings. Although equal in essence to God the Father, He submitted to Him—without feeling cheated or robbed—setting aside His identity and reputation to assume the form of a human (Phil. 2:6–8).

1 Peter 2:22–23 describes Christ's submitted life as sinless, with no deceit. He is accused and insulted, but does not accuse or insult in return. He suffers unfairly, but does not threaten. A wife following the example of Christ can view submission as God's plan without feeling cheated or robbed of dignity, significance, or purpose. Her submission does not imply inferiority or superiority, but rather, trust in God.

A wife will probably, at some time, face accusations and insults from her loved one that stir up defensiveness. Being misunderstood and taken for granted can ignite the mind with silent or spoken threats. For example, a family tends to overlook the many details a wife and mother attends to daily. Yet they may critically take notice when one of the tiniest details fails to meet their expectations. In the midst of the conflict, a woman may want to consider the threat of a boycott. Conversely, Christ—the wife's example in submission—does not threaten when He suffers. 1 Peter 2:23 reveals the secret of Jesus' response in unjust situations. He commits Himself to Him who judges righteously. A wife is to do the same. Rather than react to the situation or accusation, she is to shift her attention to the character of God and respond to Him. She can trust God to work all things together for good as she loves Him and aligns herself with His purposes (Rom. 8:28).

LIMITS TO SUBMISSION

Read Colossians 3:18 and Acts 5:26–29

Should a wife always, unquestionably, submit to her husband, no matter what he asks of her? Colossians 3:18 explains that a wife submits to her husband as is fitting in the Lord, meaning as long as his requests do not conflict with Scripture. The 1 Peter 3:1 instruction for wives to submit to husbands refers back to 1 Peter 2:13–15, comparing a wife's submission to a believer's submission to civil government. Just as Christian citizens submit to civil government, a wife submits to her husband. The challenge of submitting to ungodly civil government is addressed in Acts 5. The captain and officers strictly forbid Peter and the other disciples to teach in the name of Jesus, when God had clearly instructed them to preach and teach. Peter responds by explaining their obligation to obey God rather than men. Likewise, when a husband requests that a wife do something contrary to Scripture, the wife should respectfully explain that her desire to please her husband is limited by the Word of God.

When the Babylonian government decreed that everyone worship the golden image, Meshach, Shadrach, and Abednego refused to comply with the law of the land. They explained that God forbid them to worship an image (Dan. 3:6–30). When the king decreed that all citizens must pray only to him, Daniel respectfully explained that he could not comply with the request because it violated the commands of God (Dan. 6:3–22). When Pharaoh commanded the midwives to murder all Jewish baby boys, the midwives did not comply because murder violates God's commands (Exod. 1:15–17). In each of these challenges, God honored believers who feared Him more than they feared men. When a husband asks his wife to lie, cheat, steal, practice fornication, get an abortion, or perform any other act contrary to Scripture, she should respectfully and lovingly explain her perspective, and then obey God.

DIVINE HIERARCHY

Read Isaiah 14:12–15, 1 Corinthians 11:3, and Ephesians 5:22

Have you ever heard young children tell their brother or sister, "You're not my boss?" They are echoing the struggle that has existed since the beginning of time—a struggle over authority. It started when Satan rebelled against God's authority by declaring he would become like God (Isa. 14:14). The serpent whispers to Eve the hellish words that question God's authority (Gen. 3:1). Man then rebels and has ever since questioned both God's authority and any other that rules over him (Gen. 3:6–7). Man's depraved nature desires autonomy.

God reiterates the divine hierarchy He originally set up in the Garden of Eden by stating that He is the head of Christ; Christ is the head of man; man is the head of woman (1 Cor. 11:3). Woman's natural reaction is to question God's design that man be her head. Why does he get to be in charge? Is it because man is more intelligent? Or does he possess more wisdom? The answer is a resounding "no." It has nothing to do with inferiority or superiority, but is simply God's divine choice for the family.

In today's politically correct society, adhering to His structure for family roles is no longer acceptable. Most people would agree, however, that any successful team needs a coach. The coach is not necessarily better than his players, but is designated as the person in charge, for the good of the entire team. The harmony of a great marriage starts with both spouses obediently accepting their God-designed roles. The husband exercises servant leadership and the wife completes her husband by empowering him with her wisdom and intuition. Neither spouse is inferior or superior, but both work together according to God's plan to build a family for His glory.

FOR EDIFICATION

Read 2 Corinthians 10:8 and 1 Corinthians 8:1

The authority God assigns to us over someone else is not to be used for our own benefit, but for the good of the one under it. For example, Paul states that his apostolic authority was given to him for the edification, not for the destruction, of the people he was leading (v. 8). To edify someone is to build them up (1 Cor. 8:1). It is an architectural term that implies a constructive design of integrity and stability.

Direction that a husband gives should benefit his wife and family. For example, there have been times when I insisted that my wife go to the doctor or stop what she is doing and rest. She may have preferred to ignore her symptoms or continue to serve others, but I have the responsibility to strengthen her by protecting her from physical harm.

Similarly, a husband's purchases should not be centered solely on his personal pleasures but should include a desire to lovingly provide for his wife. He may have a job opportunity that would advance his career, but as the spiritual leader, he must factor in the impact this change would have on the amount of time he would be able to devote to prayer and worship with his family.

A husband can also build his wife up through his words, actions, and responses. Encouraging comments, using terms and tones of endearment, and sharing the workload around the house will help edify your wife. Rather than accentuating her faults, look for all the good she does. For the next twenty four hours, make a list of her admirable traits and deeds. Then take time to share the list, and let her know how much you love and appreciate her. Make it a habit to praise your wife in front of your children and friends. These gestures of honor and respect will fortify her emotionally.

God-given authority carries the huge responsibility of building and stabilizing the spiritual, physical, emotional, and financial well being of those under that authority.

SWIFT TO HEAR

Read James 1:19 and Proverbs 15:1

Have you ever been around someone who talks so much that you can't get a word in? This type of personality lends itself to speak much and listen little. All of us desire to express our thoughts and opinions in order to make them known, but we must do so only after we have been swift to hear (v.19). This principle particularly applies when disputes and differences surface. We must be careful to listen.

When someone speaks sharply or accuses us falsely, we tend to react by lashing out quickly. As children of God, we are to be quick to hear what His Word says and obey it. We can trust God to work out His will through us only when we are patient and long suffering. As a husband or wife, we must resist the temptation to react quickly but instead, take time to listen to our spouse's side of the issue. Otherwise, we can easily speak words we regret and that cannot be taken back. Rather than concentrating on defending ourselves, our goal should be to get to the truth of the issue.

Notice the progression in James 1:19. If we are swift to hear what the other has to say, slow to respond because we are evaluating it by God's truth, then we will be slow to get angry. When we follow this progression, we will offer a soft answer, turning away wrath (Prov. 15:1). Always be willing to listen to what your spouse has to say and carefully weigh the words with a heart inclined to God. Be slow to respond and slow to wrath. Start practicing this principle today and experience the peace that results.

HARMONY

Read Genesis 2:25 and 3:21

"Turn to page 256 in your hymnal and sing with us, Victory in Jesus." As soon as the words roll out of the song leader's mouth, my four boys turn and stare at me. I instantly know what they are thinking, "Dad, you're not going to sing, are you?" It is not unusual for me to hear the words, "It's a good thing you can preach because you sure can't sing!" Someone recently told me my singing was like being in jail, behind several bars and searching for the key. When you are out of harmony, you are not only out of tune yourself, but your voice hinders everyone else from singing in harmony.

When God summarizes the first marriage by stating that the man and woman were naked and not ashamed, He is concluding that the relationship was in complete harmony! As He is allowed to orchestrate a marriage, man and woman live in tune with each other physically, emotionally, and spiritually. As a result, there is no guilt, fear, or shame. How wonderful to be so in tune with each other that you can reveal your inmost desires and thoughts without fear of rejection.

When sin entered the picture, Adam and Eve started conducting their own orchestra. Shame, guilt, and fear marred the relationship and their harmonious love song became discordant. God desires that the lost harmony in marriage be restored. He lovingly pictures the solution to the problem in Genesis 3:21 when He clothes Adam and Eve with coats of animal skin. This act of grace portrays mankind's reconciliation to God through the shed blood of Jesus Christ. For harmony to be restored in your marriage, you must surrender to Jesus as master conductor, allowing His divine wisdom to prevail in every area of your life. Is your marriage out of harmony? If so, as a couple surrender your lives and marriage totally to Him today.

THE GUY THAT RATES HIGH

Read Song of Solomon 1:3

I am waiting in a lengthy line at the airport for the skycap to check our luggage. A vehicle pulls to the curb. A man hops out and unloads a suitcase for the young lady who is with him. He reminds her to call as soon as she reaches her destination. They say goodbye and declare how much they will miss each other. The young woman steps into line behind me. We slowly inch our way forward, observing the people around us. The line behind us continues to grow. After several long minutes, the car pulls back to the curb. With concern, the young lady calls out, "What is it? Is something wrong?" The man flashes a wide grin and calls out, "No, I just wanted to say goodbye one more time." By now, there are four other women in our line. They all express admiration, "Wow! How sweet! You better hang on to him! He's a keeper! It's obvious how he feels!" Each one is impressed because the man's thoughtfulness is evident and unusual.

God explains in verse 3 that all the virgins love Solomon because they recognize the quality of his character. A husband's thoughtfulness is the character trait that not only quickly wins the affection and adoration of all the ladies, but causes a wife to recognize her husband as a highly rated prize.

RESPONDING TO AN ANGRY MAN

Read 1 Samuel 25:14–35 and Proverbs 15:1

or months, David's men have protected Nabal and his property. When David reasonably asks for provisions from Nabal's abundance, Nabal insults and belittles him (vv. 14–15). David is tired, hungry, and mad. He prepares for revenge (v. 22). Alarmed at the danger, Nabal's servants turn to Abigail, realizing she is a woman of wisdom and understanding. Rather than panic, Abigail responds quickly and reverently to David's needs. She proves her sincerity with an act of kindness as she generously offers food to his men (v. 18). She shows utmost respect for David's position and integrity (vv. 23–24). She is willing to take the blame and humbly asks permission to plead her case. As Abigail approaches David, she considers the hurt of Nabal's insults and self-centeredness so she can relate to David's perspective. She speaks honestly about the injustice (v. 25). She again honors David when she points out how she has seen the Lord work in his life (v. 26). Abigail asks forgiveness for the actions of her husband, and then pronounces a blessing upon David. Her words emphasize the insignificance of this incident as compared with the plans God has for David's life. Her request is so humble, sincere, and honoring that David responds with gratitude. He recognizes that her sound advice has protected him from a tragic mistake (v. 35).

Abigail not only responds with empathy for David's hurt, but with a godly understanding that reaches beyond it, encompassing the whole truth of the matter. Likewise, when we seek to comprehend the pain felt by an angry spouse or loved one, when we are respectful and honor them, when we humbly proclaim God's favor and blessings, we are striving to turn wrath away with a soft answer (Prov. 15:1). How are you responding to the angry person in your life? Ask God to give you insight to respond according to His wisdom.

LOVE LESSON: RIGHT THINKING

Read Titus 2:3–4

We occasionally hear the complaint that a couple is not "in love" anymore. They claim to be committed to one another, but no longer have feelings for each other. Have you ever considered how couples in the Bible could flourish in arranged marriages? For example, Isaac and Rebekah had never even met before their wedding. They certainly had not developed feelings for each other. If God could work in the lives of two total strangers to grow a bond of adoring affection, He can rejuvenate love in the lives of a married couple.

The foundation for the relationship is covenant (agape) love—committing to do what is best for my spouse, no matter what my spouse does for me. It is a decision of the will, modeled after and based upon the love Christ shows to His bride.

The love referred to in Titus 2:4 is not agape love, but a specific and intense type of phileo love between husband and wife. It is emotional in nature, and cannot be commanded or willed into existence. According to Titus, older women are to teach or train young wives to love in this way. If women are instructed to teach this love, it follows that it can be learned. The feelings of love can be rekindled.

One aspect of phileo love is based on qualities that one finds admirable, attractive, and appealing in another person. It is developed through right thinking. When we are alert to watch for acts of kindness and positive characteristics displayed by our mate, each one becomes a treasure. Reflecting on these benefits increases the perceived value of our spouse. This right thinking is a habit that must be developed. When we then convey appreciation for an action, or admiration for an inner quality, it generates warm feelings in the recipient. Lesson 1 in rekindling feelings of love is this: be alert to and thankful for admirable character traits in your spouse.

LOVE LESSON: COMRADESHIP

Read Titus 2:3–4 and Genesis 2:8, 3:8

*T*itus 2 instructs older women to teach younger women to love their husbands. The phileo love noted in Titus 2:4 is an emotional family love that can be taught and learned. Spouses who view their marriages as boring or emotionless can learn to rekindle loving feelings. Another aspect of phileo love is friendship that involves enjoying one another's company. It is a fondness that requires pleasurable interaction. Ed Wheat says the interaction is achieved in three ways: by being together in the room (comradeship), by breaking bread together (companionship), and by talking together (communication).[6] The common prefix and prevailing thought in each of these elements is "com," meaning together.

Comradeship develops when couples share activities like hobbies, projects, or ministry. In high school, I participated on a drama team that presented a musical play. Our team members had many and varied talents, personalities, and responsibilities, but everyone had a common goal—to present a quality production. It required long, hard hours, but we cooperated and had fun. We memorized lines together, brainstormed for ideas for props, and even splashed color on anyone who got in the way while painting backdrops. After the final production, we all hugged and sincerely expressed the fulfillment we individually experienced as a result of our joint activity. We had become forever friends.

From the beginning of time, God designed man and woman to bond by experiencing life together. Adam was lonely because he did not have a human friend with whom to enjoy the awesomeness of creation. God placed him and Eve in the garden so they could be in the same "room" to share activities. Eden means "enclosed place of pleasure." Scripture implies that they daily took walks and explored the garden together (Gen 3:8).

Learn to do things together. What activities do you enjoy as a couple? What new projects could you add to your life together? What time robber can you cut from your schedule to free yourselves for more interaction?

LOVE LESSON: COMPANIONSHIP AND COMMUNICATION

Read Titus 2:3–5

*I*n Titus 2, older women trained younger women to love their husbands by teaching them how to incorporate phileo love into family life. A major aspect of phileo is companionship, encouraging connection by sharing meals. The word "companion" actually means to break bread together. In our culture, one of a newlywed couple's first traditions is to feed each other a piece of wedding cake. This pictures a lifetime of sharing meals. Husbands and wives are meant to eat together.

As the older women trained the younger women to manage a household, preparing meals would have been a major lesson (v. 5). Proverbs 31 commends women who prepare meals for their families (Prov. 31:14–15). Beyond nutritional benefits, enjoying food together relaxes tension and promotes communication. When our family goes out to eat, we love ordering different entrees so we can share bites from each other's plates. We have fun. We find pleasure in seeing one another enjoy food. Whether we dine at home or out, the conversation is lively. Meal time is our opportunity to talk about the day and discuss progress or achievements. Eating together encourages communication, the third element of phileo love.

Numerous seminars have been taught and scores of books written on communication techniques, but the aspect of interaction that incites fondness is not dependent on methods. Communication that produces affection requires sharing from your heart, beneath the surface level. Sharing dreams, aspirations, and hopes binds the hearts of a couple. Admitting struggles and fears opens the door for heartfelt communication. This may seem risky, since our hearts are vulnerable and exposed, but it is worth the potential relationship connection that may be nurtured.

When is the last time you shared a romantic meal together? Do you have a dream or goal that needs encouragement? Are you facing struggles that could be faced with more fortitude if you had a comforting hug? Talk them over with your spouse.

THE BODY AND THE HEAD

Read Ephesians 5:22–24

Scripture repeatedly uses the words "head" and "body" to describe roles in marriage—husband as the head and wife as the body. In an extensive study of the original New Testament word for "head" conducted by Dr. Wayne Grudem, he discovered the dominant meaning of the word is to have "authority over" or to lead.[7] Secular and biblical feminists reject the idea that there should be any chain of command in marriage. Biblical feminists would have us believe husband and wife roles are negated since the Bible states there is no difference between male or female—we are all one in Christ (Gal. 3:28). Of course, this speaks of our position in Christ, not our God ordained roles in the family.

God uses the analogy of head and body since it metaphorically pictures the roles of husband and wife. If my body begins to act independently of my head, I am said to be suffering from some sort of convulsions. If my head directs my body to act and it does not respond, there is paralysis taking place. If a wife acts independent of her husband, she will cause convulsive marital chaos. If she does not respond to her husband's leadership, the marriage will be in a state of paralysis. Also, the head or husband must take initiative or the body cannot respond. The responsibility for initiative and leadership is ultimately the husband's, but the related actions must always be coordinated. There is no sense of inferiority suggested by this design for marriage. The wife is not less than her husband; she is different.[8]

We are fearfully and wonderfully made by the master designer to carry out the roles He has ordained for husband and wife. To rebel against His plan is to rebel against God.

HOLD HER

Read Song of Solomon 3:1–5

*S*everal years ago, some close friends of ours filed for divorce. When we explained the situation to our young boys, they were confused: "We don't understand. They were always happy whenever we were with them." I asked our sons what they would do if they were married and their wives got upset with them, or even treated them unkindly. Without hesitation, my youngest and normally quiet son Philip confidently declared, "I would hold her." What a profound response!

When I am stressed or worried, an understanding hug immediately comforts my heart. How could a four-year-old know the security a woman senses when her husband's strong arms gently wrap around her? I asked Philip why he would "hold her." He explained that is what Dad always says in the ceremony concluding our marriage conference weekends. As in a wedding, Sam leads couples to repeat their marriage vows: "To have and to hold from this day forward." Unlike many married couples, our son took those words literally.

Song of Solomon chapter three illustrates the security and comfort of holding a loved one. During their engagement period, the Shulamite bride dreams Solomon is gone (v. 1). Desiring to be re-united, she looks all over the city to locate him (v. 3). When she finds him, she holds him and does not let go (v. 4). Through this Scripture, God is emphasizing the security and comfort a wife receives from being held by her husband. Wrap your arms around your bride in a gentle embrace, and whisper how much you love her.

RED-ALERT WARNING

Read 1 John 1:8–9, Galatians 6:1–2, and James 5:16

I read about a pastor who not only sought God, but was thriving in his relationship with Him. As a result, he inspired and enlightened his congregation from the overflow of the fresh fellowship he experienced daily. He adored his wife and family. As his church grew, routine disciplines developed that required attention for time-consuming details. Eventually, the urgency to hear from God was tragically replaced with structure and methods. The once passionate pastor gradually grew bored and dissatisfied, until he was distracted by a very attractive woman who added excitement to his life. Over the next three years, he became more involved with her and less invested in his ministry and family. He experienced guilt and considered going to deacons or another pastor for help, but determined that by following a plan he had used in counseling, he could conquer this challenge himself. Because his efforts were fueled by pride and personal ability rather than confession, repentance, and dependence upon Jesus Christ, the lure of sin conquered him. In time, he deserted his family and ministry.

All Christian men and women are susceptible to sin. Whenever there is a tendency to hide the slightest detail of our life from our spouse or other Christians, we, like the pastor, are not only deceiving loved ones, but we are deceiving ourselves (v. 8). According to God's Word, confession—admitting the truth without excuses or justification—is the first step (v. 9). Confession is required for victory. James urges Christians to not only confess to Jesus, but to other believers who will lovingly lead in restoring the fallen individual to Christ (James 5:16, Gal. 6:1–2). We must recognize the decision to handle sin on our own as a red alert warning that we are choosing a path of pride instead of humbly obeying God. We must be quick to admit seemingly "insignificant" wrongs before they are nurtured into destructive choices we would never have thought possible.

TAKE A WALK

Read Genesis 3:8 and Song of Solomon 2:10–16

*G*od the Creator prepares a fascinating world and beautiful garden so Adam and Eve can delight in Him through the pleasure of His creation. As they contemplate the blessings and wonders, they marvel at His creativity, power, and love. He walks with them as they enjoy His fellowship and creation.

In Song of Solomon 2:10–13, Solomon invites his fiancée to take a walk with him so they can enjoy both nature and time together. God uses Solomon to show us the intimacy that develops when we walk together and take time to notice the beauty of the flowers, the voices of the animals, and the fragrance of the fruit. Solomon strengthens their bond by setting aside distractions to concentrate on his bride-to-be (v. 14). The casual walk allows the couple to discuss potential personal problems in a non-confrontational environment (v. 15). Because Solomon takes time to focus on his fiancée as he enjoys the surrounding beauty, she can confidently declare her security in the relationship (v. 16).

Sam and I walk together to the top of the bluff near our home as often as our schedule allows. We always pause to gaze at the amazing view that pronounces the power and wonder of our Creator. We take time to pray for each other, for our family, and for our ministry. I cherish these walks because my confidence grows as I witness Sam's communication with and dependence on the Lord. He confirms his love for me with his undivided attention. Our walks, like Adam and Eve's or Solomon and his Shulamite bride's, strengthen our bond with God and each other.

WORTH THE COST

Read Proverbs 31:10, Genesis 29:20, 31:6–9, 16, and Ephesians 5:25–28

Wives are expensive! Solomon says the price of a virtuous wife is far above rubies (v. 10). Jacob sees such great value in Rachel that he is not resentful or weary in his responsibilities as a future husband (Gen. 29:20). He feels she is worth the high cost of seven additional years of labor. No complaints from Jacob. He focuses on the prize of her virtues and their future together rather than the turmoil of his labor. Loving a wife unselfishly, as God instructs in Ephesians chapter five, yields joyful anticipation instead of weariness in well doing.

Husbands are expected to provide for the family (Gen. 2:15, 1 Tim 5:8). When job requirements are taxing or unfair, a man can get weary and depressed. This can negatively impact the family—the very ones for whom the husband is toiling. Jacob worked for a cheater who repeatedly rewrote the job description and lowered his wages, but Jacob did not give up (Gen. 31:6–9). He fulfilled his responsibilities in order to provide for his family (Gen. 31:16). If your work seems to be a never ending drag, if you are weary in fulfilling your role as a husband, follow the example God provides in Jacob. Focus on your prize, on the qualities that first attracted you to your wife. Concentrate on her strengths. Determine ways to make her happy, to help her feel loved and cherished. Plan activities, vacations, and future goals together and joyfully anticipate their fulfillment. Time will fly by for you, just as it did for Jacob.

THE GREAT CANCER

Read Malachi 2:11–16

The dictionary defines cancer as, "A malignant tumor of potentially unlimited growth that expands locally by invasion and systemically by metastasis."[9] In simple terms, it is a tumor that arises within the body and destructively spreads until death occurs. Divorce in America has become a terrible spiritual cancer. Its tentacles extend and touch everyone in society! Whether or not you have personally experienced divorce, you most likely know someone who has. The divorce rate, which was only 3 percent in 1870, now hovers around 50 percent. Divorced adults are the most rapidly growing marriage category in America. The proportion of adults currently divorced more than tripled from 1970 to 1996, from 3 percent of the adult population to 10 percent.[10] A distraught couple can go on the internet and easily facilitate a divorce for less than 300 dollars.

A major reason the divorce rate hasn't increased even more is because many couples are now choosing cohabitation over marriage. Today in America, fewer than 25 percent of families are traditional (father and mother living with their children). Nearly half of American children will sleep tonight in homes without a father. No wonder God states that He hates divorce (v. 16). Its effects are devastating to the family unit and society.

Malachi 2:16 does not mean God hates people who are divorced, but rather that divorce distorts and destroys His intended family structure. God even has allowances for divorce in Scripture, but He never commands or commends it. If you have been through a divorce and plan to re-marry, God wants you to make sure you have taken care of any baggage from your previous marriage and insure that the new union is dedicated to His glory. Spouses must maintain tender hearts that are quick to repent of sinful actions and attitudes to avoid the cancer of divorce. Make a fresh commitment that divorce will never be an option in your marriage.

WHAT IS MARRIAGE?

Read Malachi 2:11– 16

Never has there been so much confusion over defining marriage. Is marriage a relationship between a man and woman? Should marriage also include two people of the same sex? Why all the concern? Understanding the answer is foundational to maintaining the integrity of the family unit and the stability of society.

The original 1828 Webster's Dictionary defined marriage as: "A contract both civil and religious, by which the parties engage to live in mutual affection and fidelity, till death shall separate them. Marriage was instituted by God Himself for the purpose of preventing the promiscuous intercourse of the sexes, for promoting domestic felicity, and for securing the maintenance and education of children."[11] In a recent Collegiate Webster's Dictionary, marriage has been redefined as: "(1) The state of being united to a person of the opposite sex as husband or wife in a consensual and contractual relationship recognized by law (2) The state of being united to a person of the same sex in a relationship like that of a traditional marriage—an intimate or close union."[12] What a major definition change in fewer than 200 years! Turning to Scripture, we must ask how God defines marriage.

In Malachi 2, the men of Judah had profaned (made common) the holy institution of God (marriage) by not only taking on additional wives of strange gods, but also by treating the wives of their youth treacherously (vv. 11, 14). God declares He will cut these men off and no longer accept their offerings (vv. 12–13). Being clueless, these men ask God, "Why?" (v. 14). In answering their question, He defines marriage with two significant words, "companion" and "covenant" (v. 14c), indirectly declaring it a "covenant of companionship between a man and a woman."[13] The devotions for the next several days will attempt to give a clear understanding of God's definition of marriage.

GOD IS WITNESS

Read Malachi 2:11–16, Matthew 19:6, and Ephesians 5:32

To convict someone in a court of law normally requires an eye witness to the crime that occurred. The men of Judah ask God why He will not accept their offerings and worship (v. 14a). In answering them, God states He was a "witness" between these men and the wives of their youth—a witness of their faithless behavior (v. 14b). The word "witness" means legal accuser. God reminds these men that He was not only present during the marriage ceremony, but as Jesus states in Matthew 19:6, was actually the one who divinely joined them together in a one-flesh relationship. He was there when they took their vows, and also observed their treacherous behavior.

When living in a society of moral relativism and tolerance, it is vitally important to understand that God's ever-seeing eye is always present. He witnesses all that we do! In marriage, we can easily be deceived into thinking we can sin against our mate without God holding us accountable. These sins could range from the extreme of adultery to that of a harsh word or unkind behavior. Whatever it might be, we must continually realize that God is watching. He is the one who will hold us accountable for every interaction we have with our spouse. God designed Christian marriage to represent the union between Christ and the church (Eph. 5:32). This understanding should constrain us to love our mates unconditionally as Christ has loved us. God is witness!

PHYSICAL COMPANIONS

Read 1 Peter 3:7 and Malachi 2:14

*I*n a previous devotion, marriage was defined from Scripture as a "covenant of companionship between a man and a woman." The word translated as "companion" means spouse, wife, or marriage partner. God is reminding the men of Judah that their need for a companion is only to be met through the wife of their youth.

The most obvious way married couples experience companionship is by physically being with each other. However, even though most couples get married with the intention of "being together," a lack of physical companionship is often what promotes distance, disillusionment, and even divorce.

Husbands are commanded to "dwell with" their wives (v. 7). The word "dwell" means to take up residence or actually live with someone. Living with a spouse requires not only residing in the same home, but also participating in activities such as projects, chores, planning vacations, meals, and sharing dreams and goals. In other words, you should enjoy each other's company. The verse continues by noting that the husband is to live with his wife in an understanding way. A husband is commanded to physically live with and spend time with his wife so he will understand her. It is impossible to truly understand someone with whom you never spend significant time. For example, you cannot have a true understanding of God if you never invest time in Bible study and prayer. You might know about Him, but you will not actually know Him unless you spend time with Him. It is the same with marriage partners.

Busyness, schedules, careers, and children can take a serious toll on couples who do not continually carve out special time for each other. Maintaining physical companionship within marriage will require mutual adjustments. Make a commitment to enhance your physical companionship by allotting and protecting your time with each other.

EMOTIONAL COMPANIONS

Read Genesis 2:18–25

*E*motional companionship originated with the Trinity. God the Father, God the Son, and God the Holy Spirit have always existed in community with love, respect, and admiration emanating from one member of the Godhead to the others. This is the character of God. Because man is made in His image, he is a social creature with a strong longing for emotional companionship. That is why God declares it is not good that man should be alone (v. 18).

The first marriage exhibited God's intent for emotional companionship. Adam and Eve lived in paradise where every need in their life was met. They found their soul's delight in God. As long as their security and significance was in Him—as long as the basis for their identity was their relationship with God, they, like the Trinity, overflowed with love, gratitude, and respect. They lived in worship, a state of gratitude for the creation accompanied by wonder of the creator. As a result, they were thankful for each other. They completely trusted God and lived in joyful dependence upon Him. Their relationship with God was the basis of the emotional bond between the two of them. Genesis describes their relationship as "naked" and without shame (v. 25).

Although the term "naked" obviously establishes that the couple was not covered physically with clothes, it also implies that they were not covered emotionally with pretense. To be naked emotionally suggests an atmosphere of transparency in which the couple was fully known by each other, yet they were still completely loved and accepted. Since there was no shame, no humiliation, no defensiveness, no competition, no urgency to prove oneself, no fear of rejection, they lived in an atmosphere of gratitude, devotion, and liberty where they could love unconditionally.

The Genesis account demonstrates the divine plan for every marital relationship—that a husband and wife be completely transparent or emotionally naked with one another. Each spouse should have the liberty to share dreams without fear of ridicule and to admit struggles without fear of condemnation or rejection.

SPIRITUAL COMPANIONS: SUBMISSIVE LOVE

Read Ephesians 5:22–25 and Genesis 2:15, 18

*L*ike the three members of the Trinity, a husband and wife are equal in essence, but different in function. The husband leads by providing and protecting in all areas of life, while the wife completes him by empowering and enabling him to fulfill God's purposes for their lives (Gen. 2:15, 18).

Before Paul expounds on specific roles in marriage, he reminds husbands and wives that their companionship is to first orbit around God, then around each other, so they will overflow with His joy, peace, and love as they serve one another (Eph. 5:18–21). Paul continues by explaining that marriage is to be patterned after Christ and His bride, the church. The husband, as protector and provider, is to lovingly lead his bride in the same way Christ lovingly leads His bride. The wife is to picture the bride of Christ as she lovingly, out of devotion, yields to the leadership of her husband, empowering and enabling him to accomplish the will of God (vv. 22–33).

Paul addresses the role of spiritual companion by instructing the wife to submit to her own husband (v. 22). Submission has nothing to do with inferiority or superiority. Submission is voluntary allegiance or loyalty that requires adapting to another's needs. The wife is a nurturer who empowers, enables, and encourages her husband according to his specific needs. In all areas of life, foremost in her mind should be the thought, "How can I help him? How can I serve him?" A wife also exercises spiritual companionship when she humbly, respectfully, and lovingly conveys her perspective related to decisions. To withhold it may deny her husband the wisdom and talents God wishes to add to his life. A wise and considerate husband will welcome his wife's viewpoint and objectively reflect on it.

The wife must focus on her relationship with God, continually worshipping, so she will be energized to be a spiritual companion who will complement her husband.

SPIRITUAL COMPANIONS: COVENANT LOVE

Read Malachi 2:14 and Ephesians 5:22–33

Yesterday we looked at the spiritual companionship of the wife through submissive love. The spiritual companionship of the husband with his wife is designated by the word "head" in Scripture (v. 23). This is an awesome responsibility! Every husband must realize it is not a question of whether he is the head of his wife—Scripture states this as a fact. The question is rather what kind of head he is?

As a spiritual head and companion, the husband's main responsibility is to emulate the love Jesus demonstrates for His bride, the church (v. 25). The verse emphasizes that love is expressed through sacrifice. Sacrificial love says, "I'm willing to die to myself for the good of the one I entered into covenant with." The husband's role is not to dominate, control, or make his wife his servant. The husband's responsibility is to serve and lead her with love. Every decision he makes should be based on what is best for her, no matter the cost to him. Christ literally gave His life for His bride. Most husbands will never have the opportunity to die physically for their wives, although they should be willing to do so. Sometimes, however it is more difficult for a husband to sacrifice his agenda, time, comforts, recreation, and habits than it is to literally die.

As a companion who sacrifices, a husband is considerate of his wife's needs, always alert to pitch in and help with chores around the house or with the children. He is willing to give up activities with the guys in order to free her to do something she wants to do. He sacrifices his time and energy to provide for his wife. He makes time to listen to her. Activities with her take priority over sports, TV, hunting, and other recreation.

SPIRITUAL COMPANIONS: CLEANSING LOVE

Read Ephesians 5:25–26

Paul teaches that the goal of Christ's sacrifice is His bride's holiness (v. 26a). The apostle Paul uses the word "sanctify" to convey how this takes place. To be sanctified means to be set apart for God and for His special use and purposes. When a person becomes a Christian, that person is positioned into a relationship with Christ. He or she now belongs to Christ, is identified with Christ, and is called by His name. "This is a wonderful thing. This is what the Lord Jesus Christ has done with the church. The same occurs when a man finds his affections and his love set apart upon one girl out of thousands. He chooses her for himself, and he selects her from all the others. 'She is to be mine," he says. So he separates her, isolates her, 'sanctifies' her, puts her there quite on her own. He wants her for himself."[14]

Paul uses the word "cleanse" to describe how the bride of Christ will be made holy (v. 26b). This refers to a continuous and continual process of purification. How is this accomplished? Paul says it is done through the repeated "washing of water with the word." He is saying that the Bible, the "Word," is the cleansing agent that purifies us from the power and pollution of sin. Jesus said we are made clean through the words He had spoken (John 15:3). If the husband is to emulate Christ's headship with the church, he must cleanse his wife and sanctify her by washing her regularly and repeatedly in the Word of God, purifying their marriage relationship with Scripture. A husband is to lead his wife spiritually by reading and studying the Bible with her regularly. This requires him to personally dedicate time to read, meditate, and memorize it himself. Husband, are you cleansing your marriage by daily washing your wife in the Word?

GREAT EXPENSE

Read Malachi 2:14c, Ephesians 5:1, 25, and Hebrews 9:22

*G*rasping the meaning of covenant is essential to building a marriage that glorifies God. In our biblical definition, He uses covenant in conjunction with companion to fully describe the relationship between a husband and wife.

Author Clay Trumbull states, "It is a peculiarity of the primitive compact of blood friendship that he who would enter into it must be ready to make a complete surrender of himself, in loving trust, to him with whom he covenants. He must, in fact, so love and trust, as to be willing to merge his separate individuality in the dual personality of which he becomes an integral part. Just as we sign a contract to make it legally binding today, a covenant in Bible days was legalized by the shedding of blood."[15] The church enters into covenant with Jesus Christ through the greatest expense ever paid—His shed blood (Heb. 9:22). Upon entering into covenant with Jesus, we are joined in union with Him.

Similarly, the marriage covenant requires a great expense—the death of self in merging two independent individuals into a new family held together by the love of God through Jesus Christ. Dying to self is a biblical concept that requires sacrificing personal desires and ambitions in order to glorify Christ and serve mankind (Gal. 5:24, Luke 9:23). This means spouses must eliminate a contractual mindset which asserts, "I'll do my part as long as you do your part." This kind of thinking portrays a legalistic rather than a covenant relationship based on God's grace. We must be careful to avoid having an unwritten list of expectations for our mate that determines our acceptance of him or her. We are to unconditionally love each other in the covenant love of God. Our attitude concerning our mate should be, "I'll love and serve you even if you don't love and serve me." This requires the greatest expense—the daily death of self!

GREAT EXPECTATIONS

Read Malachi 2:14 and Romans 8:35–39

Not only does a covenant relationship involve great expense, but also great expectations. Reflect back for a moment on your wedding ceremony. You probably repeated vows similar to these: "For better or worse, for richer or poorer, in sickness or in health, till death do we part." You made a commitment, God being your witness, to live with your mate until separated by death. This is a great expectation in a day in which more marriages end in divorce than those that do not. That's why marriage is not to be entered into lightly; it is sacred and involves a covenant to live together forever.

How can we make this kind of promise to someone and see it through? In Romans 8:35–39, the Apostle Paul rhetorically states that the love of Christ is so strong that nothing can sever it. His love is so powerful that no trials, no enemies, no earthly powers, or nothing in all of creation can separate us from it. This binding, supernatural covenant love is available to every husband and wife who put their trust in Jesus Christ! Just as nothing will separate us from God's love, we can have a marriage that can withstand distress, peril, tribulation, persecution, famine, and all other attacks, if we allow the love of God to be the oil that continually lubricates the relationship.

If you have broken covenant through a divorce, it is essential to make this marriage one that is glorifying to God. Insure that sins are confessed and repented of so you can walk in the light of God's blessing. Every marriage covenant involves a great expectation—till death do we part. Whisper now to your spouse, "I'll always love you, and never ever leave you." Hug and kiss!

MARCH 16

A SOLID FOUNDATION

Read Psalm 127:1 and 1 Corinthians 3:11

*Y*ears ago, we relocated our family into an old farmhouse in Wingate, North Carolina. Moving in on a cool fall day, I went over to the thermostat and turned on the heat. As we continued to unload the truck, we noticed the house was getting no warmer. I could hear the unit running, but there was no heat blowing out of the floor vents into the house.

Investigating the problem, I noticed near the unit outside there was a door leading into the crawl space. After crawling on my knees about ten feet under the house, I was met by two big glaring eyes! Jerking away and hitting my head on the floor joist above, I regained my composure and discovered that friends of the stray cat—which almost put me into cardiac arrest—had torn the ducting loose from the floor vents so they could crawl up and stay warm. Working to make repairs, I noticed the house was sitting on stacks of large rocks situated in strategic locations. Years of wear had caused some of the rocks to fall and move away from the support, leaving the floor sagging in those spots. The slightest shift in the foundation had caused cracks to form in the walls, and the door jambs to relocate. I was reminded that the structural integrity of the house depends on the integrity of its foundation. Similarly, where there is no foundation of faith in God, there is no stability in a marriage. Every home must be founded securely on the solid rock of Jesus Christ in order to maintain stability (Mathew 7:24–25). Jesus Christ is the bedrock of our faith and the foundation of a godly family (1 Cor. 3:11). When distractions and busy lives shift Jesus to the sidelines, cracks and sags develop in our family relationships. Renovate the cracks in the walls, reinforce the sags in the floors, and repair the damaged doors of your relationship by re-centering your marriage on Him.

March 17

Spiritual Weapons

Read Psalm 127:1 and Ephesians 6:10–18

Have you ever anxiously awaited the arrival of your child returning home safely at night? It's getting late, and you go to the window and peek to see if the headlights of his or her car are coming down the street. At this moment of concern, we realize we are not in control; we must depend upon God for the safety of our children. In the self-sufficient society in which we live, many families attempt to fortify their home through their own physical efforts. Many believe that a big bank account, a good security system, or some other tangible aspect will provide protection. God wants us to understand that to protect our homes we must guard them with not only physical—but more importantly—spiritual weapons. Satan is out to destroy our faith and our families. The Psalmist uses the word "except" or "unless" to stress the urgency and need to depend upon God to watch over and keep our families safe from the enemy.

Even though God is our ultimate fortification, He has appropriated spiritual weapons to help us protect our families. They include prayer, the precepts and promises of His Word, and the power of the Holy Spirit. Prayer protects and stabilizes the home. The precepts and promises of God's Word purify the home. And the anointing of the Holy Spirit brings God's sweet presence into the home. Daily pray together for your marriage and family. Daily read, meditate upon, and claim the promises in God's Word. Daily ask God to empower you to walk in the Spirit so that you will not fulfill the lust of the flesh (Gal. 5:16). How are you doing in each of these three areas? Commit to fortify your home with God's spiritual weapons.

FRAMED WITH WORSHIP

Read Psalm 127:2

*R*eflecting back to my childhood, I have precious memories of my mother coming into my bedroom at night, hugging and kissing me, then whispering, "Sweet dreams!" Her loving reassurance set the tone for a good night's sleep. God desires that His children have sweet rest as we abide in His embracing love. Verse two speaks of the person who lacks restful sleep because he invests his energy looking for peace and rest in all the wrong places. His life is consumed with so many cares, worries, and anxieties that he has insomnia. Just like a structural home needs sound framing to stand against the natural forces that come against it, a marriage needs the right structure to prevent the cares of this world from damaging it. Our homes need to be framed with worship.

Adam and Eve had the perfect marriage until they lost their frame of mind. A.W. Tozer aptly states, "The real tragedy in the Garden of Eden was that Adam and Eve lost their purpose. They forgot who they were. They suffered from what I will refer to as spiritual amnesia…God made man in His own image and blew in him the breath of life to live in His presence and worship Him … this is our supreme purpose."[16] Sin interrupted the sweet communion where Adam and Eve could rest. They forgot the purpose for which they were created—worship! Ever since, man has sought to find meaning and purpose in all the wrong places (idols), resulting in a life filled with worry, confusion, and anxiety. Sweet rest in our individual lives and marriages is rooted in worshipping God. Jesus reiterates this truth when He invites all who are loaded down with the weight of this world to come to Him and receive His rest (Matt. 11:28). Frame your marriage and family with worship. Take a few minutes and give God all the glory, honor, and praise. He is worthy.

GODLY FURNITURE

Read 1 John 2:15–17, Hebrews 13:5, and 1 Timothy 6:6–10

We are not to fall in love with and decorate our homes with the ungodly furniture of the world (v. 15). Its furnishings include the desires of the flesh, the desires of the eyes, and taking pride in possessions (v.16). All of the world's aspects are temporal and pass away, whereas God's spiritual realities abide forever (v.17).

There are several pieces of worldly furniture we must replace in order to truly have a spiritually decorated home that pleases God. We must remove the chairs of controversy and add chairs of contentment. Without godly contentment, controversy is inevitable. God warns us that happiness is not found in possessions, power, or position. Rather it is found in a person—Jesus Christ! Timothy says where there is godliness with contentment, there is great gain. Those who pursue the desires of flesh and eyes fall into temptation, ruin, and destruction (1 Tim. 6:6–10).

Next, we must replace the doors of compromise with doors of commitment. We must be careful not to be seduced by the world's standards of moral relativism. How sad it would be if the word "Ichabod" (the glory of God has departed) was inscribed over the doors of our homes because we have compromised His commands. He instructs us not to bring an abomination into our house because it will consume and destroy us (Deut. 7:26).

Finally, we must replace airwaves of confusion with sweet sounds of communication! Make it a priority to take time to interact with each other and your children. Be careful not to let the television, Facebook, or other distractions consume your time. Communication that enhances relationships is more likely to occur through playing games together, taking a walk, or participating in other activities that promote personal connection. Intentionally decorate your home with these pieces of spiritual furniture and see how it is filled with God's love and peace.

GOD'S FAVOR

Read Psalm 127:3–5

*W*alking with my four little boys into the restaurant, people began to stare at me with expressions that insinuated, "You poor soul; you've been cursed." Never in the history of America has parenting become more politically incorrect! According to a 2000 census, the average number of children in families with children was 1.86.[17] There are now more households with dogs (43 million) than children.[18] Unfortunately, many people see children as more of an inconvenience than a blessing.

The word "heritage" in verse three denotes children as a gift from God. He is the giver of life. If God has chosen to bless you with children, they are His favor upon you—a blessing, not a curse! In verses 4–5, God compares children to arrows and states that a man who has his quiver full is happy. The word picture describes a mighty man in battle fighting with a bow and a full quiver. It implies that this man is happy when the quiver is full, since it provides many arrows to shoot at his enemy. The more the better!

Children are like these arrows. Parents must polish them and point them in the direction God intends (Prov. 22:6). Properly training your children and developing their God-given talents demonstrates their value to you, themselves, and others. When observing your children, remember that although they may require polishing and pointing, God has favored you with His blessing. They are precious gifts, worthy of excellent care and diligent attention.

RESOLVING CONTENTIONS

Read 1 Corinthians 1:10–17 and 2:1–5

Sometimes couples come to us for advice and direction because of contentions in their home. They disagree about disciplining the children, finances, household duties, what church to attend, and priorities. Both spouses present logical, convincing points of view, but their perspectives conflict. They can't seem to find a way to agree. Paul faced a similar scenario within the Corinthian church. This group of Christians was also experiencing contentions (v. 11). Various people had different views concerning different teachers, and each was backed by logical arguments. Defending the views had become the focus. Individuals were so intent on proving their arguments that the issue of teachers became more important than the truths they were declaring (vv. 12–13). Paul challenged the contenders to look beyond the logic of words and arguments because the message of Christ and the cross was what really mattered (vv. 17–18). He reminded the believers that he set aside excellence of speech and persuasive arguments to concentrate on the character and truth of Jesus Christ (1 Cor. 2:1–4). His focus on the Lord was so intent that the power of God was demonstrated in his life. God expects believers to concentrate on Jesus rather than on proving their arguments, so their faith will demonstrate His power (v. 5).

The same principle applies to Christian couples with conflicting views. God pleads with spouses to have the same mind, to be in agreement, as Paul urged in verse 10. A husband and wife can reach agreement when they both seek God's point of view. Priorities align and contentions are resolved when a couple focuses on the character and purposes of Jesus. Then, the Holy Spirit abounds in the marriage and displays the power of God to friends and family.

A CROWN

Read Proverbs 12:4 and 1 Peter 3:1

When I was a child, my friends and I would often play a game called king of the hill. We would draw a crown on a piece of paper, color it, cut it out, and staple it together. Whoever could stay on top of the hill won the right to wear the crown. It denoted both the authority and nobility of the one who wore it! Since those days, I've learned that as a little boy grows into manhood and marries a special young lady, she becomes his crown. Every husband desires to be able to brag about how special his wife is—her character, her beauty, how industrious and prudent she is, and of course how tasty her meals are.

Unfortunately, sometimes a husband would rather not mention his wife in conversation. She is not his crown, but a source of constant misery, like an incurable disease infecting his bones (Proverbs 12:4). Her house is always a mess. She has a loose tongue and is known to gossip. She lacks discretion, or isn't prudent with the checkbook. He may be ashamed to introduce her to his friends or business associates. Not long ago, after preaching on this passage, an elderly woman approached me after the service and said, "My marriage ended more than 30 years ago, and tonight God showed me that one source of our problems was that I was not a crown to my husband." She recognized that her lack of virtue had marred their relationship. Even though a wife might want to justify her faults because of her husband's lack of godliness, she is commanded by God to live virtuously before Him (1 Peter 3:1–2). A virtuous life is a disciplined life, continually focused on God. Crown your husband with your excellence!

THE UNSEEN STRAND

Read James 1:25

An old Scandinavian proverb tells of a spider that travels down on a single thread from the lofty rafters of a barn. It seeks out a busy corner where there are plenty of insects to feed upon. After weaving a web across the corner, the spider prospers and becomes very fat. One day as it crosses the web, it notices an ostensibly stray strand reaching upward to the unseen. Forgetting the importance of this single thread, he snaps it and his whole world crashes in on him!

James 1:25 speaks of someone who looks into the perfect law of liberty. "Looking into" means to stoop down and intently inspect. When casually observing the stray strand, the spider forgot that it was the source of the strength for its entire web. He did not stop to reflect upon its significance, and how it was holding his world in place. As a Christian husband and wife, we must look intently into the perfect law that gives freedom. This may seem like a paradox since the law implies restraint, seemingly a lack of freedom. The law is perfect, however, because it rests on the finished work of Christ. His truth sets us free (John 8:32).

As the months and years pass by in marriage, we like the spider can become prosperous and lazy on our journey, forgetting that the strength of our relationship rests totally upon the unseen hand of God. We must continually stop, look intently, and re-evaluate our relationship in light of His Word. During counseling sessions, when addressing marital problems, many couples make statements that are contrary to the Word in order to justify their wrong attitudes and actions. Without realizing it, they are being forgetful hearers rather than effectual doers (v. 25). A good marriage requires continual adjustment and inspection in light of biblical truth. Marriage is a work in progress. When the intensity of our relationship with God becomes casual or diminished so that we overlook the source of our strength, our world is about to cave in!

ROMANTIC GETAWAYS

Read Song of Solomon 2:10–13, 4:7–10, and 7:11–13

*P*erhaps the greatest romantic of all time is King Solomon. Throughout his beautiful love song, he continually woos his bride to himself. He certainly understands the importance and necessity of developing a climate of romance in his marriage. Dr. Ed Wheat states, "If you are not romantically in love with your marriage partner, you are missing something wonderful, no matter how sincere your commitment to that person may be. Even contentment can be dull and drab in comparison with the joy God planned for you with your marriage partner!"[19]

One way Solomon romances his wife is by taking her on romantic getaways. In Song of Solomon 2:10, we see him compelling his sweetheart to come with him on a springtime vacation. He wants her to set time aside with him to listen to the singing of the birds, to smell the flowers, and taste the new, sweet, tender fruit. In two other occurrences (4:8, 7:11), he invites her to the mountains and to a countryside village. We might say that Solomon took a lot of honeymoons. We could easily and justifiably exclaim, "He could afford to; He was rich!" The point is not how elaborate the retreat is, but rather to simply get away and spend special time with each other. A picnic, taking a drive in the mountains, or spending the night in a hotel across town breaks the routine and demonstrates to your mate that he or she is not only highly valued, but that you desire his or her company in a secluded place. The rewards will well outweigh the costs. Don't procrastinate; plan some romantic getaways today!

ROMANTIC TALK

Read Song of Solomon 1:15, 4:1–2, and 6:4–5

Solomon continues the romantic wooing of his new bride by talking to her in terms and tones of endearment. He understands the deep longing of his wife to hear expressions from his lips that enrapture her heart with love talk. He uses the word "fair" twenty times to describe his wife's outer countenance. The word "fair" means of excellent beauty. He is saying, "Honey you're not just pretty, but your beauty is inspiring!" He proudly implies possessiveness when he repeatedly uses the phrase, "my love." The word "love" would possibly correspond to the word "darling" today. To paraphrase, he is saying, "Baby, you are my cherished darling, the object of my attraction."

Solomon doesn't stop there, but goes on to offer words of praise. He describes her eyes as doves, a reference to sexual purity and virginity (v. 4:1a). He continues by drawing a comparison between her hair and the hair of goats that live on mount Gilead (v. 4:1b). This may not seem to be a compliment, but he is saying she has rich, dark black hair that glistens in the sun, like the renowned goats. In the next verse, he admires her teeth as sparkling white—none are missing and they are all even. As husbands, we are to follow this biblical example in cultivating romantic love. We must understand that God did not intend for romantic talk to stop at the altar when we said "I do." He continually woos His bride to Him through "love talk" in His word. He whispers to our souls through His sweet Spirit, conveying love, concern, and deep care. We should follow not only Solomon's, but also the master bridegroom's example by romancing our wife every day with words that make her feel special, secure, and unconditionally loved.

ROMANTIC FRAGRANCE

Read Song of Solomon 1:3, 1:12–14, 3:6, and 4:10

I just walked in from giving our dog, Duke, a bath. What a chore! He weighs about 160 pounds. He has skin allergies, and on these hot, humid days, he itches unbearably. He claws and scratches his body until his skin is sore and stinky. Duke wants lots of attention, but when he reeks like this, no one wants to even walk by him, much less pet him. After his bath, he smells like a normal dog for about a week. We all rub his belly and scratch behind his ears. The attention he receives varies according to the scent he emits.

In contrast, when you hold a freshly bathed and powdered baby in your arms, you instinctively want to draw close and kiss him all over his sweet smelling head. The smell triggers affection.

Throughout the Song of Solomon, God points out the significance of fragrance in romantic relationships. In chapter one, the bride is aware that her spikenard attracts the attention of the king (vv. 12–15). She compares him to pleasant spices and sweet smelling flowers. The groom's processional to escort the bride to the palace (v. 3:6) is enveloped in expensively perfumed incense intended to attract the bride to her groom. In another instance, Solomon declares that the aromas of the ointments gently drifting from his bride are more enticing than all other spices (v. 4:10).

Our Creator amazingly designed and planned our physical beings to delight in a variety of senses that stir up romance. His thoughtfulness and love are evident in the details of pleasure that He designed for us. Don't miss the blessings of lotions, powders, bath oils, and perfumes. God wants you to savor the fragrance of your mate (v. 1:3).

ROMANTIC GIFTS

Read Song of Solomon 1:10–11 and Ezekiel 16:8–13

Solomon not only cultivates romantic love with his bride through romantic getaways and romantic talk, but also by enhancing her natural, created beauty with ornaments. In these verses we see that he gives gifts including jewels and chains of gold and silver. He not only praises her beauty with his words, but increases her beauty with his gifts.

In Ezekiel 16, God describes His relationship with the children of Israel as a married one (Ezek. 16:3–8). He goes on to describe how He conveyed His love to His bride by clothing and bathing her (vv. 9–10). He put bracelets upon her hands, chains upon her neck, and earrings in her ears (vv. 11–13). God, as the perfect groom, uses these metaphors to describe how He woos His bride by enhancing her natural, created beauty with accessories.

Every husband should take heed to these godly examples in Scripture. A wife probably expects a gift on certain dates (anniversary, birthday), but it is most special when it is not anticipated … when she is surprised by it. The unexpected gift conveys that you were thinking of her when you were not with her. Although Solomon was rich and could afford costly gifts, creativity in gift selection and presentation can be far more romantic than its expense. It could be as simple and modest as handpicked daffodils or a beautiful card which includes a love poem written by your hand. Continually look for new ways to enhance your wife's natural beauty through the giving of special gifts that say "I love you."

ROMANCE ROBBERS: CHILDREN

Read Song of Solomon 2:15

*S*olomon and his Shulamite bride are aware of potential "romance robbers" and compare them to "little foxes" that would come and eat the tender grapes from the vineyard (v. 15). Every marriage experiences "little foxes" that can steal romance from the relationship. We must diligently guard against these intrusions. For couples who have children, a prevalent romance robber can be their precious little ones! Children require much attention and time that can interrupt one's schedule at any given moment. When our four boys were small, I would put them in bed and explain that Dad was releasing alligators in the hallway. If they were to get up and come to Daddy and Mommy's door, the alligators would eat them. The only time they wouldn't get eaten is if they went to the bathroom. They had an "alligator pass" to go to the bathroom. You might be asking, "Did you really say that?" Well, no, but there were many times I wanted to! As our boys grew older and became teenagers, they began to roam the house at all hours of the night. Sometimes they would come to our bedroom door and yell, "Hey, Mom and Dad, what are you doing in there? Can we come in?"

Romantic getaways are one way to help solve this problem. Also to protect against intrusion from your children during a potentially romantic evening at home, you must explain the need for Mom and Dad to have special time together. Then set boundaries for your children. They need to understand that the husband-wife relationship is the priority in your home. Don't assume your children already know this, because they don't! You must train them to respect your time together, and even let them be part of a romantic evening. Have them light the candles, play soft music, and serve you cheese and crackers for a private date. Your children can be part of the beginning of an exciting, enchanting evening without spoiling the tender grapes!

ROMANCE ROBBERS: EXHAUSTION

Read Matthew 11:28–30 and Luke 10:38

For the past two weeks, I have been exhausted! I've been traveling, preaching, preparing, planning, and dealing with the everyday routines of life. To make matters even more wearisome, I contracted a bacterial infection that zapped my energy. It's not uncommon for a man or woman to become physically, mentally, or even spiritually depleted due to high demands placed upon them. The Bible uses many different descriptive words for this condition: famished, parched, faint, overcome, and weary. In case we feel this status is unspiritual, we need to remember that Jesus often spoke of being weary (John 4:6). Paul referred to weariness resulting from his intense, passionate service for God (2 Cor. 11:27).

When I become exhausted, I frequently exhibit several specific attitudes. I become edgy, short-tempered, and just plain hard to be around. I desire to isolate myself from those around me in an attempt to regain my strength. Obviously, this condition does not cultivate a climate for romance, but rather hinders any tender expression toward my wife. After several days or even a week of exhaustion, I can easily become depressed, discouraged, and ready to just give up! Many spouses lack the excitement and thrill of romantic love due to a continued state of weariness. To avoid this romance robber, we must intentionally step away from activity and make time for rest. When weary, Jesus would leave the crowds and go to Mary and Martha's house to get away and relax (Luke 10:38). He extends a wonderful invitation to come and snuggle up in his arms for this needed rest (Matt. 11:28–30). Jesus can encourage and restore us like no one else. In addition to setting aside rest time, we must evaluate our schedules, make needed changes, learn to say "no" as appropriate, and take care of our bodies through exercise and proper eating habits. Be careful not to use up all your energy and leave only the "scraps" for your spouse.

ROMANCE ROBBERS: GUILT

Read John 21:15–19 and 2 Corinthians 12:10

*G*uilt is another "fox" that robs the creativity and passion needed for romance. Guilt from premarital or extramarital affairs, addictions, or financial failure can plague a marriage. The guilty spouse has witnessed the hurt caused by his or her selfishness and bears the burdensome weight of righting the wrong. This person feels too worthless to merit affection, so thoughts of romance are defeated before they are even initiated.

After denying Jesus, Peter was so filled with guilt that he abandoned his life as a disciple and hid in a fishing career. Jesus addresses the guilt issue when he twice asks Peter if he possesses a committed love (agapao) for Him (vv. 15-16). Peter feels so guilty he can only admit affection (phileo) for the Lord (vv. 15-17). He does not trust himself because his failures have proved that his love was not fully committed. When Jesus questions Peter the third time and asks if he has affectionate love for Him, Peter is grieved. He pronounces then that Jesus knows everything about him. Jesus explains that Peter's failures are now victory. As a youth, Peter decisively operated in his own determination and strength, but now he will be so surrendered to the will of God that he will trust Him with challenges even when he has no strength or abilities of his own. Jesus expresses that now Peter is ready to allow Him to live his life when he concludes by instructing, "Follow me (v. 19)." From this point forward, Peter's life abounds in power and victory.

These Scriptures remind guilt-laden spouses that while they cannot trust themselves, they can completely trust the redeeming power of God. From this point forward they can humbly follow Him in all challenges. The relief of redemption will free guilty individuals to love and serve in His power, with new potential for romance in their marriage.

ROMANCE ROBBERS: UN-FORGIVENESS

Read Song of Solomon 2:15, Ephesians 4:32, and Hebrews 12:15

A common and tremendously destructive romance robber is un-forgiveness. This "little fox" will destroy not only romance, but also the marriage itself. A harsh word, a cutting remark, or a hateful response sows the seeds for fruit in the relationship that is covered with thorns. If not dealt with, spouses will become like two porcupines trying to nestle up against each other, unable to be intimate because of constant irritation. Many times, we falsely assume un-forgiveness will disappear with time, not realizing that it turns to roots of bitterness that continually defile our spouse (Heb. 12:15). Whenever we intentionally ignore our mate or can't speak peaceably with him or her, we should perform a spiritual examination. We need to pray, asking God to search our hearts for sinful attitudes. When He reveals them, we should immediately confess and repent. True repentance will lead us not only to restore our relationship with God, but also to mend the hurts with our spouse. Once forgiveness has occurred, the doors of romance are flung open and the stage for dramatic love is set. One of the most exciting romantic times we can experience in marriage is coming together intimately after being distanced because of un-forgiveness. We must capture the little fox of un-forgiveness before it roots around and digs up the tender vines of our relationship! Be tenderhearted and forgiving, even as God for Christ's sake has forgiven us (Eph. 4:32).

MIXED MOTIVES

**Read 1 Chronicles 28:9, 2 Corinthians 10:4–5,
and 1 Corinthians 4:4–5**

Have you ever done the right thing for the wrong reason? Maybe it's treating someone a certain way to gain favor for a future benefit. Perhaps as a wife, you fix your husband his favorite dessert not because you want to show your love, but so he will be more generous when you go shopping the next day. Or as a husband, you help your wife wash the dishes knowing that tomorrow you want to play golf. Helping her will ease your conscience! These are mixed motives.

Solomon is urged to serve God with a perfect heart because He knows the motives behind every thought (v. 9). A realization of this truth should compel us in two ways. In 2 Corinthians 10:5, God instructs us to "cast down" imaginations and thoughts that rise against the knowledge of Him. The word "cast" means to forcefully demolish the wrong imaginations or motives of our heart. We must make a conscious effort to destroy each one. Next, we must take every thought captive to the obedience of Christ, examining it to prevent further wrong motives. If we have already embraced a wrong motive and acted upon it, we should confess it as sin and repent (1 John 1:9). Sometimes we may not even know we have mixed motives. Paul describes this situation in 1 Corinthians 4:4–5 where he states that although his conscience is clear, there could be hidden motives that he is not aware of. Since we possibly face the same challenge, we must ask God to search our hearts (Psalm 139:23).

As a husband and wife, we should be introspective concerning our motives toward each other. The love of God should always be the constraining motivation for our actions.

MY PERSONAL PRIEST

Read Hebrews 4:14–5:3

I have had days of despair when I felt like I could not do anything right. I felt like a failure as a spouse, a parent, and a Christian. I knew Jesus had been tempted in all the ways that I had, and He understood my struggles. Yet even knowing all this, I still insisted on my own way (v. 4:15). I knew He loved, accepted, and forgave me, but the thought of approaching a majestic, righteous God made my failures loom even larger. I wanted to shy away. I did not want to face Him. Where was the confidence declared in verse 16?

A study of the Old Testament priests adjusted my thinking. These men were appointed to offer gifts and sacrifices for the sins of the individuals they ministered to (v. 5:1). The reason for going to a priest was not to receive strength to withstand sin. Rather, the priest served as a mediator between the sinner and Holy God so the unworthy one could have access to Him. The priest could relate to the struggles of the people and have compassion because he himself was subject to weakness and sin (v. 2). He even had to offer sacrifices for his own sins (v. 3).

Numerous passages exhort us to pray—about everything, without ceasing, diligently, in faith believing, when we have needs, when we are in trouble. These verses, however, call us to pray specifically when we have sinned, for that is when we need mercy (v. 16). Mercy is the act of withholding punishment that is deserved. We are not just told to come for mercy; we are instructed to come boldly. There is no reason to shy away. As a matter of fact, to do so because of guilt or shame rejects Jesus' role as our great High Priest, the One who offered the ultimate sacrifice so we would be cleansed to approach the Father with no hesitation, fully conscious of acceptance.

Have you have failed as a spouse, parent, or friend? Come boldly for mercy to Jesus, your great High Priest.

THE MIND OF THE HIGH PRIEST

Read Hebrews 4:14–5:2 and Philippians 2:5

*H*ave you ever noticed that when people diet and lose a significant amount of weight, they sometimes view others who are overweight with contempt? Likewise, when God convicts me of a sin I have been blind to, I become so intent on changing my lifestyle that I campaign for everyone, especially my spouse, to do the same. A victory over sin can quickly mushroom to pride when I feel that God now views me more favorably than my mate.

As I consider the previous devotion, I remember the mercy and sympathy that flows from Jesus, my personal High Priest. I am grateful for the relief I experience in knowing that He compassionately understands and sympathizes with my struggles. He is patient with my weaknesses. He understands the guilt that sometimes debilitates me. Since Philippians 2:5 urges believers to have the mind of Christ, I should have patient compassion for weaknesses in my spouse's life. Our mates should be able to trust that they can come to us confidently and boldly, knowing we will not have contempt, but will identify with their struggles (Heb. 5:2). "When I remind myself of my sins against God and of His forgiving and generous grace toward me, I give the gospel an opportunity to reshape my perspective and to put me in a frame of mind wherein I actually desire to give this same grace."[20]

Pray that God will reveal haughty attitudes and replace them with a gentleness that exercises sympathetic concern for the struggles your spouse faces.

OPEN WIDE

Read Psalm 81

s a little boy, I remember dreading the day of my dental check-up. I knew when I sat down in that intimidating chair, the command I greatly feared would be given—open wide! I hesitated to obey since I knew the dentist would begin probing with a funny looking mirror, start scraping my teeth, and ask questions I couldn't answer since my mouth was crammed full with his hand.

Years later, when I read Psalm 81 and came across verse ten, I was struck by God's command to the children of Israel to open their mouth wide. Of course His purpose was much different than the dentist's. He wants His children to open wide to make a big request to a big God! He reminds Israel of His past blessings and that He is their source of future good (vv. 1–10). He wants them to remember that it was Him alone who delivered them from the bondage of Egypt and sustained them during their journeys through the wilderness. They are His chosen people, set apart to serve Him and enjoy intimate fellowship. Sadly, we see in verse eleven the word "but." Even though God had proven strong on their behalf, Israel does not hearken to His voice and no longer cries out to Him! He bemoans the failure of His people to obey and walk in His ways (v. 13). God's heart cry to His children is to obey Him, and call out to Him for their every need (vv. 13–16).

God is the source of all good gifts. He is our deliverer, our sustainer, and desires that we ask great things of Him. Whatever situation or circumstance you are facing, remember His past blessings, open your mouth wide, and cry out to Him!

APRIL 5

PANIC

Read Psalm 11

Last night, we heard of another random victim targeted and slain by a mystery sniper. Even though the location may be miles from our hometown, hearing of shootings and terrorist attacks subconsciously stirs anxiety. We also heard a news commentary about 13 young teenage boys who, late one night, beat an innocent man to death. One parent responded, "Boys will be boys." A recent report addressed the pageant board's attempt to deny Miss America's right to promote abstinence when she tours and speaks to young people. Another commentary told of a high school dance where chaperones and leaders admitted more than 200 drunken students. These influences and trends among youth generate deep alarm in my heart. This morning, we received an e-mail from a friend who may be laid off from his job any day. We have been personally affected by the economy, as churches seem to be tightening up on the number of conferences they host. If we allow our minds to drift to the cost of paying for our sons' college education, panic can quickly shatter our sense of stability. Anxious thoughts from so many directions quickly escalate when considering how difficult it is to protect and provide for one's family.

In Psalm 11, the writer is faced with the same temptation to listen to the hopelessness surrounding him. It appears the very foundations of society and the family are about to be destroyed (v. 3). The psalmist resists the temptation to flee and reminds himself of his source of stability. He declares that he consciously places his faith in the Lord (v. 1). He reminds himself that although he is helpless, the Lord still reigns in power (v. 4). The Lord is aware of the turmoil in the world and will prevail over wickedness (vv. 5–6). In the midst of a potential panic attack, the psalmist finds peace and strength. We, too, can choose to trust in the Lord and focus on His attributes and righteousness. Resist panic before it destroys your peace.

APRIL 6

STILL EXCITED

Read Deuteronomy 34:7

Recently I was talking to a preacher friend who is in his sixties. During our conversation, he said he wanted to share something that would both encourage me and be insightful in marriage. Upon my eager acceptance of his offer, he stated, "I want to let you know that my wife still turns me on and my sex drive hasn't lessened." I responded, "I am glad to hear the good news!"

Over the course of our thirty-five years together, my wife and I have discussed this issue many times. Sometimes we joke about it and other times we are very serious. Many couples, when approaching the big 40, begin to wonder if they will be able to enjoy each other sexually in the later years as much as they did in their twenties and thirties. Looking at today's passage, God shares with us that even at 120 years old, Moses had good eyesight and all of his natural forces (this would include his sexual drive) were not diminished! To paraphrase this in the context of marriage—his wife still looked good and still turned him on! As time passes, the initial chemical bonding that sparked and sustained attraction to one another begins to fade. This is how God has physiologically made us. As we age together, however, husband and wife can grow into a much deeper, more intimate relationship both emotionally and spiritually. The physical expression of sexual intercourse is the natural outworking of our growing intimacy. Our enjoyment as husband and wife becomes richer and even more fulfilling with age. Barring health problems, a couple can look forward to an exhilarating sexual oneness well into their eighties, or even beyond! Pause and thank God for His gift.

THE LAZY BUM

**Read Proverbs 18:9, 6:6–11, 10:4–5, 20:4, 26:16,
and 1 Timothy 5:8**

Solomon compares a lazy person to someone who is a destroyer, someone who completely wastes the land as in a war of great destruction (v. 9). Paul states that a lazy husband who fails to provide for his family is worse than an unbeliever (1 Tim. 5:8). A slothful person becomes poor, causes shame, makes excuses, and ends up begging (Prov. 10:4–5, 20:4). Ironically, this person does nothing himself, but often voices a critical opinion of others' efforts (Prov. 26:16). When one spouse is irresponsible, the other becomes burdened with more than his or her share of the work. The overload stirs resentment, disgust, and frustration that can decimate the relationship.

God also shows disgust for slothfulness when He addresses the lazy person as a sluggard (Prov. 6:6). In His amazing love, however, the Father offers helpful advice to overcome this sin. He advises the sluggard to study the ants. Ants do not have a supervisor or ruler to force them to work diligently (v. 7). They exercise good work habits on their own, and aggressively respond to opportunities as they become available (v. 8). They do not wait around for a better option or procrastinate until needs pressure them to action. They prepare for the future while they can. Unlike the ant, a lazy man sleeps and slumbers, unprepared, until needs creep up on him like an armed bandit (vv. 9–11). An ant makes no excuses, but consistently and faithfully works. Be sensitive not to promote disgust or destroy your family's future with laziness, but rather inspire your spouse and children with love as you diligently labor for their good.

A Hound Dog Marriage

Read Philippians 2:14 and Genesis 3:11–13

The story is told of a preacher who paid a visit to an elderly man who was sitting on the front porch of his run down shack. Situated beside the man was an old hound dog, moaning and groaning. When the preacher asked what was wrong, the man told him the dog was lying on a nail. The preacher responded with the obvious question, "Why doesn't he get up off of it?" The country gentleman looked straight at the preacher and said, "Well, I guess it just don't hurt badly enough!"

Have you ever met someone who prefers to stay on top of the nail and complain rather than move off of it? This type of person seems to find energy in murmuring, groaning, and disputing (doubting truth). The habitual complainer takes an "outside-in" approach to problems, always looking for the source and solution outside himself. One major principle I have learned in marriage is that complaining and blaming will not inspire my spouse to change! The best way I can effect change in her is to change me. I cannot control her, but I do have control over myself and my thoughts. When Adam and Eve sinned, the first thing they did was to complain and blame (Gen. 3:11–13). Adam blamed his wife and even indirectly blamed God since He gave the woman to him. Eve immediately blamed the serpent. Adam and Eve should have done what we should do whenever we are tempted to murmur, complain, or dispute. We need to examine ourselves! Adam and Eve each ought to have confessed, "God, I have sinned against You; forgive me." This approach demonstrates taking an "inside-out" look at problems, honestly admitting what needs to change in us. Avoid a hound dog marriage. Get up off the nail, and look at the condition of your heart.

THE TRIGGER OF OFFENSE

Read Luke 17:1–4, 2 Timothy 2:24–26, Matthew 24:10, and 1 Peter 5:5

*J*esus emphatically states to His disciples that every one of them will face the stumbling block of offense. It's not a question of if they will be offended, but rather when (v. 1). Jesus even declares that in the last days many people will be offended (Matt. 24:10).

The word translated as "offense" is the Greek term *skandalon*. It originally referred to the part of a trap to which bait is attached.[21] When someone is offended, he or she becomes like an animal lured into a snare. Paul sheds more insight into what happens to an offended person when he urges Timothy to gently correct people who are quarreling with or are offended at one another (2 Tim. 2:24–26). The verses insinuate that a person who has been offended is deceived to the point where God must grant him repentance before he can even realize he is captured in this deadly trap. The individual is unsuspectingly lured into it because the trigger of offense is covered and hidden by the deceptive bait called pride! Pride concentrates on the unfairness of the hurt and emphasizes one's right to be defensive. Pride builds resentment and justifies revenge. The bitterness becomes so consuming that the offended person is taken captive in the snare of the devil to do his will (2 Tim. 2:26). Satan's will is to cause Christians to express hatred and bitterness, leading to the disintegration of marriages, families, and churches.

To protect our marriages against the entrapment of offense, we must stay alert to incidents that offend us so we can respond with forgiveness. We can protect loved ones from our own offensive behavior by clothing ourselves with humility and love. God promises He will give grace to the humble, but will resist the proud. (1 Pet. 5:5). Have you offended or been offended by someone?

WOE TO HIM

Read Luke 17:1–2 and Matthew 18:3–10

As Jesus continues His teaching regarding offense, He adds a stern warning by saying it would be better to have a millstone hung around your neck and be thrown into the sea than to cause one of His children to be offended (v. 2). In the culture of the day, this type of punishment was often used for heinous crimes! This warning is also mentioned two other places in the gospels (Matt. 18:6, Mark 9:42). In Matthew 18:10, Jesus says that God has guardian angels who report directly to Him when someone offends His children.

To offend is to cause resentment and wounded feelings through insensitivity, insolence, or contemptuous rudeness. God is not saying it is wrong to share the truth if we are motivated by love (Eph. 4:15). In order to awaken them to truth, Jesus often made statements to the Pharisees that were offensive, but He spoke out of concern for their well being. When we hurt someone intentionally or even unknowingly, without regard for him or her, we offend!

It is a terrible thing to cause another believer to be taken captive in Satan's entrapment of offense (see yesterday's devotion), but it is just as serious to allow ourselves to be enslaved by it. Jesus illustrates this danger with allegorical warnings to cut off our hands, feet, and eyes when they lead us to be offended (Matt 18:8–9). Warren Wiersbe explains, "Christ is not speaking literally when He commands us to 'cut off' the members of the body that cause us to sin, for sin comes from the heart, not the hands and feet. He is telling us to deal with our sins drastically, completely, and mercilessly, the way a surgeon deals with a cancerous growth."[22]

We must continually be on guard not to offend our spouse, or brothers and sisters. God will hold us accountable!

A STRONG CITY

Read Proverbs 18:19, 1 Corinthians 13:1–5, and Hebrews 12:15

Have you ever been deeply hurt by someone you love? Perhaps you have opened up to this person and have been transparent and intimate. Your walls are down and the gates of your heart are wide open when a dart of criticism or rejection unexpectedly pierces you. Husbands and wives seem to be prime candidates for this type of wounding. Two people who at one point in their lives loved each other so much they said, "Till death do we part," are now so deeply hurt that they never want to speak to or see each other again. Where did it all start? How did they move from intimacy to hatred? God gives us a hint in a profound word picture concerning offense.

When people are offended, they become like a strong city. They begin to construct walls of protection to prevent further hurt. The disastrous result is that they not only keep the perceived enemy outside, but they are taken prisoner inside the very walls they have constructed. They then begin to filter all of life, including God Himself, through their pain. Roots of bitterness spring up and extend their reach. As a result, un-forgiveness not only controls the life of the offended person, but also affects others who come in contact with him or her (Heb. 12:15).

Individuals in this situation cannot love unconditionally because they are seeking their own protection. They become like a vacuum cleaner, always sucking in but never giving out. Over time, the love that once compelled one spouse to care for the other deteriorates to defensiveness, then betrayal, and even hatred (Matt. 24:10). This progression can only be stopped when God grants repentance that leads to an acknowledgement of the truth—that a person is enslaved in a trap of the devil (2 Tim. 2:25–26). If you are bitter and offended at your mate, confess your sin and humbly forgive.

REBUKING

**Read Luke 17:1–10, Matthew 18:6–15,
and Proverbs 18:19**

The first step to reconciliation between two offended parties is for the offended one to rebuke the one who offended him (v. 3). The word "rebuke" sounds harsh, but in this context it means to lovingly confront the person who offended you by explaining your perspective. The purpose of the conversation is to clear up any distortion of truth that may have been communicated. From there, the process of restoration through forgiveness can proceed. The question often arises, "Why should I approach the offender if he is the one who hurt me?" It is possible that the individual does not even know he committed an offense, and the relationship would not be reconciled if the one offended did not bring it to his attention. Once the offender realizes what he has done, he can seek forgiveness.

For example, John usually arrives at home after work promptly at 5:30. As an expression of love and devotion, his wife Susan has supper prepared and on the table. Today, John decides to stop by the driving range and hit some golf balls. Forgetting the time, he arrives home at 6:30. He is insensitive to the fact that he has hurt his wife's feelings. Susan doesn't say anything about it, but she is irritated. As she silently contemplates the inconveniences she was subjected to, her heart begins to nibble at the bait of pride on the trigger of the trap of offense. When Susan avoids rebuking John, she fortifies herself against further hurt and creates distance in their relationship (Prov. 18:19). In order for reconciliation to begin, she must lovingly confront him about what he has done.

Many times, a major marriage problem results from a minor offense which has festered over months or years without resolution. We must guard our relationships from the trap of offense that destroys thousands of couples every year. If your spouse has offended you, lovingly confront him or her so you can experience true reconciliation.

IF HE REPENTS

Read Luke 17:1–10 and Matthew 18:15–18

Are we required to forgive someone when he or she has not asked for forgiveness? God's forgiveness is clearly seen to be conditional! The Bible teaches that we cannot receive forgiveness of our sins without repentance (Luke 13:3, Luke 24:47, Acts 17:30). Since we are to model our forgiveness after God's, there are conditions to that forgiveness (Eph. 4:32). Although we are never to harbor bitterness, our forgiveness of an offender is based first on his or her repentance (v. 3).

In Matthew 18, Jesus teaches what to do when a brother or sister offends you. The offended party is first to go to the offender privately, then with one or two witnesses (vv. 15–17). If confession and repentance take place at any stage in the process, the matter is settled. If the offender refuses to repent, you are to bring the matter before the church. If the sinner neglects to hear the church, you are to consider him or her as an unbeliever. Church discipline is based on the condition of repentance. God's loving goal is reconciliation. It is dependent upon genuine repentance and forgiveness.

There is much confusion today concerning repentance. The word "repent" comes from the Greek word *metanoeo*, which means to change one's mind. Godly repentance is not regret. Regret is having sorrowful feelings for what you have done. Repentance may involve regret, but always must include an acknowledgment of sin. God gives us insight into the meaning of repentance in Isaiah 55:7. A truly repentant person will turn from his or her own thoughts and ways, which are sinful, to God's thoughts and ways, which are holy. Repentance is not about making excuses or simply saying, "I'm sorry." It requires honestly admitting wrong thoughts and attitudes, and making lifestyle changes accordingly.

Husbands and wives must be willing to humbly acknowledge sin, genuinely repent, and graciously forgive in order to remain in an intimate relationship!

FORGIVENESS IS A PROMISE

**Read Ephesians 4:32, Isaiah 43:25,
and Jeremiah 31:34**

One of the hardest things we can do is forgive our mate for the hurt he or she has caused. In Ephesians 4:32, God provides a perfect model for us to follow. We are commanded to forgive in the same way He demonstrates forgiveness to us. Just how does He forgive? Isaiah 43:25 and Jeremiah 31:34 both declare God's promise to "not remember" our sins. Isn't it wonderful to know He does not base forgiveness on our merit or on a feeling, but rather on a promise backed by the sacrifice His Son paid to cover our sins? I have heard some people ask, "How can God forget our sins?" He doesn't. Obviously an omniscient God cannot forget, but He can choose to "not remember." Just as an accountant may clear the financial record of a debt so no balance is due, God clears the sin from His accounts payable. Jay Adams explains, "To not remember is simply a graphic way of saying, 'I will not bring up these matters to you or others in the future. I will bury them and not exhume the bones to beat you over the head with them. I will never use these sins against you.'"[23] When we forgive someone, we need to follow God's example in the threefold promise, "I will not bring up this sin to the one who offended me, to others, or to myself." Biblical forgiveness begins the process of reconciliation between the offended parties and offers opportunity for an even richer relationship than previously experienced. Is there someone you need to forgive? Have you offered forgiveness to someone who has offended you, but repeatedly remind yourself of the details related to the wrongdoings? If so, make a new commitment that refuses to retrieve those memories.

FERVENT LOVE

Read 1 Peter 4:8

Should a husband and wife rebuke, repent, and forgive each other over each offense that happens in their marriage? If so, much of our time would be spent repairing every little matter that causes irritation! Fortunately, God has made a provision for handling all the minor offenses we commit toward one another. But how do we distinguish between sins requiring rebuke and the ones which do not? Those that do not break fellowship or lead to an unreconciled relationship are to be covered by fervent love (v. 8).

The word "fervent" means to stretch. It refers to an athlete who extends his muscles in preparation for a race. It is this "stretched out and extended love" that we are commanded to demonstrate to one another. God is stating that fervent love is a prerequisite to the exercise of all Christian virtues. It is to be modeled after His love, which is patient, long-suffering, and keeps no account of wrongs. This love never fails (1 Cor.13).

If we exercise fervent love, the glorious result is that it covers a multitude of sins. This doesn't mean that it cleanses the offender's sin, but because of it we will dismiss minor offenses instead of musing over them or sharing them with others. As a married couple, we must continually manifest fervent love to our spouse, eliminating the need to bring up every little offense. Since we have the great potential to daily commit many sins against our mate, God's provision of "fervent love" allows us to be gracious—to look for and expect the best and maintain intimate oneness. When we love each other this way, it's like pulling up the covers on a cold winter's night, snuggling close and only thinking about how blessed we are to have our spouse next to us.

BEAR THEIR BURDENS

Read Romans 15:1–7

*M*y husband is efficient and organized. I tend to vacillate from one task to the next to the next, until I turn in circles. My husband concentrates so intently on the job before him that he may overlook the people near him. I will set aside my chores and get involved with whoever is around me, even if it means leaving tasks unfinished. This is just one example of how my husband and I approach life differently. Some of my strengths are his weaknesses, but some of my weaknesses are his strengths. And I know that my weaknesses probably frustrate him at times.

Today's Scripture passage instructs people who are strong to bear the weaknesses of others (v. 1). The word "bear" means to pick up and carry a weight. Rather than being irritated by the inconvenience and just tolerating the weaknesses, Christians are to be concerned for their friends and encourage them with positive comments (v. 2). My husband praises me for my strengths and works with me to get my tasks done. He encourages me to set aside the less important chores and admires the things I do for him. He is sensitive not to put pressure on me.

Individuals who struggle in certain areas discover hope when the Scriptures remind them of the patience and encouragement of the Lord (v. 4). Hope exists because weaker Christians have the opportunity to greatly improve as they allow the Lord to empower them. Jesus, who is longsuffering and full of comfort, will help more mature Christians to not only endure the weaknesses of others, but to gently offer reassuring direction that produces harmony (vv. 3, 5). As husbands and wives promote unity by supporting each other through edification and empathy, they follow Christ's example and glorify the Father (v. 6). Jesus accepted us with all our weaknesses. He strengthens us with His life. We should be willing to accept, embrace, and strengthen our spouses (v. 7). Are there burdens you need to bear for your husband or wife today?

BITTER ENVYING AND STRIFE

Read James 3:13–18

*J*ealousy is a resentful attitude toward one who is believed to enjoy an advantage. A husband with a strenuous job may resent that his wife can spend more time enjoying the children. A wife may be envious of a husband who gets to associate with adults while she watches the children day after day without a break. A husband may resent his wife spending "her" money on nice clothes while "his" is designated to pay bills. A husband may be irritated that he has to work in the hot sun to mow the lawn while a wife is irritated because she has to work inside. As spouses dwell on the other person's advantages, they tend to justify their resentment and boast of the reasoning behind the justifications. Eventually, their attitudes mushroom into bitter envy.

Being argumentative incites strife in the same way. Sometimes, I catch myself feeling extremely intent on proving I am right about the most trivial detail. I waste precious energy by delving into elaborate detail because I want my husband to recognize I am correct, and he is mistaken. I might want to prove that we received the phone call on Wednesday instead of Thursday, or that I was the one who picked up the dry cleaning last time. I may be right or I may be forgetting the detail that proves me wrong, but winning a trivial argument is not worth the cost of division.

James 3:14 explains that envy and strife are arrogant, and do not represent truth. Envy and strife come from the devil, who distorts truth with confusion and evil (vv. 15–16). God's perspective, however, is pure, peaceable, gentle, willing to yield, without partiality or hypocrisy (v. 17). The result is not strife and bitterness, but righteousness and peace. Recognize envy and strife in their early stages of jealousy and being argumentative. Look to Jesus to replace them with pure, peaceful wisdom from above.

COMFORTABLE

Read Colossians 3:23–24 and Ecclesiastes 9:9–10

*I*sn't it wonderful after a long day to return home, flop down in your favorite chair, and snuggle up under a cozy quilt? It's one of those rare times when everything's going okay, no one's sick, the bills are paid, and you can just relax. In those situations, it's easy for us to enter into a "comfort zone." If we aren't careful, however, comfortable times are when we are most vulnerable to the seductive plans of Satan. He will whisper, "Take it easy; you're doing just as well as everybody else. Your marriage is all right; the kids are okay. Relax."

I often ask couples at our conferences to raise their hands if they want an average marriage. Usually they look around to see how others respond, then make their decision. I remind them of the startling fact that the average marriage ends up in divorce. I challenge them, "If you don't want to be a statistic, you must do more than the average couple does to have a great marriage!" "Average" has been defined as the best of the worse and the worst of the best. To avoid it, we must not become spiritually comfortable. God urges us to do all we do heartily, as unto Him (v. 23–24). This means we are to passionately pursue God in every area of life.

It is interesting that after instructing us to celebrate our spouse all the days of our life, God commands us to do whatever we do with all our might (Eccl. 9:9–10). We must be careful not to be lulled asleep in just an okay relationship. Rather, we must work on our marriages with all our might so they sparkle and reflect the glory of God! Attend a marriage conference. Read a Christian book on marriage. Plan a special date. Don't compare your relationship to those around you; rather compare your marriage to the highest standard—Christ and His bride!

DON'T LEAVE HOME WITHOUT IT

Read Exodus 33:13–17, Psalm 91, Psalm 22:3, and Isaiah 57:15

God promises Moses that His presence will go with him and the people of Israel as they journey. In His presence, the people will find His rest (v. 14). God will empower them. They will succeed. They will not worry or fear. Psalm 91 describes in detail the protection that is available to those who dwell in the presence of God. Like Moses, the psalmist recognizes the blessed security of God's presence. Moses understands the tremendous need of God's presence as he declares that if He does not grant His presence, he does not want to proceed (v. 15). He is willing to give up his 40-year quest, just to insure the presence of God is with him. Moses realizes that the Israelites will be no different than the rest of the surrounding pagan nations if God's presence is not with them (v. 16).

The presence of God is also vitally important and to be desired in your marriage. The benefits are immense and valuable. But how do we obtain the presence of God? Isaiah 57:15 explains that God dwells with the person who has a contrite, humble spirit. This person erases all arrogance by focusing on the greatness of God rather than the importance of self. Isaiah, like Moses, realizes and admits his inadequacy and need for the Lord. He greatly desires the presence of the Lord and refuses to go anywhere without it. Psalm 22:3 announces that God inhabits the praises of Israel. He lives in the praises of His people who allow the depths of their souls to be fascinated with Him. Declaring the goodness and greatness of God's many attributes attracts His presence. He will grant His presence to the family who humbly realizes they need Him, and honors Him through praise. Commit as a couple that you will not move or act without the presence of the Lord in your marriage and family. Don't leave home without it.

DON'T LET THEM SLIP

Read Hebrews 1:1–2:1

At the end of a demanding day, do you ever pause to reflect and realize how little you thought about the Lord, much less relied upon Him? The power of His Words slips away from us as we are engulfed with routine "busyness."

The Scriptures for today remind us how our majestic, holy God communicates with mankind. In the past, He proclaimed through His prophets, but now He speaks through His Son. Like a lawyer who extols the qualifications of his expert witness in order to move jurors to pay attention and accept what they hear, the author of Hebrews recites the divine credentials of Jesus. If believers trusted the authority of the prophets, mere humans, enough to acknowledge the message God spoke through them, how much more should we embrace the Words of the One who purifies us from our sins, possesses the power to sustain the universe, and radiates the glory of God? The author continues to exalt the uniqueness of Jesus by contrasting His superior attributes to those of angels. Angels magnificently serve like flames of fire, but King Jesus rules forever in righteousness. He is the Creator who never changes and sits in a position of honor bestowed by God Himself. His preeminence demands that we heed what God communicates through Him. If we will daily take time to worship and embrace the overwhelming credentials of the Son of God, we will be compelled to pay attention to His Words of life. If we fail to do this, His gospel message and the impact it has on how we respond to our spouses and families will drift from us.

Ponder His magnificence as you read His Word today. Don't let His truth slip away.

IT'S CONTAGIOUS

Read Romans 15:8–13

As we returned to our hotel room from breakfast, we noticed a young Filipino cleaning lady coming out of our door. When she realized the room was ours, she was ecstatic. She followed us back into the room and excitedly told us she had been reading Sam's Bible each morning. She explained that she had to get up at 3:30 to catch a bus to travel two hours to work each day, and did not get to read before she left. She grabbed Sam's Bible and showed us the verses she had read that day. She enthusiastically declared that they were promises meant for her and for us. Her eyes sparkled. Joy flowed from her being and refreshed us. We had many peaceful relaxing moments on our trip. We feasted on tasty meals and basked in the incredible beauty of the countryside around us, but this encounter with Darlina was one of the highlights of our trip! Through her, we received energy and refreshing from the Holy Spirit. Her joy was contagious.

Joy is defined as the delight of anticipation in seeing one's hope fulfilled. Romans 15:13 teaches that believing the promises of God is the source of joy. Once joy is stirred, it abounds in hope and affects the lives of those around us. Of all the people I want to "infect" with the joy of my heart, my spouse and children are at the top of the list. At home, however, I have a tendency to be so focused on my responsibilities that I do not concentrate on the trustworthiness of God's love. Andrew Murray says, "Joy is not a luxury or a mere accessory in the Christian life. It is the sign that we are really living in God's wonderful love, and that that love satisfies us."[24] As I anticipate the promises in our verse today, joy will be generated in my life, and my family will be refreshed!

REGRETS

Read Joel 2:12–27

*I*n my marriage, I have regrets. I regret some things I said to my spouse. I regret some things I have neglected. I regret wasting time with unimportant activities. I regret certain financial decisions. I wish I could spray these regrets with pesticide and rid my mind of these irritating bugs. 1 Corinthians 6:9–11 addresses more intense regrets generated from past sins of adultery, homosexuality, stealing, addictions, and extortion. The devastating effects of these sins, like a swarm of locusts, can devour the fruits of peace, joy, and trust in a marriage for years to come.

In the scripture for today, the Israelites are experiencing the severe but deserved judgment of God. The prophet, Joel, reminds them that the mercy of God is great enough to overcome the devastation and regrets. The "pesticide" he instructs them to use is repentance. He urges believers to mourn over their sins as they return to God and His way of thinking (v. 12). He declares it is futile to become consumed with expressing outward frustration, but urges individuals with regrets to surrender their hearts to the Lord (v. 13). God's unfailing love is so extensive that He may relent from judgment and grant a reprieve (v 14). He wants His people to ask Him for help (v. 17). He promises to refresh. What a great relief to know that as we replace our old, sinful way of thinking with His righteous mindset, He vows to replace regrets with new blessings (v. 19)! God promises to overshadow the embarrassment and sorrow with gladness and joy. He promised the Israelites that once they repented, He would drive their enemies away and bless His land with abundant provision (vv 20-24). He will restore the years that the locusts of sin devoured (v. 25). He will make up for lost time. He will replace what was destroyed. Such mercy, such generosity, such unfailing love produces hope and rejoicing. (vv. 26–27). Stop dwelling on regrets and start repenting.

YOU ONLY

Read Amos 3:1–6 and Genesis 4:1

*E*very Christian marriage ceremony includes sacred vows between two people who agree to walk only with the other for the rest of their lives. This agreement is preceded by first meeting and getting to know each other. After all, how could you possibly walk together except that you are in agreement (v. 3)?

God uses the Hebrew word "yada" in verse two to picture the intimate relationship between Himself and the nation of Israel. This is the same word He uses (knew) to portray the intimacy in marriage between Adam and Eve (Gen. 4:1). He adds special emphasis to the word by stating "you only" in Amos 3:2. This language reveals that Israel was the only one chosen to walk in agreement with Him as His bride. What a tremendous privilege! But with every privilege comes responsibility. To whom much is given, much will be required (Luke 12:48). Through a series of seven rhetorical questions (vv. 3–6), Amos reminds Israel that each effect has a cause. The people had broken their covenant with God, yet they expected to continue to walk in agreement with Him, enjoying His presence and fellowship without repentance and reformation. Agreement would only come through reconciliation with God.

Couples who initially agree to share their lives often find themselves miles apart in the months or years that follow. Disagreements can cause distance in a relationship that makes spouses who were once in agreement feel totally incompatible. Repentance will only come as they humble themselves and agree that intimacy with God has to be the common path in their walk together. Once their vertical relationship is in agreement with Him, their horizontal relationship can be restored with each other! Are you walking in agreement with God in your marriage?

THE PROMISE OF TODAY

Read Hebrews 3:5–15

*M*arriage has daily challenges. Two people with different perspectives continually attempt to coordinate their lives. The choices of one spouse affect the other. Decisions that impact another person can be complicated and confusing. Thankfully, we do not have to depend on our own schemes and wisdom since God promises to speak to us if we will hear Him (v. 7). Today, we have a choice to either listen or refuse to listen to the voice of God.

Moses faced challenges in coordinating the households of the children of Israel, but he was faithful, trusting in God's future promises because He spoke to him personally and regularly (v. 5). We, too, can confidently hold fast to hope because God will speak to us today. We may have responded harshly to our spouse yesterday. We may have made selfish decisions. But, we can hear from God today and choose from this point forward to obey. He may not answer the question that is foremost on our heart. He may not speak what we expect Him to. He may require a tough sacrifice or a humbling repentance. He may remind us of His promises. He may repeat the same message we have refused to listen to for years, but He will speak. We can listen and respond today. The question is, will we? Open your heart to God as a couple, and ask Him to speak truth into your marriage. He can give you wisdom to resolve any conflicts, struggles, or circumstances you may be facing. He will speak to you today!

THE WARNING OF TODAY

Read Hebrews 3:7–19

After my son brought in the chicken from the grill and I began to enjoy a few bites, I asked him if he had turned off the gas. He explained that he had left it on in case the remaining chicken wasn't done. He promised to take care of it as soon as we finished eating. I knew I should prompt him to turn it off, but decided to wait and not interrupt our meal. Several hours later, I went to the grill and saw that it was still on. Because I procrastinated, we wasted fuel and would have a higher gas bill to pay.

We are instructed to immediately respond when God speaks so we will avoid harm and not miss His blessings (vv. 8–11). Andrew Murray says, "There is nothing so hardening as delay. The believer, who answers the To-day of the Holy Ghost with the To-morrow of some more convenient season, knows not how he is hardening his heart; the delay, instead of making the surrender and obedience and faith easy, makes it more difficult."[25]

Often, the most tempting directives to delay are those involving our spouse and family. God prompts us to forgive or apologize, but we wait until we build up our courage. He urges us to sit down and pay attention to our spouse, but we decide to finish the household chores first. We reason that our spouse will understand if we attend to other things first. When we do not immediately respond to the Holy Spirit's direction, we are conveying to God that we can better allocate our time than He can. To procrastinate regarding what He wants exhibits an evil heart of unbelief (v. 12). Even though this tries His patience, God is faithful to warn us (v. 8–9). Notice the urgency evident as He uses the word "today" three different times (vv. 3:7, 13, 15). God repeatedly challenges us to respond today. Are you delaying obedience to Him in some matter?

THE DUTY FOR TODAY

Read Hebrews 3:12–14

Hebrews 3:12–14 references the responsibility fellow believers have toward one another. As brothers and sisters in Christ, love should be exhibited as a concern for the well being of one another. This care is greatly intensified in marriage because of the deeper bond and stronger commitment. When these verses challenge us to exhort one another daily, we are to especially and most importantly do so with our spouse. Exhortation is not criticism. It is not soothing guilt or sugar-coating wrong behavior. Exhortation is a warning or urgent appeal that simultaneously causes someone to consider their hope in God. Exhortation involves considering a situation in light of God's attributes and power. As we live life with our mates, we are to inspire them by expressing confidence in the character and purposes of Jesus in all they do.

God issues a strong warning to exhort because He realizes our tendency to drift away from the fact that He is living and present in the midst of our circumstances. When people are enveloped in activity, crisis, or stress, they are so personally involved that they might not realize they are thinking and acting as though God does not exist. A husband or wife who is focusing on the Lord can recognize a spouse's unbelief when the spouse might be blinded. For the good of the family, for the good of the body of Christ, whenever we recognize this lack of faith, we need to encourage our husband or wife to trust in the living God. The longer individuals think and act in unbelief, the more blind or deceived they become, until eventually their hearts are hardened to the voice of God. Out of love, care, and concern that our spouse experiences the fullness of the Lord's blessings, it is our obligation to daily exhort him or her to live according to His majesty.

THERE IS HOPE

Read Ecclesiastes 9:4 and 1 Timothy 1:1

*S*tatistics tell us that suicide is one of the leading causes of death in America.

"A divorced male is 2.5 to 3 times more likely to commit suicide than the average male."[26]

The main reason a person becomes suicidal is that they have lost all hope.

In today's verse, Solomon—the wisest man who ever lived—makes a profound statement concerning those who are alive, "There is hope." If you are experiencing a struggling marriage and you are still alive, there is hope. If you are financially strapped and you are alive, there is hope. If you are having problems with your children that seem insurmountable, and you are alive, there is hope. If you are physically impaired and you are alive, there is hope.

Solomon illustrates this living hope by using the analogy of a living dog and a dead lion. A dog was the most despised animal of that day (1 Sam. 17:43), whereas a lion was the most respected (Prov. 30:30). Solomon points out that even though greatly valued, a dead lion has no potential, but even when despised and rejected, a living dog has hope. Although we might not be as talented, gifted, or intellectual as someone who has gone before us, his or her opportunity in this life has passed, yet our hope and potential remain.

The activities and perspectives of this temporal natural world are meaningless, but the supernatural purposes of God are eternally fulfilling. He desires for each of us to experience abundant life through Jesus living within us. When we do not know Christ or have not surrendered totally to His life living in us, our hope diminishes into the dead emptiness of this world. With Jesus as our Lord and Savior, no matter what challenge or problem we may face—even if we are the most despised of all people—there is always hope (1 Tim. 1:1).

TO BUY OR NOT TO BUY

Read Luke 14:28-30 and Proverbs 31:11–12

Recently, a young wife called seeking counsel. She had searched for a lost item in her husband's truck and discovered a stack of collection notices including bills for back taxes totaling $300,000. For years, he had ignored tax obligations and had hidden bills from extravagant purchases. She was understandably hurt, scared, and mad.

Another friend maxed out the credit cards and ran up high accounts at local stores. She justified her spending with the intention to work out a payment plan, but one charge at a time slowly piled into a mountain of bills that created stress in her marriage. The husband added to their problems when he sought relief in the listening ear of another woman.

The problem with overspending is that it sneaks in and becomes a habit justified with endless excuses. "That bargain is too good to resist, I will not have another chance. This purchase will enhance my life, I need it. This item will pay for itself. My friend owns one and says that it's great, or it doesn't cost that much." Budgeting is common sense, but requires discipline (Luke 14:28-30). Understanding God's view of money provides spouses with the incentive to avoid excuses and exercise self control in their spending. Christians are expected to manage resources according to His purpose and for His glory (Gen 1:28, 1 Cor. 4:2).

Money management directly impacts family relationships. Proverbs 31:11–12 describes the honorable woman as one her husband trusts to make wise decisions because she conscientiously avoids filling his life with stress and frustration. Although the passage describes the traits of a wife, a trustworthy husband should also be sensitive to make reasonable purchases that will not incur anxiety from unnecessary debt. Eliminate stress in your marriage by developing a budget that is agreeable to both of you. If you have never taken a biblical financial class, commit to find one and enroll together. This will unite your thinking and help you develop a plan that is pleasing to God.

START TODAY

Read Psalm 119:60 and Ecclesiastes 5:4

One of the most debilitating thoughts in our Christian life is, "Why do today what I can do tomorrow?" A story is told of the devil and his demons discussing how they can destroy families. One little demon speaks up and says, "I know what we can do. Let's get pornography, alcohol, and drugs into homes and schools." The devil responds, "No, we are already doing that and it is working quite well. We need to think of something new." Another demon speaks up and suggests, "Let's get husbands and wives so busy they don't have time for each other." The devil impatiently replies, "We are already making great strides in that area. We need a fresh idea." A shy little demon raises his hand and says, "I know what we can do; let's whisper in their ear to have family devotions, for husbands and wives to pray with each other, and spend time together." All the other demons shouted, "Are you crazy? We don't want them to do these things." The shy little demon continues, "Let me finish, tell them to do these things and then, whisper in their ear, start tomorrow." The devil does not care how many marriage seminars we intend to attend, or how many times we intend to go to church, as long as we do not actually start doing these things today.

If God has shown you through His Spirit to start tithing, develop a budget, or read a book on parenting, begin today! Deadlines turn good intentions into commitments. True obedience is demonstrated through immediate response. By setting a deadline (a specific time to act) for what God has shown us, we can turn good intentions into commitments, and be greatly blessed. Are you procrastinating over a directive from God?

TENDING THE SHEEP

Read John 21:15–19

*J*esus gave Peter an assignment. Tend My sheep. Provide what they need. Give them the food of My Word. Protect them from the spiritual nutrition robber, the devil. All three times before Jesus instructs Peter to minister to His sheep, He inquires about Peter's love for Him. Before an assignment like this, the question you would expect is, "Do you really love My sheep?" When Peter was young, he achieved much through his own energy and strength, but the challenge to effectively feed Jesus' sheep would require much more (v. 18). Peter needed to establish that he loved the Lord with all of his heart, with all of his understanding, with all of his being. Ministering to self-centered, demanding, needy human sheep would present heart-rending difficulties. An intimate relationship with the Lord would provide the divine compassion and fortitude Peter would need for this calling.

Spouses are like sheep. They need lots of attentive care. They tend to get stuck in thickets. They allow the gnats and bugs of life to annoy and eat away at the tender parts of their mind. They need nurture. Wild, hateful, growling enemies will attack, so they need a safe, loving haven where they can find comfort. Sheep are dumb creatures that tend to wander. Spouses may not be intellectually challenged, but there are times when they don't think straight.

What a task! Tending to a spouse requires unending compassion, wisdom, sensitivity, patience, and energy. We must remember that human talents, abilities, experience, study, and techniques are not the keys to effective care. Rather, passionate, steady, confident love for and from Jesus will empower a husband or wife to effectively minister to a spouse. Is your love for Jesus factual or intimate? Is it steady or random? Do you seek Him out of duty or devotion? Do you truly love Him with every fiber of your being? Your marriage depends on it.

NO NEED TO HALT

Read Psalms 37:1–40

*D*etailed reports of another horrifying school massacre hit the airwaves. A friend asked if watching the news prompted me to live in fear. No doubt, if I lived in that community, I would dread the thought of my child returning to school. Her question stirred memories of the reactions of people during the aftermath of 9/11. For months, people refused to fly or travel by mass transit. Others avoided crowds because any large gathering provided a tempting target for a terrorist. A sense of shock, helplessness, and even panic invaded the lives of all Americans. Not knowing what to do in response paralyzed us. But I also remember President Bush's admonition during those days. He urged citizens to resume their normal activities, since bringing routine life to a halt would accomplish the enemy's purpose.

Psalms 37 instructs us in the same way. Repeatedly, the passage warns us not to fret because of evildoers and what they might do (vv. 1, 7, 8). It describes the activity of terrorists (vv. 12, 14, 21, 32, and 35), but also specifically instructs believers in their everyday routine of life. We are to trust in the Lord, do good deeds, and carry on our usual activities (v. 3). The wrongs of the enemy may force us to take action, but our focus should be on the Lord's strength, faithfulness, and love so that we will trust Him. We are to delight in His character (v. 4). Concentrating on and being confident in Him will relieve the tendency to fret. Fretting fuels evil and harm (v. 8), but delighting in the Lord results in His fulfilling the desires of our hearts (v. 4). We are to commit our routine life to Him who controls all things (v. 5). He can be trusted. He and His people will be victorious (vv. 38–40). Are you fretting over evil-doers? Choose to trust God instead.

A PERFECT HEART

Read 2 Chronicles 16:9 and Psalm 130:1–8

A few days ago, Sam requested that I print a report of our ministry's finances for the previous quarter in order to identify aspects in which we had been negligent or careless. He noted a benefit supplied by the ministry that we had not considered when we tithed. He instructed me to include extra with our tithe for the next few weeks until the difference was met. He explained that he was examining his life for any sin that could be hindering God's blessings on our finances and ministry. We prayed together, asking Him to reveal areas of our lives that we needed to change.

We knew that God could reveal a problem which would require an adjustment that was out of our comfort zone. We might have to repent from something we really wanted to do. I was apprehensive. Then I walked by a counter where my memory verse for the week was displayed. 2 Chronicles 16:9 relieved my concern. Sam was striving to have a perfect heart before God, and the Lord promises to show Himself strong on Sam's behalf. The next day I read Psalm 130. We had cried out to the Lord, asking Him to reveal what we needed to know (Psalm 130:1–2). When we first prayed, I was worried about how God might correct us. But God's correction is redemptive, not punitive. Rather than mark down a record of our wrongs and defeat us, He grants forgiveness so that we will respect Him (Psalm 130:3–4). Now I wait for the Lord to answer our prayer and I find hope in His word (Psalm 130:5). I anxiously await His revelation. I can hope in Him, not only because He is merciful, but because He will redeem us from any sin He reveals (Psalm 130:6–8).

BEWARE

Read Joshua 9:3–16

Several years ago, the Lord directed us to sell our Christian theater to start a family ministry outreach. We contacted an agent who specialized in selling established theaters. He was from another state, and told us he was a Christian. After sharing details about his family and health problems, he told us he had a reputable buyer. He explained all the contracts and gave us a down payment from his client. Out of sincere concern, we prayed for the agent, his family, and the problems he was facing. We blessed him and sent a gift for his wife. The purchaser moved in and took over the theater, but never paid us again. During the process of seeking payments, we discovered the agent had "conned" us. The buyer had a reputation of deception and dishonesty. The agent knew that if he appealed to our sympathy, we would trust him and contract with him so he would receive his commission. He deceived us.

In Joshua 9, a group of people from nearby Gibeon plotted a scheme to appeal to Joshua's kind heart so he would make a covenant with them (Joshua 9:3–6). The strangers—like our agent—acknowledged a respect for God, then mixed truth with lies as they poured out their story (vv. 9–11). They presented heart-rending, but false evidence to entice him to sympathize with their problems (vv. 12–13). The men of Israel dismissed the hesitancy within their hearts when they accepted the skimpy evidence as credentials (vv. 7, 14). Joshua and his leaders based their decision on the "facts" before them, and did not consult the One who knows the deep and secret things (v. 9:14, Daniel 2:22). Joshua responded in compassion and agreed to the covenant.

We learned, like Joshua, that we must not only consider the evidence, but also consult our all-knowing God. Beware of people who appeal in His name with intent to manipulate. If we consult the Lord, He can protect us and our families from deception.

CONFUSION

Read Psalm 35

In our previous devotion, I described how God used the situation with a dishonest sales agent to remind us to consult Him in every transaction. When the sales agent and purchaser deceived us and refused to make the payments agreed upon in our contract, we were forced to take the purchaser to court to retrieve our equipment and remove him from the building. We had already learned a valuable lesson when we trusted these strangers without consulting the Lord concerning their character and intentions. At a Bible study I attended weekly, I requested prayer for God's grace and deliverance in this matter. He used the Bible study leader and specific Scriptures we discussed to bring comfort and assurance. Psalm 35 described our situation (v. 7). As a group, we rejoiced in the compassion and power of God to deliver us (vv. 10–12). We requested that the Lord rescue us from this destruction (v. 17) and that He be glorified in the process (v. 18). We realized what we were facing in dealing with liars (vv. 19–21). We were limited in our resources to defend ourselves in court, so we declared our dependence upon the Lord (vv. 22–25). He directed us to pray that our adversary be confused and brought to shame (v. 26). In court, the purchaser contradicted his own testimony numerous times. God confused him so that he could not keep his lies believable. He was shamed. We were amazed and continue to rejoice to this day at how specifically God answered the very prayer that He showed us to pray (v. 27). Utterly depending on the Lord brings confusion to the adversary, while flooding believers with joy and confidence.

A FAITHFUL STEWARD

Read Genesis 1:28 and 1 Corinthians 4:2

*M*oney management is an area that is often neglected by couples before marriage, but it is one of the greatest sources of potential conflict. Couples who reported arguing about finances at least once a week have a 30 percent higher chance of getting a divorce. Statistics show that as many as 70 percent of divorcing couples attribute the breakdown of their marriages to arguments related to finances.[27]

How we manage our money is so significant that God frequently addresses the topic in His Word. Sixteen out of thirty eight of the Jesus' parables deal with it. More is said in the New Testament about money than heaven and hell combined. There is five times more said about money than prayer.[28]

Establishing a biblical understanding of money is essential to a strong marriage. Wise and godly financial management will not only serve to protect your future from unneeded stress, but will better equip you to respond to the tasks to which God calls you.

God commands man to be a faithful steward over all His creation (Gen. 1:28). A steward is someone entrusted with another's wealth or property, charged with managing it in the owner's best interest.[29] As stewards, we are commanded by God to faithfully manage all things according to His purpose and for His glory (1 Cor. 4:2). A faithful steward clearly understands that he owns nothing and God owns everything! He does exactly as the Master directs. This includes not only our time and talents, but also the treasure (money) He entrusts to us. Will you as a couple commit to faithfully steward the resources God blesses you with in your marriage?

TEMPORAL OR ETERNAL PERSPECTIVE

**Read Matthew 13:44, Matthew 6:19–21,
Philippians 3: 7–8, and 1 Timothy 6:10**

Throughout the Bible, God teaches that to be a faithful steward of His money, one must have an eternal rather than temporal perspective. Jesus profoundly illustrates this truth in the parable of the hidden treasure (v. 44). The man in this parable realizes the kingdom of God is a treasure far more valuable than all temporal possessions. "In his joy," he sells everything to buy what is eternal and priceless. From this teaching, Jesus wants us to understand that when money is spent on earthly treasure, it has only temporary value. When it is invested in heavenly treasure, it takes on eternal worth and brings joy to the one who has rightly invested.

In another command, Jesus reasons that how we use our money indicates whether our heart is inclined toward God or toward the things of this world (Matt. 6:19–21, 24). We will either use the money He supplies for our purposes (our glory) or for God's purposes (His glory). Where we put our money clearly unveils the allegiance of our heart! God desires that we treasure Jesus (the eternal) above the temporal things of this world (Phil. 3:7–8). If a couple has an eternal perspective, they will use their money according to God's purposes and plans. If a couple has a temporal view, they will use their money to accumulate the riches of this world, which will inevitably lead them down a road of many sorrows (1 Tim. 6:10). If you want a quick look at which perspective you have, review your check book and credit card statements. Do you tithe and support missionaries? Do you give to those in need? The facts will reveal where your heart is, whether your perspective is temporal or eternal.

Will you as a couple commit to having an eternal perspective with your finances, to use the resources God gives you to help further His kingdom?

OBEDIENT RECEIVING

Read Philippians 4:19

*H*ave you ever had a child beg, "It's hot, I neeeeeeed a Popsicle. Please may I have a Popsicle!" The child is totally convinced that life would be unbearable without a Popsicle. He or she even politely offers the words, "please" and "may I." But you, the wiser more experienced adult, realize that a third Popsicle in a span of two hours—twenty minutes before meal time—would be unhealthy.

We serve a God who created and holds title to everything! Those who have a personal relationship with Him through Jesus Christ have access to His holdings and can claim the promise in today's verse that God will supply all their need. His plan is that we receive all we need through Him, our loving Father. He does not say He will supply a little bit or part of our needs, but all. The question arises, "What is my need?" We can confidently affirm that food, shelter, and clothing are needs. We might even stretch them to include transportation, a vacation, or retirement. Wayne Coleman defines a need as "the total physical cost to physically perform the spiritual will of God"[30] in your life.

Since God has a different "spiritual will" for every person, our physical needs will vary. For one person, it may require large sums of money while for another it may be minimal. Whatever it is, we should submit to God in receiving provision for that need. He defines our need as we commune with Him and He reveals His will to us. If we attempt to define it ourselves, we are acting self-sufficiently, independent of God. Prayerfully seek the Lord as husband and wife and ask Him to show you exactly what you need to perform His will for you and your family. Confidently commit those needs to the Lord for His provision. He will faithfully fulfill them, and may also graciously grant blessings abundantly beyond your needs.

PROVISION OF THE NEED

Read Philippians 4:19 and John 10:10

Children know they do not receive candy from their parents any time they ask. If denied, the nature of the child is to seek another source. If not previously warned, a child may leap at an opportunity to accept goodies from a stranger. We shudder at the danger.

As Christian adults, there are two basic sources through which we receive provision—God and Satan. When we look to and wait on God to supply our need, we live in freedom as we pursue His will (v. 19). When through self-sufficiency or indifference to God we allow Satan to supply our need, we end up in bondage through debt and enslavement to man (Prov. 22:7, Deut. 15:6). To freely pursue the "spiritual will" of God, we must submit to the principle of correctly receiving His provision for our needs.

To avoid risky receiving, we must submit in four keys ways. First, we submit to God's definition of the need. This requires constant communion with Him as we strive to discern between what is a strong desire and what is a genuine need. Second, we must submit to God's provision for the need. Many times He may supply in a different way than we expect. We may need transportation and trust God to supply money for a car, but He chooses to supply the actual vehicle or a ride rather than finances. Third, we must submit to God's timing related to the need. He is never early or late; He is an "on time" God! We must be patient and trust Him. Finally, we must submit to His method of meeting the need. God will, many times, surprise us in the way He supplies. It may be through a person, an organization, or even through what we might call chance—actually God's sovereignty. The key is to set aside personal plans and desires that may be overshadowing what He wants, and be willing to sacrifice them as He directs. Desire what He wants more than what you want. Trust Him. His riches are vast and His grace is abundant!

OBEDIENT GIVING

Read James 2:17, Luke 6:38, and 2 Corinthians 8:1–9

*G*od commands His children to be faithful stewards through whom He can channel His resources, for His glory. When we give as God directs, we exercise both obedience and faith. Faith without works is dead (James 2:17). Giving to meet the needs of others as God prompts us shows that our faith is alive and real. If we receive from Him and do not practice giving, then we are like the Dead Sea. It takes in millions of tons of water every hour, but has no outlet. As a result, it becomes stagnant and as the name suggests … dead.

Jesus teaches that giving and receiving actually comprise one experience rather than two (Luke 6:38). He promises that those who give will receive in the same measure that they gave. Giving becomes a cycle. Givers receive so they can give more. Our motive in giving, however, is not to receive, but to point others to the generosity and faithfulness of God. We gratefully repeat what He did for us.

God has a plan for every dollar even before we receive it. Our responsibility is to determine how He wants us to use it. Just like obedient receiving, obedient giving becomes an act of worship! The Macedonians understood the grace of giving as an act of worship (2 Cor. 8:1–9). These early Christians experienced great joy because they "first gave themselves to the Lord" (2 Cor. 8:5). They surrendered in faith to God and gave sacrificially according to His will. Our purpose in giving is not to receive, but rather to experience and expose God in both realms. This is our act of worship.

The local church you attend should be your first priority in giving (1 Cor. 16:1–2). The more you prosper, the more your generosity should abound.

DON'T LIGHT THAT FIRE

Read Proverbs 16:27–28 and Judges 14:17–15:5

When someone faces irritations in marriage, it's common for him or her to complain to a friend. The complaints are normally backed up with details of the absent spouse's conversations or actions. The spouse who is complaining typically is not seeking a solution, just sympathy for his or her plight. Sometimes friends compare notes on the shortcomings of their spouses so they can relate to one another. Others describe their mate's secret quirks so they can amuse their friends. Some individuals seek to nurture closeness with friends by discussing family details such as wages, job situations, and in-law problems.

Proverbs 16:28 warns that such "whispering" separates close friends. This especially applies to spouses. The marriage relationship is built on trust, and "whispering" or gossiping destroys it.

In Judges chapter 14, Samson challenged the Philistine wedding guests with a riddle (v. 12). When they threatened his new bride, she pressed him to tell her the answer, and then secretly disclosed it to the guests (v. 17). The betrayal angered Samson so much that he separated from her and went back to his father's house (v. 19). The couple completely separates when Samson's bride marries his best man (v. 20). The story ends when Samson catches 300 foxes, ties them together in pairs, lights torches on their tails, and turns them loose in the Philistines' fields, vineyards, and olive groves (vv. 15:4–5). Telling private details resulted in a fire of massive destruction.

In Proverbs 16, a whisperer is compared to an ungodly man who digs up evil about others (v. 27). The gossip burns on his lips like a fire. He is also compared to a harsh man who sows strife or spreads dissension (v. 28). These terms are the same root words as those used to describe the inferno ignited by Samson and the flaming foxes. Sharing a spouse's little secrets may seem innocent or amusing, but has the potential to burn the relationship. Don't light that fire.

DON'T SELL HIM OUT

Read Judges 16:4–21 and 1 Timothy 6:10

At a recent marriage conference, a young wife shared her dilemma with me. The company she worked for was requiring her to relocate, but her husband did not want to change jobs. I explained that God intended for the wife to help her husband in fulfilling His purposes for him. In God's plan, wives adapt to the husband's schedule, career, income, personality, and special needs (Eph. 5:24). But she said, "My job pays more!" I told her that a man's self worth is often linked to his job and career, especially if God has directed him to the job. Her husband's significance and dignity were worth more than money. She replied, "You don't understand; I make a lot more money than him." Now I understood; money, not her husband's dignity or significance, was the deciding factor.

In Judges 16, Delilah faced a similar challenge. God had specifically called Samson to be judge over Israel. Samson dearly loved Delilah (v. 4). But Delilah had the opportunity to make a lot of money—thousands of dollars (v. 5). She pushed for what she wanted until she wore him down (vv. 16–17). Delilah made her money, but Samson lost his significance and dignity (vv. 18–21). She cared more about the money than she cared about her man. Delilah actions proved that her love for money (1 Tim. 6:10) was an evil desire. It pierced Samson's life and brought many sorrows.

Money should not be the deciding factor in our decisions. God has promised that if we seek His kingdom first, He will supply all of our needs (Matt. 6:31–33). Money itself is neither good nor bad, but it can be the root cause of many marriage problems if we love it more than God. When you trust Him to supply your income in His way, you are free to edify and support your mate. Base your decisions on Scripture, and what is best for the good of your loved one.

FOOLISH TALKING

Read Ephesians 5:4 and Colossians 4:6

One of my father's favorite TV shows was "All in the Family." At the time, it was fun and humorous to listen to Archie Bunker call his wife "Dingbat" or his son-in-law "Meathead." Thankfully, when I married my wife Debbie, God had taught me not to make teasingly degrading comments about her. Sadly, when ministering in conferences, I often hear comments from one husband to another that get a laugh at the expense of his wife. It all seems innocent, but is it?

In Ephesians 5:4, God warns against sins of the tongue—which actually are sins of the heart! Our words reveal the temperature of our heart to those listening to our speech. Warren Wiersbe states, "Two indications of a person's character are what makes him laugh and what makes him weep."[31] The reference to "foolish talking" does not refer to innocent humor, but to speech that is not edifying to another. This is the kind of vulgar language you would expect to hear from a foolish person. Paul continues by including the word, "jesting" or "crude joking," which is found nowhere else in the New Testament. It refers to individuals who are so quick-witted that they can easily turn a clean conversation into a coarse or even filthy dialogue. Of course, the gift of having a quick wit is a blessing, but it can be a curse if not controlled by the Holy Spirit. God continues by saying this kind of speech is inappropriate for His people. Rather than speak this way, we should give thanks. We should season our speech as with salt, to build up and minister grace to the hearer (Col. 4:6).

A husband and wife should be very careful not to use foolish talking or jesting with regard to one another. They also should not take part in conversations with others who engage in this type of humor (Eph. 5:7). Refuse to be involved in such discourse. Seek to edify your spouse!

4:8 YOUR MATE

Read Philippians 4:6–8

After the honeymoon, when day to day routine sets in, most couples will start to notice annoying habits in their spouses. These tendencies can range from a nervous habit of shaking a leg whenever he or she sits, to leaving dirty clothes on the floor, to repeatedly comparing the spouse with mom or dad. Some spouses wake up grouchy. Others space out each night in front of the television. When we are in a hurry or under pressure, these annoying habits are even more bothersome. If we allow ourselves to think about how inconsiderate or how ridiculous the habit is, our frustration grows. We may even reinforce our point of view by comparing our misfortunes with others who have similar challenges with their mates. Before long, we can write an essay paper on the challenges of dealing with the habit. Focusing on it builds tension in our relationship. We are tempted to scream, clench our fist, or even throw something.

In Philippians, Paul offers a solution. He instructs the believers in finding the peace of God (vv. 6–7). Then in verse eight, he tells them how to think. He directs them to consider what is true, not blown out of proportion. Consider what is honest and just. Losing your temper is not just. Paul urges believers to concentrate on what is pure and lovely. Think about what attracted you to your mate. Remember the things that are of good report—what you would encourage him or her to include on a resume. Paul says that if there is anything virtuous or worth praising, think about these things. We should apply these instructions to our mates so we will think good, kind, loving, respectful thoughts about them. Shifting our thinking in this direction will decrease tension and increase appreciation. Next time you feel the urge to express frustration to your spouse, try Philippians 4:8 instead!

THE TEST

Read Genesis 22:1–11 and 15:18

Covenants do not stand unchallenged. They will be tested. Covenant relationships that withstand tests emerge much stronger. God was loyally committed to the covenant He had made with Abraham (Gen. 15:18), but He tested Abraham's devotion when He commanded him to sacrifice something more precious than his own life, the life of his son (v. 2).

Can you imagine? Any godly father prizes the life of his son over his own. To sacrifice his son required total surrender and trust in the One with whom he had covenanted. Through faith, Abraham took Isaac to Mount Moriah (vv. 3–4). Abraham demonstrated trust in God when he told his servants that he and his son were going to worship on the mountain and they would return (v. 5). As Abraham stretches out his hand to slay his son, an angel of the Lord calls to him from heaven and tells him not to harm the child. He passed God's test (v. 12).

In this passage, Abraham proves his trust in God yet again, no matter the cost! He had trusted God earlier, when He instructed him to leave his homeland and relocate his family. Now he trusts God when he obediently takes steps to offer Isaac on Mount Moriah. The covenant relationship is built on trust.

Marriage is patterned after the covenant relationship God has with us. Marriage can get tricky, however, because it involves two sinful people who will fail each other at times. This can be a huge test if the failures cause trust issues to surface—matters which must be resolved. The path to resolution involves climbing the mountain together, laying your lives and what you care about before God, and worshipping Him. When you both sincerely surrender, the re-building of trust can begin. You can descend the mountain in unity, much stronger in your faith and tighter in your covenant bond. Are there trust issues in your relationship that need to be resolved?

LEAVING AN INHERITANCE

Read Proverbs 13:22

*G*od's plan is that a family not be enslaved by debt, but rather that a father leaves an inheritance to his children, giving them a head start financially. The inheritance from a Jewish father was often land. It provided security for his son's future family to have a place to live, free from the burden of monthly payments or interest. The firstborn was given a double portion because he was not only to have enough for his future family, but also to take care of his parents in their old age. The inheritance passed to a daughter was known as the dowry. It was typically seven years wages, paid to the bride's father for the bride. Through that process, a father would have an inheritance to leave his daughter without depleting the amount he gave his sons. A son's inheritance would be cut off for any of the following sins: idol worship, defiling one's wife, blasphemy, and any capital crimes such as murder, rape, adultery, sodomy, or others.

Unfortunately, in our culture it is common for a young couple to start marriage with college loans, credit card debt, and other financial encumbrances that create much stress. Most parents do not have resources to leave their children, as they lived most of their married life in debt. These realities, plus the expectations of young couples to have a lifestyle equivalent to their parents or peers, can potentially add tremendous conflict to a marriage.

As a couple, commit to a biblically based financial plan. In doing so, you will protect your marriage and family from being enslaved to debt, and you will be able to leave an inheritance to your children.

LOVE TURNED SOUR

**Read 1 Samuel 18:20, 27–28, 2 Samuel 3:13-16, 6:16–23,
and Philippians 2:3**

Saul's daughter, Michal, recognizes David's integrity and strong character and deeply loves him (1 Sam. 18:20). David risks his life killing 200 Philistines to prove he is worthy to marry Michal and become the king's son-in-law (1 Sam. 18:27). Michal's love and adoration for David are evident to everyone when they get married (1 Sam. 18:28). When Saul attempts to kill David, Michal proves her loving loyalty when she warns him, helps him escape, and boldly diverts the enemy. When Saul gives Michal to another man, David sends men to bring her back (2 Sam. 3:13–16). The couple loves each other enough to risk their lives and fight for their love. Their love is deep.

One day, however, David embarrasses Michal. She disagrees with his behavior. In her opinion, he acts undignified and disgraces their royal position (2 Sam. 6:16). When a wife is surprised by unexpected behavior, it is tempting to deem a husband's motives to be wrong and unacceptable. David does not live up to Michal's expectations, so in her pride she judges his motives with sarcasm (2 Sam. 6:20). She feels that God accepts her and her reasoning above the actions of her husband. Rather than giving him the benefit of the doubt, she swiftly condemns him without hearing his side of the story. Her deep, committed love turns sour to the point that she despises David. He comes home ready to bless her, but humbles her instead when he explains the godly intent of his heart (2 Sam. 6:21–23).

Regretfully, there have been times when I determined my husband's motives without hearing his perspective. I am humbled as the Lord reveals the wickedness of my judgmental pride. I am sorry for the undeserved hurt I inflicted. Always give your spouse the benefit of the doubt. Allow opportunity for them to explain their intentions. Let God be the judge. Don't let critical pride sour your love.

MINE

Read Song of Solomon 5:9–6:3

*W*hen my four-year-old niece was visiting her grandmother, she walked through the entire house pointing to many different things and asking, "Is this mine, Grandma?" At first her grandmother was puzzled about this sudden obsession to know what belonged to her. Since my niece lives with three teenagers, she was accustomed to their pointing out their belongings to her, with instructions not to touch. In her mind, everything interesting belonged to someone else and was off limits. She felt deprived. She needed the security and stability of her own possessions. Her grandmother pointed out several items she could claim as her own. She liked being in control of her own possessions. She felt secure because she knew that no one would take them from her.

In today's passage, the Shulamite bride experiences similar anxiety with her new groom. He is King of Israel. Everyone demands his time and attention. He is surrounded by beautiful, dignified ladies of the kingdom. At the beginning of their relationship, she is unsure that a simple country girl like her could continually captivate the heart of the king. The daughters of Jerusalem ask her what is so special about her husband (v. 9). She replies with an admirable and detailed description of his attributes (vv. 10–16). She claims him as her lover and friend. When the daughters of Jerusalem question his whereabouts (v. 1), she allegorically explains that he is fulfilling his responsibilities (feeding) to the citizens (flock) of the kingdom (v. 2). She concludes by saying, "I am my beloved's, and my beloved is mine." Describing his qualities and explaining her understanding of his work makes her realize how special their relationship is. A husband and wife know each other in ways no one else can claim. They share life events, memories, dreams, and secrets that belong only to them as a couple. Both spouses can then experience security and stability as they confidently claim one another as "mine." Say to your spouse "You are mine," followed by a big hug and kiss!

THE POSSESSIVENESS OF CHRIST

Read John 17:6–26

*Y*esterday's devotion concluded that as a spouse, I experience security and stability by claiming my mate as "mine." Christ also claims possession of His bride with the word "mine" (v. 10). Understanding the importance of this concept from His perspective helps us practice the principle in our own marriage.

Christ understands that His bride is a special gift from God the Father (v. 6). He cherishes His gift and develops intimacy with her by opening His heart and sharing what is most important to Him. He explains the words the Father has personally revealed to Him. His life also proves to His bride that He has an intimate relationship with the Father (vv. 7–8). This stirs her to a deeper relationship with the Father that they can share together. Christ is concerned for His bride, so He diligently prays for her (v. 9). Christ recognizes the preciousness of His possession, and understands that He shares ownership with the Father (v. 10). He is proud of His possession. He exercises responsibility to care for her (vv. 11–12) and His overwhelming desire is that she experiences the same joy He has known (v. 13). Christ enjoys sharing with His bride and giving to her (v. 22). He conveys that she is special to Him by making arrangements to be with her (v. 24).

Christ expresses selfless possessiveness. He fulfills His responsibility to point His bride to the Father, and His thoughts and actions exhibit authentic care and concern for her welfare. He achieves all of this because He Himself is completely surrendered to the will of the Father. What a profound example for us to follow in claiming our spouse as "mine."

THE WHOLE DUTY OF MAN

Read Ecclesiastes 1:2, 12:13, and Proverbs 2:1–6, 24:3-4

The title of the book, Ecclesiastes, simply means "preacher." Solomon, the preacher of this sermon implores man to understand that power, prestige, pleasure, and popularity cannot fill the vacuum that is within man. God created us to be filled with Him, to worship Him and Him alone! When we attempt to fill the void with anything other than God, our efforts are vain (v. 2).

The preacher ends his sermon with a powerful conclusion—to fear God and keep His commandments is the whole duty of man (12:13). This does not refer to a reaction that is the result of being afraid, but a reverence that acknowledges the holiness and power of a sovereign God. God's original intent and purpose is for man to fear Him, obey Him, and glorify Him through worshipping Him. Our chief concern and care should be to fear God and obey His commandments every moment He grants us breath. No other pursuit or ambition in life equates with this duty of man.

A careful investigation of the Bible reveals that the instruction to fear God is woven all throughout Scripture. There are more than 150 specific references to the fear of God and hundreds of indirect ones. A man's character and conduct are rooted in the fear of God (Prov. 16:6). Our worship and service must be founded in our fear of God (Ps. 2:11, 5:7). Intimacy with Him is reserved for those who walk in the fear of God (Ps. 25:14). We are commanded to pursue holiness in the fear of God (2 Cor. 7:1). The success of the Proverbs 31 woman is attributed to her fear of God (Prov. 31:30). Proverbs 24:3–4 names three ingredients necessary to build a godly home: wisdom, understanding, and knowledge. These essential ingredients are all rooted in the fear of God (Prov. 2:5–6, 9:10). We cannot escape the crucial importance of the need in our lives, families, and nation to fear God! Over the next few days of devotions, we will investigate exactly what that means, and how to build a God-fearing family.

THE SOUL OF GODLINESS

Read Job 1:1 and 2 Corinthians 6:14–7:1

As a little boy attending church, I would often hear someone described as a God-fearing person. Today, however, it is rare to hear someone referred to in that way.

Throughout the Bible, we see many examples of God-fearing men. Job is described as a man who feared the Lord and turned away from evil (v. 1). When Abraham obeyed by willingly offering Isaac as a sacrifice, God acknowledged that Abraham feared Him (Gen. 22:12). God instructed Moses to only appoint leaders who feared Him (Ex. 18:21). The New Testament church is depicted in Acts 9:31 as multiplying as they walked in the fear of God.

What exactly does it mean to fear God? John Murray states, "The fear of God is the soul of godliness ... the fear which constrains adoration and love ... It consists of awe, reverence, honor, and worship, and all of these on the highest level of exercise. It is the reflex in our consciousness of the transcendent majesty and holiness of God."[32] Albert Martin explains, "Take away the soul from the body and all you have left in a few days is a stinking carcass. Take away the fear of God from any expression of godliness and all you have left is the stinking carcass of barren religiosity."[33]

Without the fear of God, godliness will not be pursued (Prov. 16:6). A life, home, or nation that lacks the fear of God becomes an ungodly entity! He emphatically promises to live and walk with us as our powerful Father and God if we will be separate and holy (2 Cor. 6:16–18). The pursuit of holiness is the direct result of a heart that fears God (2 Cor. 7:1). The fear of God is the soul of godliness.

TERROR OR DREAD

Read Genesis 3:8–10 and Hebrews 12:28–29

*M*y wife Debbie, like most women, is scared to death of snakes. If she walked into her closet and a snake slithered out, she would be overcome with a sense of terror or dread of what the object of her fear (the snake) could do to her.

This type of fear is first illustrated in the Bible after Adam and Eve disobey God. They had previously enjoyed sweet communion with Him, but now they hide when God calls (v. 9 –10). Why? God had warned Adam that if he ate of the tree of the knowledge of good and evil, he would surely die (Gen. 2:17). Unlike my wife, Adam deserved punishment. His terror and dread was real not only because chastisement was justified, but because he realized the power of the One who would exercise wrath against him. The God with whom Adam had previously communed is now a terror and dread. Should all persons fear God in this manner? John Murray aptly observes, *"It is the essence of impiety not to be afraid of God when there is reason to be afraid … The Scripture throughout prescribes the necessity of this fear of God under all circumstances in which our sinful situation makes us liable to God's righteous judgment."*[34]

Jesus warns not to fear people—who can kill the body, but cannot kill the soul—but rather fear God who is able to destroy both soul and body in hell (Matt. 10:28). To the non-Christian, the terror or dread of God is that of spending eternity separated from His presence in a literal hell. The basis for this type of fear is rooted in understanding the holiness of God against sin. Because He is both holy and just, He will not tolerate sin in His presence.

Even though a Christian does not have to fear eternal separation, he still must realize that God will discipline him if he continually practices sin (Heb. 12:5–8). This chastisement not only affects him, but its consequences can cause innocent family members to suffer. How important to incorporate this aspect of the fear of God into your life!

OUR AWESOME GOD

Read Isaiah 40:12–18, Psalm 147:4, and Jeremiah 5:22

On our twenty-fifth anniversary trip to Hawaii, we often took time to sit near the ocean as the darkness of night approached to observe the awesomeness of God's creation. We were amazed at the powerful waves splashing onto the rocks, and the brilliance of the stars intensified by the darkness of our obscure location. As we gazed out into the vast horizon, I was reminded of the immensity and wonder of creation (Isa. 40:12–18). God can hold the oceans in His hand, whereas we can barely hold a tablespoon. We can measure nine inches across the span of our palm, but our incredible God measures the heavens with His. He even numbers the stars and calls them all by name (Psalm 147:4). It is no wonder that we are challenged to find anyone that can even begin to compare to Jehovah God (Isa. 40:18).

Even though a terror or dread due to our sinfulness is an essential part of the fear of God (yesterday's devotion), the dominant aspect described in Scripture includes a reverence and fascination at the awesomeness of God. Jerry Bridges aptly states, "A profound sense of awe toward God is undoubtedly the dominant element in the attitude or set of emotions that the Bible calls the fear of God."[35] Webster's dictionary defines "awe" as an emotion combining dread, veneration, and wonder that is inspired by Deity. The awe we are describing is not that of an awesome food or amazing sporting event, but rather a deep reverence directed specifically toward a holy God. We only experience this type of fear by being in the presence of someone who is in a high position of worth and dignity. That ultimate someone is God Almighty. Take a few minutes and reflect together on the wonders of God. Praise Him for His greatness!

A FOREVER FAMILY

Read Deuteronomy 5:22–6:9, Exodus 20:18-21, Isaiah 29:13, and Jeremiah 9:23–24

The time has finally arrived to enter into the land of promise. Encamped on the plains of Moab, the anticipation is high among God's chosen people. Before entry into the land that flows with milk and honey, however, Moses reminds the Israelites of their response to the law given forty years earlier (Deut. 5:22–28). God had given them a test, to help them realize their lack of reverent fear for the Lord. (Exod. 20:18–21). Before they enter the land, God cries out to them to fear Him, so that His blessings might be upon them and their children "forever." He is indirectly stating that a heart that fears God is the hinge upon which the door to building a forever family swings (Deut. 5:29).

In the verses that follow, God admonishes His people—and especially parents—to abide in His fear (Deut. 5:30–6:9). Verse four emphasizes the need to continually recognize God in our life and family. In order to correctly acknowledge God, we must properly understand who He is. Unfortunately, our image of Him is often distorted. Arthur Pink states in his book, The Attributes of God, "The heathen outside Christendom form gods out of wood and stone while the millions of heathens inside Christendom manufacture a god out of their own carnal minds!"[36] God points out this same problem in Isaiah 29:13, when He describes His people as giving Him lip service while their hearts are totally distracted and their fear of Him is taught by men. We must not have a distorted view of God (Jer. 9:23–24). He knows we will worship and serve Him in the image we have of Him. Studying and understanding the biblical qualities of God is vital to having a marriage and family that fears Him and receives His forever blessings. Plan to read a book together on the attributes of God.

PRACTICING HIS PRESENCE

**Read Psalm 139:7–12, Proverbs 16:6, Jeremiah 16:17,
Psalm 44:21, and 1 Chronicles 28:9**

My son had just turned sixteen, and was very excited about getting his driver's license. Before letting him drive alone I pointed out, "I won't know everywhere you go or see everything you do, but I know Someone who sees everywhere you go and knows all you do—God!" I told him I had asked God to tell me everything. By admonishing my son in this manner, I was instilling him with the second important key to walking in the fear of God—the continual practice of His presence! The fear of the Lord includes the continual realization of the ever-watching eye of a Holy God.

In Psalm 139, King David states there is no place in heaven or on earth where he could escape God's presence (vv. 7–12). J.I. Packer states, "Living becomes an awesome business when you realize that you spend every moment of your life in the sight or company of an omniscient, omnipresent creator."[37] When A.W. Tozer was asked what the most profound word in the dictionary is, he answered, "God." He went on to say, "The most profound fact is 'God is' and the most profound experience is 'God is here.'"[38] Realizing that God is omnipresent is a vital aspect of the fear of the Lord that causes men to depart from evil (Prov. 16:6). God not only sees and hears all that we do and say, but also knows our inner thoughts (Ps. 44:21) and motivations of our heart (1 Chr. 28:9). Integrity begins in living all of life in the conscious awareness of God's continual presence.

Practicing the presence of God in our marriages will constrain us to treat our spouse with kindness and tenderheartedness, and to forgive when he or she sins against us. It will keep us from pornography, adultery, and other sinful sexual practices. This important aspect of the fear of God will literally usher His glory into our relationships.

GOD OUR PASSION

**Read Deuteronomy 6:5–6, Revelation 3:15–16,
Matthew 6:24, and Psalm 27:4**

Another ingredient in becoming God-fearing is to be passionate in our relationship with Him. The little word "all" appears three times in verse five. God is emphasizing that He does not want a little bit of us; He doesn't want us to be lukewarm. He desires our all (Rev. 3:15–16). He must be our passion!

After graduating from college, I became involved in a multi-level marketing business. My goal was to become financially independent by my thirtieth birthday. To accomplish my dream, I was told that I must be obsessed with my business. I daily contacted new prospects, held nightly meetings, and wore out several vehicles. My new endeavor consumed my thoughts and actions. I filtered all decisions through my business perspective and it quickly became the driving force of my life! About five years later, when God called me into ministry, I continued to fervently pursue my business as well as my new direction. The Lord began to speak to me about my misplaced priorities. He convicted me, "Do you love me as passionately as you love your business?" My answer was, "Of course God, you know I love you!" He challenged me, "Then why don't you spend as much time with Me—witnessing, praying, and studying the Word—as you do pursuing your financial dream?" I immediately had to confess to God that He was right. I could not wholeheartedly serve two masters at the same time (Matt. 6:24). Even though you may not have been called to serve in full-time ministry, God still desires to be the first love in your life and marriage!

King David describes his passion as a thirst for the living God (Ps 42:2). In Psalm 27:4, he declares his longing to be in the presence of God as his most compelling desire. Walking in the fear of the Lord requires a zeal for Him that supersedes all others. Do you passionately pursue God above every other love in your life? Only when He is the central priority can all other priorities—including your spouse, family, and career—fall into proper alignment.

THE MASTER'S DESIGN

Read Psalm 139:13–16 and Ecclesiastes 4:11

*M*y husband Sam has been out of town for several days. The temperature is dropping outside. When I crawl into bed alone, my body is already chilled and the sheets feel like they have been stored in the refrigerator. I pile on extra blankets, but it still seems like hours before I warm up. This makes me miss Sam even more. When he is home, I look forward to snuggling up to his warm body, even though he automatically jumps when I first touch him. I tell him that God expects him to hug me until we reach equal body temperature, so we will truly and totally be one-flesh (Eccl. 4:11). Even though he complains that I lower his body temperature by about four degrees, I think my interpretation of God's plan for "one temperature" makes sense.

God has amazingly designed our bodies to become one-flesh in many ways other than temperature. He created a chemical called oxytocin to be released through the sense of touch. Oxytocin creates an emotional bond of intimacy and a desire for affectionate touch. Each time a couple holds hands, hugs, or kisses, the oxytocin released produces an emotional high that strengthens their emotional bond. Couples almost begin to crave each other's touch. Ceasing to touch or be together interrupts the transfer of oxytocin and causes spouses to experience withdrawal symptoms such as depression, lovesickness, and a longing to be back together.[39]

The psalmist marvels at how God intricately knits our bodies together with a remarkable plan in mind (Psalm 139:13–14). He compares God's handiwork to the work of a skilled craftsman who follows a careful pattern to weave a beautiful, colorful tapestry (v. 15). Oxytocin is one of the threads in God's design for married love. He not only created the systems of individual bodies to function independently, but He planned that we would communicate with each other chemically, to help insure that we remain faithful to one another as spouses. Pause and worship our Amazing Creator.

The Mountain

Read Joshua 14:7–14

Week after week, fading into month after month, then year after year, husbands and wives can attend church secretly dissatisfied that the supernatural presence and power of God are spoken of only as a distant possibility. They silently long for the fullness of God to be manifested in their life, family, and church, but fear being labeled weird, fanatical, or self righteous if they express a desire for more of Him. They settle for hoping that He will bless them anyway.

Caleb faced the same dilemma when he explored Canaan with the other Israelite spies. He, however, was bold and honest when he expressed the godly desires that were in his heart (v. 7). The other leaders chose faith in their own logic over belief in God (Heb. 3:19). They presented pros and cons that influenced the children of Israel to melt and shrink back into mediocrity. Caleb risked being labeled fanatical, and wholly followed the Lord (v. 8). He challenged the people to trust God and allow Him to demonstrate His power. Moses swore that the mountain Caleb had spied out would belong to him and his family forever because he boldly expressed his desires and wholly followed the Lord.

Forty-five years later, Caleb has not changed. He boldly claims this promise and announces his confidence in God (vv. 10–12). Because he is not embarrassed to declare his faith and claim the promises, Caleb receives a mountain of blessing for his family (vv. 13–14). Be bold to wholeheartedly proclaim your trust in God, and believe the promises proclaimed in His Word.

A GREAT STONE

Read Joshua 24:1–28

We recently honored Debbie's parents with a 50th wedding anniversary celebration. We remembered special times and events, and how their lives affected each of us. Since only five percent of marriages last 50 years[40], it was a great inspiration, not only to our family, but to all who were aware of the occasion. At the end of the 19th century, the average length of marriages that ended when one spouse died was 28 years. Today it is more than 45 years.[41] If a couple remains faithful to their marriage covenant, they have a good chance of reaching their golden anniversary!

After Joshua had gathered all of the children of Israel together, he challenged them to decide who they would worship. They were instructed to choose between the one true Jehovah God and the false gods of the pagan culture surrounding them. Joshua then affirmed that he and his family were committed to worship God and God alone (15). The Israelites responded that they would not forsake the Lord to serve false gods (v.16). As a memorial of this occasion, Joshua took a great stone and placed it under an oak tree so that each time they passed by and observed it, they would remember their vow to God (vv.26–27).

On Memorial Day, we remember those who gave their lives that freedom might prevail in America. As we reflect back on World War 1, Pearl Harbor, D-day, Vietnam, 9/11, and other important dates, we are inspired to preserve what so many people died for.

Tragically, along with foreign enemies, the disintegration of the traditional family is destroying the America we love so much. In a society where divorce, cohabitation, and same sex marriages have become a norm, leaving a legacy of fifty years of marriage to our children and grandchildren has a great impact. When our families observe our lasting and committed love relationship, it becomes a great stone of memorial challenging them to faithfulness and long-term commitment!

LOOKING GOOD

Read Esther 5:1, Proverbs 31:22, 30, Ephesians 5:27, and 1 Peter 3:3-5

ifferent people have asked me why I go to the trouble of applying makeup first thing each morning when I am not even going anywhere. Well, the person that I want to notice me is not just anywhere. He is living in my house, and I want to look my best for him. During the day when my husband goes to the bank or has a meeting, the women he encounters are attractively dressed, and they greet him with a pleasant smile. I do not want him to walk by lovely ladies every day and then come home to a wife who does not seem to care about what her appearance conveys to him.

The Bible bears witness that looks are important to husbands (Gen. 6:2). The Scriptures repeatedly mention the beauty of different men's wives (Abraham, Isaac, Solomon, David). Queen Esther understood the importance of looking her best for her husband (v. 1). She considered her appearance and carefully selected her clothing for a special appointment with her husband. One of the attributes of the virtuous woman is that she dresses beautifully (Prov. 31:22). Ephesians 5—which compares marriage with Christ's relationship to the church—states that He desires His bride to be beautiful in holiness, without spot, wrinkle, or blemish (v. 27). It is interesting that Christ emphasizes the importance of the church's spiritual purity by using analogous words describing an attractive outward appearance in His bride. This inner beauty not only smoothes the wrinkles and blemishes of a sinful human heart, but is the source of an external radiance that does not fade (1 Peter 3:3-4). It is the beauty secret of Esther, Ruth, Sarah, and every notable woman in the Scriptures (1 Peter 3:5). I don't want my husband to have frumpy, drab impressions of me. I want to invest time and effort to look my very best for him, but at the same time I realize the futility of obsessing over outward appearances (Proverbs 31:30). I desire to wear the glowing countenance that comes from a sacred reverence and fascination for my Lord. Wives, let's look good for our husbands, but let's begin our beauty regimens with daily worship.

THROUGH HIS STOMACH

Read Proverbs 31:14–15, Esther 5:4–7, and 1 Samuel 25:18–19

A woman came to me in tears and admitted that her family was suffering because she did not cook. For fourteen years, they had either eaten out or had microwave dinners. She discouraged her children from inviting friends to visit because she could not prepare a meal for them. Her mother shooed her out of the kitchen and never taught her to cook. That afternoon, I pulled out some cookbooks and showed her some basic recipes. We reviewed local grocery ads and charted daily menus for the next week, compiling a list as we planned. Next, we went grocery shopping and I demonstrated how to select vegetables and determine economical buys. We prepared supper together and I instructed her to call me every afternoon as she prepared meals. By the end of the week, her husband was ecstatic. He was grateful for this new demonstration of love. He not only enjoyed a hot meal each evening, but loved having leftovers to microwave at the office. The wife was so motivated by his response that she eagerly looked for other ways to delight him.

Proverbs 31:14–15 describes the virtuous wife as one who carefully plans and prepares nutritious meals for her household. These meals do not need to be elaborate or gourmet, but they do require thought and effort. The Bible also references other women who won the favor of men by preparing food for them. Before she asked for his help, Esther wisely invited the king to banquets that she specially made ready for him (vv. 4–7). Abigail loaded donkeys with food and sent them to David and his men before she presented her request (1 Sam. 25:18–19). The widow of Zarephath baked bread for Elijah (1 Kings 17:9–16). Peter's mother-in-law served food to Jesus and the apostles (Mark 1:30–31). In all of these examples, God's word confirms that lovingly providing nourishment enhances the relationship. Maybe there is truth to the old saying that one way to a man's heart is through his stomach!

UNITY

Read Psalms 133:1–3

*L*ast week, a lady who is a member at our church unexpectedly lost her husband after forty-four years of marriage. At the funeral, she told me how lonely she was. She explained that they did everything together, and talked about activities they had participated in together just two weeks earlier. After more than four decades, they still walked hand in hand everywhere they went. Their emotional bond was evident as she described how she respected and admired different aspects of his character. She told me they never went to bed angry with each other. She said she had no regrets. She declared that he died loving her, and he died knowing that she loved him. This couple dwelt in unity.

This precious widow recognizes unity as good and pleasant (v. 1), and she receives comfort from her cherished memories. The testimony of the unity she shared with her husband inspires other couples to desire the same in their relationship. Psalm 133 confirms her experience by describing the blessings of dwelling in spiritual unity. Unity brings blessings from the Lord that people living in discord will miss.

God likens unity to sacred oil trickling down the head, the beard, and the garment of Aaron (v. 2). All of Israel focused on the holiness and majesty of God as they observed Aaron's anointing. They were unified in worship. The anointing represents the consecration of Aaron. In the same way, unity consecrates believers by setting them apart for effective service to their family and community. God also compares unity with the dew of Hermon, descending upon the mountains of Zion (v. 3). This word picture portrays a refreshing source that waters the crops and produces life. Unity brings a source of vitality to a relationship. Couples are challenged to strive for unity by setting aside differences and seeking God's perspective. We experience unity when we both see things from His perspective. Dwell in unity with your mate so you can experience the strength and refreshment that God intends for your marriage.

SPEAKING TRUTH

Read Ephesians 4:22–25 and 1 Corinthians 12

I recently overheard two women expressing disgust because their husbands exaggerated details when trying to impress friends. Because of this irritating habit, the ladies felt they couldn't fully trust their mates. When the men exaggerated, the wives wanted no part in the interaction.

I have had to deal with relatives who repeatedly lied to me. Now years later, I feel an urgency to verify any information they give me before I act on it. Even though I dearly love these relatives, their past behavior strains my enjoyment of the present relationship.

Nothing creates distance between a husband and wife like lying and deceit! As children of God who have put on the new self, we are exhorted to speak the truth with our neighbor (Eph. 4:24–25). Our neighbor is someone who lives close or nearby. Our closest neighbor is obviously our spouse. The reason given in Ephesians 4:25 for speaking truth is that we are members of one another. In 1 Corinthians chapter 12, Paul describes the church as a body with many members, each working to build up the whole. If this is true for the overall body of Christ, how much more essential is it for a husband and wife?

Trust is the bridge that connects. When we speak lies, distrust invades the relationship. Without trust, the relationship crumbles and we start drifting from each other. Most marriages are not destroyed by one major lie, but by ongoing little lies and exaggerations that gradually chip away at the bond of trust. Without repentance, the deception will eventually frustrate the other partner into withdrawal. Jesus declares that the Truth will set you free (John 8:32)! Don't let your marriage be destroyed by deceit. Be sensitive to always speak honestly, in love.

WHEN STRUGGLES COME

Read James 1:2–4

One of the greatest struggles my wife and I have faced in our marriage was the financial transition we experienced when I surrendered to enter full-time ministry. Debbie had already quit her job as a systems analyst to stay at home with our sons. I resigned from my engineering position to start an inner city outreach. At the time, we received no monthly support from individuals or churches. I believed God had called me, and therefore would supply my needs! During that first year, we sold our house, our cars, and even some of our personal items to try to make ends meet. Even though we experienced the Lord's blessings in our ministry, our annual income was only around $8,000. I was confused! I questioned God as to why we were struggling financially, and He revealed a tremendous truth. Trials can do one of two things: isolate you from God and your spouse, or draw you intimately closer to Him and your husband or wife.

God urges us to consider it nothing but joy when we fall into all sorts of trials (v. 2). The word "fall" depicts a sudden change. It is as though we are on top of the mountain one minute and are plunged into a deep valley the next. We can consider it all joy knowing (having certainty) that these tests will develop perseverance in our lives (v. 3). If we will trust in the sovereign hand of God, we will grow in our faith (v. 4). The trials Debbie and I faced drew us closer to Him and to each other as we prayed, read the Word, and sought the Lord more earnestly. Since those years, we have learned to trust Him even more and have been privileged to see Him do things in and through us we never would have imagined! When struggles come, don't isolate yourself from God. Rather, use the challenges as a catalyst to bond you intimately to the Master and to each other.

AVOID TOXIC ADVICE

Read Psalm 1:1–6

A friend of mine told me that for twenty-two years of marriage, she had been more concerned about meeting her mother's expectations than filling her husband's needs. Her mother was a domineering and demanding person who hated men. She had always criticized my friend's father and husband. As a child, my friend learned that life was easier when she pacified her mother by agreeing with her. This habit extended into her married life every time her mother belittled her husband. Her marriage was tense and frustrating because she was trying to force her husband to change in order to meet her mother's unreasonable expectations and gain her approval. As my friend studied Scriptures and marriage, God showed her if she was going to be a wife who empowered and completed her husband, she needed to support rather than demean him (Eph. 5:33). The next time her mother condemned her husband, she wholeheartedly defended him. For two weeks, my friend concentrated on doing kind things for her husband, rather than trying to help him improve. She made an effort to enjoy who he was. Her marriage began to yield new life and fulfillment. They fell in love all over again.

My friend experienced the principles of Psalm 1, where God declares that the person who refuses to listen to ungodly counsel—especially scornful advice—will be happy (v. 1). Her choice to defend her husband rather than agree with her mother's poisonous criticism resulted in happiness not only in her husband, but also in her heart. My friend had a deep desire to obey God. As she meditated on His Word, she understood how she needed to adjust to God's purposes in her marriage (v. 2). She was determined to obey the Lord and encourage her husband. God prospered her marriage with the fruits of joy and love (v. 3). Her mother's negative attitude had caused a venomous dynamic within her marriage. Avoiding toxic thinking produced a relationship that was revived and healthy. What toxic advice do you need to ignore?

FOR HIM

Read 1 Corinthians 11:7–11 and Genesis 2:18

After completing college, Debbie and I moved to Kingsport, TN, to take jobs at Tennessee Eastman Company. Six years passed by and we were actively involved in church. God blessed us with two sons and a very nice home. Debbie was a homemaker and we were on course to have a "Leave it to Beaver" type family. Everything was cool and calm until God stirred my heart to surrender to His calling. After several weeks of intense prayer, accompanied with some fasting, I cautiously explained to Debbie how God was working in my life, not knowing how she would react. After the initial shock, she responded by giving me her full support and encouragement. During the next year, I quit my job, transitioned our family to a modest lifestyle, and started an inner-city ministry. As I reflect back over those years, I realize that without Debbie's support, we would not be in ministry today! My wife surrendered to God's leading in my life, submitting to my headship in our marriage and helping me to accomplish His will.

Scripture states that the man was not created for the woman, but the woman for the man (1 Cor. 11:9). Feminists today would argue that this statement is oppressive and degrading to women. A husband and wife will only have true happiness, however, as they carry out the roles God has assigned to them. Lest men get too big-headed, Paul reminds them they would not be here except through the womb of woman (v. 11). A godly wife is the glory of her husband (v. 7). The old saying, "Behind every successful man is a hard working woman," is true! A wife brings gifts, talents, insights, and abilities that balance and enhance her husband's life in a way that enables and empowers him to more effectively fulfill God's purposes. Daily thank God for the gift of your spouse. Together, build your marriage for Him.

MOTHERS-IN-LAW

Read Ruth 1 and 2, 4:13

When Ruth first becomes acquainted with her in-laws, she observes two important characteristics. Her father-in-law's name, Elimelech, means "My God is King." Ruth is so impressed with his relationship to Jehovah God that she denies her own gods and chooses to worship his God (1:15–16). Ruth realizes that the God of her in-laws is the true living God. Ruth's mother-in-law's name Naomi means "pleasantness and sweetness." Ruth characterizes her name as "friendship," and bonds with Naomi in deep, lasting companionship (1:8, 16).

When Elimelech dies, however, Naomi's disposition drastically changes. Her grief is so intense that she announces her name has changed to "Mara," meaning "bitter" (1:20). Naomi barely acknowledges the loss of Ruth's husband, and then drowns in a sea of self-pity because she considers her loss so much greater (vv. 1:12–13). Have you ever associated with people who sympathize by agreeing with your plight, but then attempt to top the difficulty by explaining personal challenges they view as unquestionably tougher than yours? How irritating and depressing this could have been for Ruth! When Ruth and Naomi finally reach Bethlehem, where Naomi should be encouraged to see her friends, she plunges into deeper despair (1:21). Instead of deliberating on her mother-in-law's negative attitudes, Ruth chooses to concentrate on the strengths that bonded her to Naomi. She sympathetically strives to understand her mother-in-law's perspective. She compassionately determines to meet her needs by performing kind deeds (2:2, 18). Ruth does not give up, but enthusiastically focuses on developing a relationship with God. This eventually softens her mother-in-law's attitude. Naomi starts praising and trusting God instead of bitterly blaming Him (2:20). When Ruth denies herself in order to show love to her depressed mother-in-law, God blesses her abundantly, far above what she could dream, in the very areas she had previously denied herself (2:11–12, 4:13). Do you need to encourage an in-law?

Giving Thanks

Read Ephesians 5:18–20 and Psalm 100:4–5

As a father who tries to lovingly provide for my four sons, I am always encouraged to hear a sincere thank you. That simple response makes me eager to give more. Just as we desire a "thank you" from our children, God calls us to give Him thanks. The word "thank" and the word "think" are from the same root word. Thankfulness proceeds out of thoughtfulness. Pondering the gracious acts of a loving God produces a heart of thanks! Giving thanks is the normal expression of a life filled with the Spirit of God (v. 18).

We are commanded not only to give thanks, but thanks for "all things," which at times can seem impossible. A couple of years ago, I personally experienced devastating loss when my sister was murdered while working in her real estate office. Our family was crushed and confused over why this had happened. How could we give thanks? Since thankfulness proceeds out of thoughtfulness, we had to expand our thoughts beyond the facts of the event to include the truths of God. Circumstances change, but His goodness and love remain steadfast and dependable (Psalm 100:5). Since God is not the author of evil, I am not expected to give Him thanks for the evil act. I express disdain for the evil act toward the author of evil. At my sister's funeral, I didn't thank God for her death (the result of an evil deed), but rather expressed gratitude for her life and the fact that she was a Christian, now rejoicing in His presence in heaven!

Since there are approximately 140 references in Scripture concerning thanking God, He obviously regards gratitude as extremely significant. An attitude of thankfulness honors Him, humbles us, and promotes contentment in our lives. It opens the door for us to draw closer to Him (Psalm 100:4). When my heart struggles to be thankful, I must fill my mind with truths about the goodness, faithfulness, mercy, and grace of our sovereign God (Eph. 5:19). The result will be heartfelt thanks (Eph 5:20).

Facing difficulties in marriage is inevitable. When we remind ourselves to view those heartaches in light of the character and faithfulness of our great God, we can give thanks.

STAY IN TOUCH

Read Romans 8:35–39 and 1 Peter 3:7

*J*obs that require extensive travel can be very taxing to a marriage relationship. Separation promotes isolation and a lack of communication. As a result, marriage partners can easily grow distant from each other. Satan will, opportunely, bombard the mind of the spouse who stays home with incorrect thoughts concerning their mate. These fantasies may range from "my spouse desires to be away from home because he or she really doesn't love me" to "my spouse is committing adultery." If the travelling spouse stays in touch, it helps eliminate these lies from taking root in the mind of the spouse who remains at home.

For example, since a wife needs loving affirmation, a travelling husband should often let her know that she is on his mind and he is looking forward to seeing her again. Christ specifically affirms His love for His bride in Romans 8:35–39. He also reinforces His love through His Word and His Spirit as we commune intimately with Him. In 1 Peter 3:7, God commands husbands to live with their wives in an understanding way. An "understanding husband" who is away from home "lives with" his wife by calling and texting as frequently as possible. When calling, he should make sure he has sufficient time to talk with his wife. He should find time each day to read Scripture and pray with her. Some men will dutifully call their wives, spend thirty seconds on the phone, and think to themselves, "I've got that done!" The wife senses this attitude, and feels insecure and unimportant. A husband must be sensitive to his wife's needs. The conversation should not just be about surface issues, but should also include intimate talk and excitement about seeing one another again. Reuniting can then be thrilling for the couple who stays in touch!

HUSBANDRY

Read Genesis 3:6 and Ephesians 5:22–33

My wife and I enjoy the opportunity to work in the yard—cutting the grass, trimming the bushes, and planting new flowers. Maintaining the yard can be hard work, but the rewards are well worth the effort. When we come up the driveway and notice the flowers blooming alongside the freshly mown lawn, we experience a sense of accomplishment that makes us feel proud.

The cultivation of plants and the domestic care of animals are often referred to as husbandry, which simply means "to care for." In Genesis 3:6, we see the first use of the word "husband" in the Bible. God is commanding Adam to dress and keep the garden—to exercise husbandry (Gen. 2:15). God also weaves the word husband throughout Scripture as a reminder for man to "take care of" his wife. In Ephesians 5:22–33, the word husband is mentioned five times as man is instructed to follow the example of Christ taking care of His bride. To "husband" a wife correctly, the husband must have an understanding of her (1 Pet. 3:7). To gain an accurate understanding of how to husband our bushes, grass, and flowers, I researched what kind of soil to use, how much water was required, the amount of sunlight or shade needed, and the correct fertilizer to apply. In nurturing his wife, the husband must observe her specific needs: the amount of rest needed, clothes required, food, shelter, likes, dislikes, dreams, and fears (v. 29). He must fertilize and water their relationship by studying and sharing the Word of God (v. 26). The wife is like a delicate flower that requires tender loving care from the gardener (her husband) in order to bloom into its intended glory (v. 27). To husband a wife is a great responsibility, but it carries with it the abundant blessing of a blossoming bride! Pray that God will reveal ways you can encourage your spouse to bloom.

PROTECT HER

Read Ruth 3:1–11

*A*man recently made arrangements to travel about two hours to our house to purchase a puppy. I arranged to meet him at a certain time, and then drive back to another location to help at an event involving our family. I had just turned into the driveway when I noticed my husband pulling in right behind me. Sam hopped out of his car and explained that even though I had four large dogs to guard me, he didn't feel comfortable leaving me by myself knowing that a stranger would be coming to our home. He instinctively desired to protect me. Recently, when I decided to travel to visit my parents, Sam took the car to the garage and instructed the attendant to check the brakes and tires. He was concerned for my safety. When church, school, family, or friends concurrently request my attention and help, Sam cautions me to limit my activities. He is protecting me from over-commitment.

Naomi conveys concern for Ruth's security and protection, and makes plans to arrange Ruth's marriage to Boaz (v. 1). Ruth follows Naomi's instructions (v. 6). When Boaz retires for the night, Ruth softly uncovers his feet and lies down. When Boaz wakes in the middle of the night and asks who she is, she humbly claims that she will serve him and requests that he cover her with his garment, since he is a close relative. As a close relative, custom dictates that he should marry her. When Ruth asks him to cover her, she is portraying a need for protection. When a Jewish man marries a woman, he throws the skirts of his talith over her to signify that he has taken her under his protection, like a mother bird gathers her little birdies under her wings to guard them from predators. God intends for a husband to protect his wife. Love your bride enough to protect her physically, emotionally, and spiritually.

PROTECT YOURSELF

Read Numbers 24:12–14, 25:1–9, and 31:15–16

My husband has a guideline for when he counsels a woman. He requires that either her husband or I attend the session. When our children were young and we occasionally hired a babysitter, he would never drive the young lady home by himself. He is very cautious to avoid situations that leave him alone with another woman. Although he has no desire for another woman, he realizes the enemy of the Christian faith frequently incites sexual attraction as a ploy to lead a believer into the trap of sin.

In Numbers 23, Israel's enemy, Balak, attempted to hire Balaam to curse the children of Israel. Balaam had previously explained to Balak that he could only speak the words that God put in his mouth. Three different times when Balaam stood to curse Israel, God protected Israel and forced a blessing from his mouth (Num. 24:12–14). Balaam was unable to harm Israel with a curse, but according to Revelation 2:14, he placed stumbling blocks before Israel that provoked their disobedience and incurred the wrath of God. This stumbling block was the allurement of the opposite sex. Balaam convinced the Moabite women to infiltrate Israel's camp (Num. 31:15–16). As long as the Israelite men were living in the blessing and favor of God, Balaam could not curse them, so he used women to lure them astray. The women of Moab attracted the attention of the Israelite men (Num. 25:1). Then, the foreign women appealed to their lusts and eventually enticed them to participate in idol worship and adultery (Num. 25:2).

The Israelite men never intended to betray the God who was blessing them, but the women tempted them beyond what they expected. I am thankful that my husband guards against this stumbling block. Love your spouse enough to protect yourself.

HIS YOKE

Read Matthew 11:28–30

Do you ever find yourself so tired that it's hard to enjoy your spouse and family? Are the stresses of your career so heavy that you feel consumed by their pressure? Are the influences and weight of the outside world crushing you? Jesus offers the solution. He invites us to bring these heavy burdens to Him, so He can exchange them for rest (v. 28).

Tradition says that as a carpenter, Jesus built yokes for beasts of burden. When the crossbar was set exactly in the middle of the yoke, the weight was distributed evenly between the two animals. When the bar was positioned with one end longer, the animal on the longer end proportionately bore the heavier weight. In today's passage, Jesus explains that when a Christian shares his cares and responsibilities with the Lord, He will provide a yoke specially designed for the Christian's particular need (v. 29). Jesus will labor on the side of the longer bar. He will bear the weight of the stress and pressure. Coming under this specially designed yoke will require the believer to walk in step with Jesus and follow His lead. Under this yoke, a Christian cannot scheme and plan his own solutions, but must learn and trust in the ways of the Lord. A believer learns the ways of the Lord by studying the life of Jesus with the purpose of recognizing His heart's intent (v. 29). The labor becomes a team effort. The Christian's responsibility is to learn of Jesus and obey Him. Jesus promises to lead and bear the heavy portion of the weight.

The result of this team effort may or may not involve a change in circumstances, but the labor will be much lighter as we yoke up with Jesus (v. 30). We will experience His rest, allowing us to more fully enjoy our life and family. Are there burdens you need to share with the Lord today?

THE HEALTH OF MY COUNTENANCE

Read Psalm 43

Do you ever experience times of despair where you can't seem to find direction from God? When I find myself under this pressure, I naturally blame the individual who is stirring up anxiety in my life. My immediate solution is for God to either deliver me or correct that person. David expresses this way of thinking in Psalm 43. He calls upon God as both his defense attorney and righteous judge (v. 1), and recognizes his deep need for help. He is confused, however, because although he acknowledges his dependence upon God by pleading for Him to conquer his enemy, he still feels distant from Him (v. 2). Then David begs God to reveal His light and truth, knowing it will lead him into God's presence (v. 3). Now, instead of directing Him how to help, David is pleading for His very presence. I love this request because it opens my heart to whatever the Lord wants to show me. Sometimes He reveals my spouse's perspective so I can be more understanding. Many times, however, after I've requested light and truth, God allows increased tension between my mate and me. That is not the solution I would plan for myself. In this case, I need to respond to what He is revealing by examining my attitude for rebellion, greed, or selfishness. I am amazed at the way God often uses interaction with the person I love most to expose sin in my life. But whatever He reveals, I, like the psalmist, can bow before His Majesty with exceeding joy knowing that it is not a specific solution that will satisfy me, but rather the presence of the Lord Himself (v. 4). There is no reason to stay depressed and defeated. When I wait on God, I can trust Him to deliver, reveal, forgive, or do whatever else He deems best. I don't need to plan His strategy, but I can have confidence because He is my stability—the health of my countenance (v. 5).

FOLLOW ME

Read John 10:10–11, 27–28, and Ephesians 5:30-31

Although we raise English mastiff dogs, I never thought I would let a dog live inside our house! And I certainly never dreamed that Debbie would be receptive to the idea. Recently we traded a female puppy for a sixteen-month-old housebroken male named Thor. Debbie, the boys, and I all fell in love with him and decided to give him a chance to live indoors. I quickly discovered that Thor wanted to be everywhere we were. If I walked into my office, he followed me. If I left to go to the kitchen, he immediately got up and tagged along. Wherever I went, he went. When I stopped to sit down, Thor laid at my feet. He began to recognize the sound of my voice, and responded when I said his name. I learned that Thor's overwhelming desire was to be with us. His life and well-being depended upon it!

Jesus, as our chief Shepherd, calls us to follow Him (v. 27). He is our Savior, our Master, and Lord. Our greatest desire should be Him. When He speaks, we should know His voice and obey Him. Jesus wants us to rest at His feet and commune continually with Him. In other words, He wants us to be content just knowing He is in control. He knows that abundant life on this earth results from our allowing Him to live His life in and through us (v. 10). We simply must follow Him.

For spouses to enjoy harmony, joy, and the bliss of marital romance, both must follow Jesus. As each partner follows Christ, our oneness with Him enhances our unity with each other (Eph. 5:30–31). We move ahead as husband and wife in the same direction because we are following the same Person. We allow Him to appropriate His life into us, and into one another! As we both stay focused on Him, we invite the grace of God to flow through our marriage, blessing each other with His unconditional love.

RESPECT

Read 1 Peter 3:5–6 and Ephesians 5:33

*S*am and I recently watched a documentary program that highlighted the effects of boxing. It stated that competitors receive so many power blows to the skull that brain damage is inevitable. Doctors usually warn boxers before the pressure and injury reach dangerous levels, but many ignore the warnings and continue to enter the ring. This is inconceivable to someone like me who avoids unnecessary pain, but the athletes who repeatedly subject themselves to this abuse explain that they do it for the respect. Their need to be highly esteemed is so intense that they are willing to risk permanent brain damage.

Through my studies of marriage, I was aware that husbands were created with a great need for respect, but I had no idea that its importance could be so consuming that some men would endure abuse in order to receive it. I want to make a sincere effort to respect my husband simply because as a man it means so much to him, but there is a more significant reason. In Ephesians 5:33, God urges wives to reverence their husbands. In 1 Peter 3:5–6, He commends Sara for her submissive attitude. Her spirit of cooperation proved that she was devoted to her husband. The passage notes that she conveyed utmost respect for Abraham in the way she talked to him, and to others about him. The word lord (v. 6) is a title of honor, expressing respect and reverence. When Sara referred to Abraham as lord, it would be similar to wives today admiring their husband's strengths and leadership, and voicing their appreciation in front of children or friends. A wife's reverence could also include reminding her husband of his accomplishments and potential. Ultimately, it consists of admiration, praise, and love. God inspires women by reminding them that if they follow Sara's example and do what is right without giving in to fearful apprehension, He will consider them honorable. He commands that a wife show respect to her husband, and promises blessing in return.

PIERCED EARS

Read Exodus 21:1–6, Psalm 40:6–8, and Isaiah 50:5-6

A Hebrew slave who served his master for seven years was free to leave his servitude and enjoy his freedom. If he was already married when he became a slave, he could take his wife with him. If his master had given him a wife during his servitude, however, he could not take her with him. The husband had a choice to make—leave without his wife and children as a free man, or remain with them in servitude. If he elected to stay, his master would take an awl and pierce his ear with it, marking him for servitude forever (Exod. 21:5–6). A slave who was a devoted Hebrew husband had to abandon his opportunity for liberty so he could share the rest of his life with his wife!

This custom is referenced when Psalm 40:6 speaks of ears that are opened. The passage prophetically pictures Jesus as the husband, who willingly leaves His freedom as the Son of God, comes to earth, makes Himself of no reputation, and takes the form of a servant because of His love for His bride. Matthew Henry explains, "God the Father disposed him to the undertaking (Isa. 50:5, 6) and then obliged him to go through with it. *My ear hast thou opened*. It is supposed to allude to the law and custom of binding servants to serve for ever by boring their ear to the doorpost."[42] Our image of a marred Jesus needs to include not only the wounds on His hands and feet, His pierced side, wounded forehead, lash marks on His back, but also the invisible wound of an idiomatically pierced earlobe. The pierced ear in Scripture serves as an awesome reminder to every husband to unconditionally love his wife through his never-ending commitment to stay with her. Husbands, next time you see someone with a pierced ear, let it be a reminder of the unending devotion God calls you to have toward your wife!

IN DEED

Read 1 John 4:19 and 3:16–18

When a lady who attended one of our conferences explained her marriage problems to me, we made an appointment later that day to discuss personal applications of God's principles to her situation. We talked about the hope that is available in His power. After pondering this, she declared, "But, you don't understand; my husband doesn't like me anymore." This made me think. What can you do to win someone's affection?

The Bible says that we love Him because He first loved us (v. 19). We love Jesus because He manifested such great love to us that we are compelled to love Him in return. This principle should apply in our relationships with others. We know that Christ loves us because He proved His love by sacrificing His life before we loved Him or even knew Him (v. 16). Likewise, we should follow His example and be willing to give our life to prove we love our spouse whether or not he or she likes us. The Scripture further explains that when we see someone in need, we should be willing to set aside our wants, our agenda, and even our possessions to help them (v. 17). This shows that our love, like the love of Christ, is genuine. To tell someone that we love them is not enough. We demonstrate our love through deeds and acts of service (v. 18). We have the opportunity to continually see needs in our spouse's life. We can show our love first by recognizing needs in his or her life and then acting in ways that will ease stress or bring blessing. To be effective, our actions should be thoughtful, and more than what is expected. A wife can fix her husband's favorite dessert or purchase surprise tickets to a special event. A husband can help with chores, fix a leaky faucet, or draw bath water for his wife. If a spouse needs space, be creative to think of ways that show you care, but do not require a response. These expressions of love can nurture affection between husband and wife, and result in a winsome, loving lifestyle that brings new life to marriage.

MARRIAGE SYMBOLS

Read Jeremiah 31:3 and Ephesians 5:27

The blockbuster movie *Lord of the Rings* uses a ring as a symbol of darkness and evil. Whoever possesses the ring is consumed by an incessant desire to serve the creator of the ring, Lord Sauron. Every time someone looks upon the ring, it brings fearful emotions. The movie centers around the struggle to destroy the ring, therefore negating its evil influence on mankind.

In the movie, the ring looks similar to a wedding ring. But, unlike the ring symbolizing darkness and death, the wedding ring symbolizes life, light, and unending love! The traditional Christian wedding has its roots not in biblical customs but rather in those of the ancient Romans. For example, the month in which most brides are married is June, named after the Roman queen of heaven and the goddess of femininity and marriage. The engagement of a bride and groom came from the Roman idea of betrothal. The groom would present a ring to his bride and upon acceptance she would wear it on the third finger of her left hand because the Romans believed that finger contained a vein that connected to the heart. At the conclusion of the ceremony, the couple would join hands and kiss.

In the traditional Jewish wedding, a bride had little or no say in the selection of her groom. She may have met him for the first time at her betrothal and the second time a year later at the consummation of the marriage. There was no exchange of rings, but there was an exchange of gifts (bride price, dowry). Today a Jewish bride wears white, not to show virginity, but to emphasize the seriousness of the occasion. During the ceremony, she receives a ring which is placed on the index finger of the right hand, the finger used to point out Scripture in the Torah.

Different symbols are used by different people in different cultures. Glenn Greenwood states, "Such symbols are acceptable to God as long as they portray the holiness and permanency and joy of the marriage covenant.[43]" Take a few minutes to tell your spouse what your ring means to you.

DUTY OR DEVOTION

Read Colossians 3:17–20 and Hebrews 12:2–3

On rare occasions when my husband has made me mad, I—being the "godly, committed" wife that I am—would continue to perform my household duties with an extra amount of vigor. I would cook supper, but I would bang the pots and pans to make sure he realized I was sacrificing to serve him. I would cook out of duty rather than devotion.

A friend told me that when her husband harshly demanded that she cut up her credit cards, she did exactly what he asked, and then threw the pieces at him. She complied out of duty, not devotion.

Pastor and author John MacArthur explains that Colossians 3:17 challenges Christians to always act consistently with who Christ is, and what He wants.[44] Verses 18–20 describe basic family relationships. Wives are instructed to submit to their husbands as long as their requests are not contrary to the Word of God. The word "submit" is translated from the Greek word *hypatasso* which means to come under the hearing of out of devotion. Children are exhorted to obey their parents in all things. The word "obey" is translated from the Greek word *hypakouo* meaning to come under the hearing of out of duty. When I serve my husband out of duty, I am viewing our relationship as parent to child rather than as husband to wife. This is not what Christ requests. Verse 17 prefaces the family instructions by challenging Christians to give thanks in everything we do. If I thank God for the food I am preparing and for my husband who earned the money for the food and home, my attitude will change to devotion. In this same passage, husbands are instructed to love their wives. When a husband expresses gratitude as he conveys consistent love and commitment to his wife, he not only increases his feelings of devotion, but stirs a desire within her to be devoted to him. Following the example of Christ by voluntarily serving out of devotion produces joy (Hebrews 12:2). Forgetting to consider Christ by serving out of duty yields resentment, weariness, and discouragement (Hebrews 12:3). It's a spouse's choice—duty with discouragement, or devotion with joy.

LET IT SNOW

Read Proverbs 25:13 and 2 Corinthians 7:11–16

Three years ago, our family planted a large garden. We had rows and rows of green beans. We had so many that we had to pick them even in the heat of the day, just to get the job done. It was scorching hot. Our throats were dry and dusty. As we picked, we dreamed of tasty snow cones. Proverbs 25:13 compares a faithfully delivered message to this type of refreshment.

Paul sent Titus to the Corinthians with a message from God. The message was filled with love and acceptance, but also called for a change in their thinking. Titus was nervous about delivering this truth because he did not know how the people would respond to it. When Titus delivered God's message, written by Paul, they respectfully received it and out of reverence for God, they obeyed (2 Cor. 7:11). Because their hearts were filled with such an intense desire to please Him, Titus was refreshed and filled with joy. As he remembered their enthusiastic response and willingness to follow God, his affection for the people increased (2 Cor. 7:15). Paul's approval and confidence in the people abounded, and he was also refreshed.

The same principles apply in Christian marriage. When God reveals truth or direction to one spouse, through prayer or meditation in His Word, he or she receives a message from Him. If the spouse shares the message and the mate receives it with respect and enthusiasm for the Lord, the spouse will be refreshed. Like Titus and the church he was ministering to, a couple will be bonded with affection because of the common aspiration to please God. Confidence in their relationship will abound, and serve to influence others for the Lord.

JUNE 20

NIP IT IN THE BUD

Read Proverbs 12:16, 14:29, 15:18, 17:14, 19:11, and 20:3

Our family enjoys watching the *Andy Griffith Show*. One of our favorite characters is Deputy Barney Fife. Barney often offers sound advice, "Nip it in the bud. Nip it, nip it, nip it in the bud." He understands the value of solving a problem before it grows into an uncontrollable nightmare. Proverbs 17:14 supports this advice. God urges us to stop contentions before they snowball into a quarrel. Strife begins like a tiny hole in a dam that allows only a trickle of water to seep through, but the pressure of anger, like the force of water, weakens the dam and eventually bursts through with destructive power. Married couples can relate to this. They are enjoying a peaceful, calm day, when one little remark trickles out, followed by a slightly more intense accusation. Then, before they realize what is happening, the couple is hammering each other with a flood of condemnations. God's answer is to nip the argument in the bud. Proverbs 20:3 explains that it is honorable for a man to stop striving. But how?

The Bible repeatedly cautions us to be slow to respond in anger (Prov. 15:18). This will help deter contentions. Discretion helps a man be slow to anger (Prov. 19:11). It goes beyond understanding the pros and cons of the petty issue that is trickling through the dam. Discretion sets aside personal interests of the moment and sees the issue from the perspective of eternity. It includes the complete truth of God's love, power, and righteousness. It also considers the Father's view of the matter, plus the value He places on the people involved. Discretion allows a person to determine whether an issue is worth pursuing, or if it could be dropped and ignored. Proverbs 19:11 continues by explaining that if discretion allows, it is honorable to overlook a transgression. Preserve the joy and calmness of your relationship by exercising discretion, and nipping quarrels in the bud.

OPPOSITES

Read Acts 18:1–3, 26, and Romans 16:3–5

*T*he old saying that "opposites attract" is very often true! Aquila was a Jewish man born in Pontus, a remote place on the shore of the Black Sea. He married Priscilla, a Roman lady of high society. Although they were from diverse cultures, their bond in marriage was apparent in their devotion to Jesus Christ.

Aquila was a missionary whose journeys led him and Priscilla to many different locations (Pontus, Rome, Corinth, and Ephesus). Picking up and relocating was a natural part of their life. Priscilla was devoted to her husband and his call from God. I often reflect upon how thankful I am for my wife. During the last twenty years, whenever God would lead us in a new direction, she willingly and supportively relocated, even after moving five times.

Aquila and Priscilla faced a difficult situation at one stage in their marriage when Aquila was expelled from Rome (Priscilla's homeland). Instead of balking against her husband, Priscilla continued to follow his lead. Their journeys eventually led them to Corinth, where they started a tent-making business. They met the apostle Paul and partnered with him in both business and mission work. Their mutual devotion and service to God moved Paul to call them his helpers in Christ Jesus. When Paul decided to go to Ephesus, they liquidated their business and joined him. They invested their money into a home where they started a church (Rom. 16:3–5). Together, Aquila and Priscilla unselfishly gave their time and resources to reach the lost and help fellow believers grow in Christ. In Romans 16:4, Paul states that this couple loved him so much that they were willing to die for him! In his final letter, he concludes with greetings to Aquila and Priscilla (2 Tim. 4:19). This husband and wife, from such diverse backgrounds, are so focused on their mission that whenever they are mentioned in the New Testament, both names are included. God can do great things through married "opposites" whose relationship is centered in Jesus Christ!

LEAVING

Read Genesis 2:21–24 and Joshua 24:14–15

We recently counseled a young couple who were struggling with health issues, complicated by emotional and financial challenges. Added to the stress was well meaning advice from not only several physicians and counselors, but also from both sets of parents. Rather than being bonded together as they sought a solution, the couple was torn apart as they heard conflicting admonitions from their respective parents. As we questioned them about the facts, then discussed Scriptures regarding decision making, seeking God, and listening to Him, the couple decided they needed to proceed in the direction they sensed God leading them, without fretting about the reaction of their parents. The immediate result was a peaceful bond since they had sought the Lord's perspective together.

God addresses this dilemma in Genesis 2:24 when he explains that there must be a "leaving" when a couple gets married. Author Dan Allender states, "Leaving means starting a whole new relationship in which the core loyalty is not to parents' priorities, traditions, or influence, but to an entirely new family that must set its own course, form, and purpose."[45]

New priorities and traditions could include relocating to a different city or church. They may involve adopting a new financial perspective, or applying a biblical method of parenting rather than a traditional standard. In each aspect of life, a couple will experience oneness if they adopt the mindset of Joshua, "As for me and my house, we will serve the Lord" (Josh 24:14). The Lord will then set their course, which is determined by His explicit purpose for their particular family unit. As husband and wife, will you resolve to honor your parents, yet allow God to direct your marriage?

UNEQUALLY YOKED

Read Job 1–2, 2 Corinthians 6:14, and 1 Corinthians 7:12–16

God is clear in His instruction to single men and women not to marry an unbeliever or be unequally yoked (2 Cor. 6:14). He allows differences in background, physical appearance, and personalities, but marrying an unbeliever is sin and can generate many sorrows.

Job learned this lesson the hard way. The Bible describes him as a perfect, upright, God-fearing man who shunned evil (Job 1:1). Scripture depicts his wife, however, as an unbelieving woman. When Satan came before God to accuse the saints, God specifically mentioned Job. After Satan made excuses about why Job followed God, God gave him free reign to destroy anything Job had, except his life. Satan took wealth and children away from him but didn't touch his wife. Perhaps Satan knew that he could employ her as a weapon against Job. In Job 2:9, his wife tells him to curse God and die. How devastating for a man who had suffered such intense loss! How should a godly husband respond in this situation? Job told her she was speaking like a foolish woman. Although Job labeled his wife as "foolish" or as an unwise non-believer, he still remained committed to his marriage. How did this God-fearing man end up marrying a non-believing wife? Many times pre-arranged marriages would result in an unbeliever married to a believer who had no choice in the marriage.

But what if a believer is married to a non-believer? Paul teaches that if any brother has an unbelieving wife who consents to live with him, he should not divorce her (1 Cor. 7:12–16). He continues by saying that the unbelieving mate can be influenced by the believing spouse (v. 14). Even though unequally yoked, through His Spirit God can empower the believing husband or wife to be a godly testimony to their unbelieving mate. If you know a couple in this situation, encourage them to stay faithful in their marriage and be a shining light to their unsaved spouse. There is hope!

BIBLICAL TREASURE HUNTING

Read Proverbs 2:1–5, 16–17

When I was a little boy I played "treasure hunt" with my brothers and sisters. Our old, two-story home provided some very secretive hiding places. One of us would hide the treasure (usually something insignificant like a pack of gum) and the others would have five minutes to find it. Before the countdown started, the one who hid the treasure gave the seekers several hints. Using the clues given, we would search the house, looking in every conceivable nook and cranny to find the hidden prize.

In today's verses, Solomon instructs his son to go treasure hunting, not for an inexpensive material item, but for three priceless prizes! He first gives his son some hints about discovering the treasure. He tells him to use his ears, heart, mouth, and eyes to find wisdom, knowledge, and understanding (vv. 1–4). Solomon, the wisest man who ever lived, knew that his son must pursue these three treasures with all of his being in order to have godly success in life! In verse four, Solomon uses two verbs, seek and search, to convey how the treasures are to be found. "Seek" implies an intense desire that manifests itself in the outward action of searching until the items are located. These treasures are so valuable that we are to relentlessly hunt for them! Acquiring and embracing them accomplishes the whole God-given duty of man—intimacy with Him, which comes through fearing the Lord (Eccl. 12:13). Obtaining these gifts will also deliver Solomon's son from the seductive woman who has forgotten her marriage covenant and forsaken her husband (vv. 16–17).

These three treasures—wisdom, knowledge, and understanding—not only facilitate God's purpose for a person's life (to reverence Him), but they also protect a marriage from infidelity. No wonder He expresses such urgency related to pursuing them. Biblical treasure hunting is vital to maintaining a godly marriage. Seek and search for wisdom, understanding, and knowledge.

THE DUTY OF THE PRIEST

Read Numbers 6:22–27

The husband is often described in Scripture as the priest of the home. One of the main duties of a priest is to bless the people who are under his spiritual care. As priest of the home, a husband is to regularly pronounce a blessing on his wife. God specifically tells the priest how to render a blessing (v. 23). In the presence of his wife, a husband should voice his desire that the Lord show favor to and protect his wife (v. 24). A wife needs to not only hear that her husband is concerned for her safety and well being, but that he has confidence in the sovereign God to watch over her. The priest also requests that the Lord cause His face to shine upon the one being blessed (v. 25). This is an appeal for God to magnify His character to this person so he or she will personally understand His goodness and greatness, and experience grace or divine enabling power. The priest prays that the favor of the Lord—His kindness and love—be evident in the person's life and that peace will abound (v. 26).

The intent of a husband speaking these desires before his wife is to inspire her to live according to the majesty and trustworthiness of the Lord (v. 27). The husband's confidence in the Lord will be transferred to the wife. As a result of receiving the blessing, the wife's dependence on and hope in the Lord will increase. Hearing her husband express loving desires for her with confidence in the Lord will generate peace in a wife's day, and affection in her heart. Through speaking blessings, a couple can truly celebrate the Lord in their marriage. Take time to bless your wife with the words found in today's passage.

CONTENTMENT

Read 1 Timothy 6:6–8, 2 Corinthians 9:8, and Hebrews 13:5

*I*n his book *Family Survival*, Steve Farrar describes a modern epidemic that is sweeping across America and destroying families by the thousands. He calls it "Affluenza," an insatiable desire to be affluent or have just a little bit more. We might say these people are looking for something they are unable to find—contentment! This lack of contentment is fueled by the bombardment of advertisements portraying happiness as attainable by having the latest gimmick or newest vehicle. Each day, the average American is exposed to 3,000 advertisements that promise happiness.[46] As a result, the typical person has four major credit cards, with an average debt of $9,000.[47] Marty Seligman, professor at the University of Pennsylvania, reports there has been a sharp increase in depression since World War II. People born after 1945 are ten times more likely to suffer depression than people born earlier.[48] The reason appears to be that even though people have a more comfortable lifestyle now, they are never content!

The word "content" means sufficiency for the necessities of life (1 Tim. 6:6–8). The contented Christian not only experiences God's sufficiency in the provision of his or her needs, but also the sufficiency of His grace in every circumstance (2 Cor. 9:8). Have you heard the saying, "It's not having what you want, but wanting what you have?" Rather than longing for what we don't have and fretting over circumstances we don't understand, contentment requires that we exercise firm belief in the sovereign grace of God, acknowledging and appreciating all He has graciously supplied. By focusing on the eternal instead of the temporal, we realize that God has a plan for each life, that He is in control, and He will supply all our needs. We can trust Him! Without such contentment, joy and peace elude our life and marriages.

DISCONTENTMENT

Read Philippians 3:1–15

*I*s there ever a time that we should be discontent? In chapter three of Paul's letter to the Philippians, he alludes to being spiritually discontent. Although Paul had accomplished so much that he could be named to the spiritual "Hall of Fame," he considered his accomplishments worthless compared to the fulfillment he had in his relationship with Christ (vv. 4–6). He continued with heartfelt expressions: "that I may win Christ," "that I may be found in Him," and "that I may know Him." Obviously, Paul's consuming passion was to know Christ more intimately every day! He determined that he would not rest content in past spiritual achievements, but would "press" toward the mark of the high calling of God in Jesus Christ (v. 14). The word "press" pictures a runner approaching the finish line that leans forward and stretches himself out with all his might to cross the finish line! Paul was discontent with anything less than the goal of total spiritual intimacy with Christ.

We counseled with a couple who, after three years of marriage, were ready to file for divorce. They explained that their first year of marriage was exceptional with no problems. That year, they enjoyed doing everything together. They had been told that the first year of marriage was the most difficult, so they thought they had it made. They were content, feeling like they were headed for the "Marriage Hall of Fame." Then, however, they started taking each other for granted. Rather than press toward the finish line of an unselfish, giving relationship, they coasted until they were eventually ready to quit. When concerned parents invited them to hear a message preached on God's fulfilling design for marriage, the couple realized they were cheating themselves by avoiding His plan. The Holy Spirit was inciting discontentment with their current spiritual condition. They determined to press toward deeper relationships with God and each other by committing to regular prayer and devotional times. Their discontentment inspired them to read Christian books on marriage and strive for God's best. In this young couple's case, discontentment served an important purpose. It saved their marriage.

OUT OF BOUNDS

Read 1 Samuel 6:13–19 and Proverbs 4:20–23

Years ago, some teenagers from our town were out joy-riding. They were all honor roll students respected by peers and teachers. They were respectable kids who withstood the peer pressures of alcohol and drugs. On this particular night, they were not causing trouble—just enjoying life. They decided to build up a little speed and hit a dip in the road that would send them airborne and fill their stomachs with the surging thrill of the unexpected. They were full of joy and considered themselves invincible. A tree tragically proved they were not invincible; their vehicle overshot the boundary of the road. Regrettably, the driver was fatally injured; two passengers were critically hurt and faced months of rehab, while only one emerged with minor cuts and bruises.

We meet many couples who are experiencing the joy of a stable marriage. They, like the teens, do not foresee problems and do not see the need to attend marriage conferences or read books to strengthen their marriage. They resemble the people of Beth-Shemesh, described in 1 Samuel 6, who also felt invincible. God's favor was shining upon them. He blessed them with the honor of receiving the ark. They were full of happiness, enjoying abundant blessings (1 Sam. 6:13). They worshipped God through sacrifices and offerings and were cautious to observe His instructions for handling the ark (1 Sam. 6:15). They were respectable people who acknowledged God in their lives. They recognized His blessings and were thankful. Verse 19 shocks readers when they learn that in the midst of such a stable life, God suddenly struck the men of Beth-Shemesh. They had been living in a comfort zone with the Lord and felt shielded and safe. Their complacency tricked them into justifying a little curiosity. They overstepped the bounds because they were not diligent to remind themselves of God's commands. All of us need to be reminded of the Lord's principles, and all of us need to examine the details of our personal lives to ensure that we don't slip out of bounds. Safeguard your marriage. Read the Bible daily. Regularly read Christian books on marriage. Set a goal to attend a marriage conference each year.

CALM DOWN

Read Psalm 131

When my spouse and I are faced with challenges or a crisis, I try to do my part in bearing the burden, but I have a tendency to over analyze. Whether we face a financial problem, a parenting problem, or a health problem, I consider all angles and possibilities. I consider every path the difficulty may travel, and decide how I will respond. This can become very complicated when I am also guessing how others will react to various hypothetical scenarios. The process is further complicated because I sometimes struggle with a desire to achieve and to be impressive. This tendency heightens the pressure to be in control. I want to understand and figure out the details. I so long for our family to succeed that I become consumed with the "what ifs." As a result, I am filled with stress.

In Psalm 131, David offers a simple solution, and God has proved to me that it works. First, David makes sure he is not demanding his rights or insisting on personal success. He is not consumed with how the challenge is affecting him personally. He declares that his heart is not haughty and his goals are not selfish (v. 1). He determines not to concern himself with complicated matters or things that are too difficult to understand. David compares himself to a child who is weaned and experiencing the calm of his mother's presence (v. 2). A nursing child depends on his mother totally, but with great urgency and intensity. The child focuses on filling his belly, fearing if he doesn't eat now, he may never get another chance. As the child is weaned, he is confident that his mother loves him and will provide what he needs. He is peaceful in her presence. He is content. When we, like David, let go of our urgent desire to figure out all the angles—when we no longer insist that God meet our needs with the intensity of a nursing child—we can confidently trust Him. As we calm down and hope in Him, He will quiet our souls with His presence.

FLATTERY

Read Proverbs 6:23–7:27

ave you ever been flattered? Flattery is when someone gives you excessive or insincere praise for the purpose of his or her own self-interest. A student might flatter his teacher to gain favor in subjective grading situations. A salesman sometimes flatters a potential buyer so that he will purchase his product. Normally when someone flatters you, you recognize it and respond with the words, "What do you want, or what are you up to?"

The Bible warns ministers and believers not to use flattery (1 Thess. 2:5, Job 32:21–22). Scripture also disapprovingly cites different types of people who flatter: the wicked (Ps. 5:9, 12:2, 36:2), the hypocrite (Ps. 78:36), and false prophets (Ezek. 12:24, Rom. 16:18). In these references, we see the flatterer described as a liar with no truth or faithfulness in his or her mouth, or as a person who speaks with a double heart. Solomon instructs his son to beware of the strange woman (the one who is not his wife) who uses the tool of flattery to entice him to commit fornication (Prov. 6:24, 7:5). This type of woman uses her smooth tongue to appeal to the male ego. God created man with a need for respect that is to be satisfied by a loving and respectful wife (Eph. 5:33, 1 Pet. 3:2). A wife who encourages and respects her husband not only fills this need in his life, but helps to construct a hedge around him that protects from the strange woman's flattery. A man preserves himself from the evil woman by treasuring and being attentive to the Word of God (Prov. 6:23–24, 7:1–5). This precaution must be taken before a man is even exposed to her so he can recognize her flattery and avoid other deceptive tools she may use (her beauty, her eyelids, her attire, her lovely bed decked with spices, vv. 13-17). Every man, no matter how strong (Prov. 7:26), must guard himself from this snare of Satan that will lead him to death and hell (Prov. 7:27). Although Solomon is addressing his son in today's passage, the warnings are just as relevant for females. Both spouses have a part in protecting their marriage from the dangers of flattery. Let the Word of God be your guide in this important area of your relationship.

RESPONDING TO CONVICTION WITH COVER UP

Read Genesis 3:6–13, 21, 2 Corinthians 5:21, and Romans 4:6-8

We used to allow our English mastiff, Duke, to lie on the floor in our downstairs family room while we watched TV. Like most mastiffs, he was content just to be where we were. One day, when we all had to go upstairs for a while, we left Duke in the basement. He became lonely and bored. For entertainment and comfort, he decided to chew on the remote. When we returned and discovered what he'd done, all we had to do was sternly say his name. He was convicted immediately. He hung his head, tucked his tail, moped over to the corner, and covered his sad eyes with his paws. Duke seemed to think that if he couldn't see us, we wouldn't know he was the culprit.

We, as humans, respond in a similar manner. As soon as Adam and Eve sinned, they realized they had corrupted their lives (v. 7). They immediately acted to cover up the wrong they had committed. Likewise, as a husband and wife, when we sin against each other, we sometimes attempt to hide our transgressions with the pretense that nothing is wrong. We reason that if we don't bring attention to the situation, our spouse will not notice. Sometimes we cover sin by trying to make up for what we did. I remember a time when I wanted Sam to overlook a wrong I had done, so I made him a surprise batch of caramel walnut brownies. He enjoyed the brownies, but deep down the offense had not been resolved.

Concealing our self-centered choices does not erase the truth or deliver us from the tendency to commit the same sin again. Hiding does not ease our guilt. We must admit the truth (vv. 12–13) and trust God. Only He can provide the remedy for our sin problem (v. 21). He cares enough to cover us with the innocent life of Jesus (2 Cor. 5:21). His covering frees us from guilt and we are blessed (Romans 4:6-8).

Are there incidences or issues that you are concealing, hoping your spouse will not notice? Experience liberty in your relationship by admitting the truth, rejoicing together that your wrongs can be covered with His forgiveness and righteousness.

HIDING FROM CONVICTION

Read Genesis 3:6–13

*W*e know a young man who broke contact with his family and ran away for several years because he was ashamed when his parents discovered he had deceived them. He was repeating Adam and Eve's behavior. When Adam and Eve were convicted of their sin, they literally hid from God (v. 8). It is common for couples facing marital problems to avoid the presence of God by omitting prayer, Bible study, and contact with other Christians. We do not want to admit our failures to God.

Adam and Eve also hid behind fear (v. 10). Couples who are troubled can allow fear to dominate their thoughts and paralyze them. They expect their turmoil to increase. They fear the embarrassment of admitting they are wrong.

Next, Adam used blame to hide behind Eve, and Eve used blame to hide behind the serpent (v. 11–12). We prove that we have inherited their cowardly nature each time we shift attention away from our own wicked ways to the influence someone else has had over us. We prefer to concentrate on the shortcomings of others rather than admit our own.

Since these methods did not work, Adam and Eve tried to hide underneath excuses. Eve excused her behavior by claiming she was deceived (v. 13). She implied that what she did was not so bad because she had a valid excuse. As spouses, we quickly make excuses for our harshness or our laziness by claiming to be under too much stress. We apologize for carelessness by explaining that we were in a hurry. We excuse self-centered forgetfulness by declaring that we just didn't think.

God did not accept Adam and Eve's excuses, but He proved He still loved them by continuing to pursue them. He desired to restore the man and his wife to their original transparent relationship with Him and each other. God has not changed. He does not want us to hide from conviction. He desires that we admit our guilt so that we can be reconciled with Him and each other.

CONVICTION AND SURFACE CONFESSION

Read Genesis 3:12–13 and Psalm 51

*M*ost Christians have been taught regarding the need to quickly confess a sin once they have committed it. Eve eventually admitted her wrong actions, but she confessed in the way we often do. She concisely acknowledged her action related to the forbidden fruit, "I ate it." She did not, however, confess that her heart had sinned against God. She had esteemed her reasoning and logic above His. She had betrayed the One who had done nothing but pour out His blessings and love on her. She had even convinced Adam to sin with her.

I have recognized this same lame tendency in my life. I remember speaking sharply to my husband. I knew the words were harsh when they came out of my mouth, so I quickly added, "I'm sorry. I shouldn't have said that." This was a surface confession because the truth was, I was selfishly thinking of myself or maybe I was actually being greedy, hateful, or arrogant. I have also caught myself admitting surface actions to God in order to ease my conscience. For example, I have been with other people and uncomfortably sat through a TV show that glorified immorality. At first, I admitted to God that I shouldn't have watched the show, but I then realized I was aware of my wrong-doing the entire time I was watching the offensive program. I demonstrated a greater respect for the people I was with than I did for God. I did not want them to think I was a "goody-goody" or a "stick in the mud."

King David understood the need to confess his heart attitude in addition to his wrong actions. He admitted to Nathan and God that he had committed adultery and murder (Psalm 51:3, 14). He also confessed his heart to God (vv. 4–6). David realized that surface confession yields surface cleansing, but thorough confession is the path to deep restoration (v. 10). When you sense God's conviction, pause and allow Him to shine His penetrating light on your attitude and your actions, so you can confess your heart and experience true forgiveness. You will be amazed at what He will do for you personally, and how your marriage will benefit.

CONVICTION AND GODLY REPENTANCE

Read Acts 3:19–20, John 14:26, and Psalm 51

Two summers ago, God planted within me an intense desire for a clean heart. I was not aware of any blatant sin, so I asked Him to reveal the dirt in my life that needed to be cleansed. He chose to use various small family conflicts and misunderstandings to reveal my wickedness. As God exposed the evil within me, I was shocked and horrified. I grieved with each exposure, but through it all, He taught me the meaning of repentance. Repentance involves a true sense of one's own guilt. The remorse is intense enough to change one's way of thinking concerning a specific sin.

Victorious repentance also includes the realization that a person is helpless to correct or prevent a particular transgression by sheer determination. After the horror of my sinfulness struck me, I would immediately design a personal program of planned responses to eliminate the possibility of falling into the same trap. My plans led me, however, into bondage to a self-made list of "do's and don'ts." God showed me that I could release my sin to Him and trust the Holy Spirit to remind me of what He had taught me (John 14:26). Trusting God to both forgive and overcome should be the concluding step to repentance.

King David knew that in order to victoriously repent, he needed the power of God (Psalm 51:1). Rather than design a personal program of reformation, he expressed intense sorrow, then asked God to uphold him (v. 12). David summarized repentance as having a broken heart that trusted the Lord to rebuild what sin had destroyed (vv. 16–19).

David expects the refreshment of joy and gladness to follow godly repentance (vv. 8, 12). The result is a combination of relief and hope that produces a fountain of joy, and the refreshment that comes from being in the presence of the Lord (Acts 3:19–20). Once David experienced the life-giving renewal of repentance, he was enabled to effectively minister to his wife (2 Sam 12). The personal revival resulting from repentance becomes an overflowing source of jubilant love that benefits our spouses and families.

BE SOFT

Read Proverbs 15:1–4, 23

A college survey reports that during incongruent communication (communication that is not in harmony or conformity with what was expected), 55 percent of what people respond to and make assumptions about takes place visually. Thirty-eight percent of what people respond to and make assumptions about takes place through the sound of your voice. Only 7 percent of what people respond to and make assumptions about takes place through the actual words said.[49] Yet when my spouse points out that I said something harshly, I respond innocently, with a much gentler tone, "All I said was …" I repeat the same words I just used, as though they are the only thing that should have an impact. Proverbs 15, however, confirms the survey results. Our spouses respond to our demeanor and tone more than they do to our words. A gentle, soft tone calms people and turns away wrath (v. 1). Mothers softly sing to screaming babies because it calms them down. Shrill, loud, forceful tones accompanied by fierce body language cause spoken words to produce grief and anger. Yelling and shaking our fist as we speak will stir up a temper. A person may have a serious rebuke to convey, but a wise person will convey it in a calm, soft manner (v. 2). A foolish person will release the same verbiage by opening his mouth and dramatically letting his emotions fly. He will convey the message with the wrong tone and actions. The Bible says that a wholesome tongue is a tree of life (v. 4). The tree of life has healing properties (Rev. 22:2). The tongue should exhibit restorative qualities that soothe hurt and misunderstanding.

Scripture presents communication principles that are not only proven by surveys, but by our everyday lives. The Holy Spirit awaits our surrender to Him, so He can gently apply the healing balm of the tree of life through our communication to the people we love—including our spouses. Speak softly today.

THE GARDEN OF THE LORD

Read Genesis 2:8 and Isaiah 51:1–3

God's original intention for the first married couple was to live in a beautiful garden called Eden. The word "Eden" in Genesis 2:8 means an enclosed place of pleasure. God placed Adam and Eve there to continually delight in His creation and His person. Like an earthly father who takes great joy in seeing his children convey abundant love to him, God the heavenly Father would be glorified by His children's exuberance when in His presence. In Isaiah 51:3, God gives us additional insight concerning the garden of the Lord. It was a place of comfort, joy, gladness, thanksgiving, and melody! In God's garden there was no anxiety, no worry, but rather His comforting presence. The sounds of rejoicing, thanksgiving, and the voices of melody permeated the air.

When sin entered the Garden of Eden, the atmosphere of overflowing love immediately changed to one of fear. Adam and Eve now covered themselves and hid from God. Because of disobedience, they were expelled into the wilderness and waste places of the surrounding world (Genesis 3:23–24).

As I reflect on these truths, I'm reminded of so many marriages that began in the garden and ended up in the wilderness. Joy turned to discouragement; laughter was replaced with tears; thanksgiving disintegrated to complaining; airwaves of melody were carried away by winds of harshness. All God requires to restore the marital garden to its original glory is for husband and wife to yield to Him. When we seek Him and place our confidence in Him, He acts on our behalf (Isaiah 51:1–2). With outstretched arms of grace, God will gladly reach down into the deep pit of a broken relationship and set it free. He desires that every marriage live in the renewed garden of the Lord through His abundant grace and mercy (Isaiah 51:3). Only here can you truly rest in the comfort of the Lord, and partake of the fruits of His garden!

THE MAN GOD SEES

Read 1 Samuel 16:1–13

While seated in the gate area at the St. Louis airport waiting for our flight to be announced, a very tall, muscular, athletic man walks by. A tired little boy trails about ten yards behind him. Sam recognizes the man as a professional football player and whispers his name to me. The impressive man strolls over to another athletic-looking man, exchanges a few words, pats the second man on the back, and continues his long-legged gait down the crowded corridor. The weary child lags along, unnoticed. The man is approached by a traveler and stops to sign an autograph. When the man returns a few minutes later, the young couple next to us fumbles in their bag, retrieves a camera, and jumps up to take a picture with him. The shy boy quickly slips behind a pole to hide from the camera. He waits as his dad flashes a wide smile to the photographer. Without speaking or acknowledging the child, the man chooses a seat behind us. The young boy sits on the floor, mumbling to himself and his toy airplane. Several more fans shake hands with the man and walk away with autographs.

Later, when our plane lands, the people in Nashville brighten as they recognize the athlete, but the Spirit of God within me tears my heart with grief. Instead of noticing the man's accomplishments and stature, I see pride and self-centeredness. I see a man who cares more about his fans than his own son.

1 Samuel 16 reminds us that God chooses servants according to their heart rather than their height. Is the world's admiration more compelling than the opportunity to serve and enjoy your family? What does God see as He observes you?

CULTIVATING ROOTS

Read Hebrews 12:14–15

When someone, especially my spouse, offends me and I suffer hurt feelings, I naturally start nurturing and fertilizing the root of bitterness. I consider how unjust, selfish, and unkind the offensive action or words appear to be. I loosen the soil around the root of the offense by rehearsing the details in my mind. I fertilize it by pondering how I can retaliate, listing the reasons why I am justified in my thinking. As I dwell on the hurt, I water the little root by imagining what the offending person is thinking. It rapidly increases in size as I imagine similar events that could happen. I now have the opportunity to cultivate the fantasized events in the same way I nurtured the original offense. Unlike my flowers and shrubs, the root of bitterness abounds in the absence of God's presence.

No wonder the Lord urges us to pursue peace and holiness when we are offended (Heb. 12:14). Without His perspective, we smother grace and deeply ground ourselves with self-righteousness and a critical spirit. In this season of cultivation, we do not seek God. Instead, we become obsessed with the wrong done to us. The fruit of our troubles spreads like a weed to defile the lives of many others (Heb. 12:15). We unintentionally react to innocent bystanders with the sharpness with which we wish to wound the offender.

God warns us to watch carefully. These roots spread uncontrollably and overtake the garden. The way to contain or stop a spreading root before it wraps around our marriage and family is to crowd it with the growth of something stronger. If we are pursuing peace and holiness (v. 14), we cannot simultaneously pursue revenge and self-justification. As soon as we recognize the root of bitterness, we need to block it by reminding ourselves that when we offended and betrayed God, He bestowed grace and forgiveness upon us (v. 15). Concentrating on His grace encourages longsuffering, which yields peace and holiness that block bitterness before it infects the relationship with our spouse and loved ones.

PEA-BRAINED

Read Song of Solomon 5:6–8

For twelve days, during our recent anniversary trip, Sam and I spent twenty four hours a day together. We hiked together, snorkeled together, ate together, prayed together, and talked heart to heart. We cherished every moment. A few days after we returned, Sam was out of town for four days. Then he left to lead a men's conference and was gone for five more days. Even though I had the company of three sons and thirteen newborn puppies, I experienced a deep sense of loneliness.

I struggle with separation from Sam because God designed us physiologically to be strongly attached to each other as husband and wife. For example, when we come together sexually, a chemical called PEA is released in our brains that acts as a natural amphetamine. When we are apart, we experience depression, lovesickness, and a longing to be back together.[50] Between spouses, this intensity actually promotes sexual faithfulness.

Perhaps this fact explains the lovesickness the Shulamite bride experiences in Song of Solomon chapter five. She is separated from her husband and cannot find him. She endangers her life as she searches for him. She declares to the daughters of Jerusalem that she is lovesick.

One of the amazing ways God designed husband and wife to become one flesh is through a natural, physiological attraction. You strengthen your bonds of love every time you have sexual relations with each other. Become PEA-brained today.

THE POWER OF A NAME

Read Genesis 2:19–23

I vividly remember the first time my wife told me we were expecting a baby. I was so excited that God was blessing us with the privilege of having a child (Psalm 127:3). We immediately started investigating the meanings of different names and began discussing which ones would best describe our son. As parents, this was our right and responsibility.

God, in His wisdom, allowed Adam the special honor of naming not only the animals, but also his wife. As Adam tackled the monumental task of descriptively naming all of the different types of animals, God began to impress on him his need to eliminate loneliness through having a companion. As the animals paraded by and he named them, he observed that each creature had a corresponding partner. Observing these pairs, Adam was awakened to desire a companion with whom he could intimately fellowship.

Assigning a name also carries a responsibility to care for the one named. God instructed man to both name and manage the animals. Parents name their children and assume charge of their provision, protection, and training. When God presented woman to Adam, he declared with great enthusiasm (some Hebrew scholars believe Adam actually sang these words), "This is now bone of my bones, flesh of my flesh; she shall be called woman" (Gen. 2:23). Adam understood that she was a unique and special gift to him from God. He gave her the most precious name he could, the Hebrew word "ishshah," which means "soft man," a derivative of his own name, "iysh." This name expressed his understanding that he was to love her, take care of her, and protect her. She was a treasure presented to him from God. Take a minute to thank the Lord for the gift He has given to you in your spouse. Husbands, reaffirm your love to your wife.

MY STRENGTH

Read Isaiah 40:28–31

*S*am and I returned from a refreshing anniversary trip to the normal, more stressful routine of catch-up. Not only did we face stacks of unopened mail, phone calls to return, massive loads of dirty laundry, tall grass, and appointments, but our garage was now occupied by thirteen newborn puppies. Because the mother could not adequately feed them, we immediately set up a feeding rotation to supplement. The schedule required me to bottle feed, burp, and clean the puppies every three hours, even through the night. As I contemplated my lack of sleep and my huge list of urgent things to do, I moved from feelings of being overwhelmed to despair and defeat. I prayed for strength.

The Lord reminded me that months ago we had prayed He would bless us with healthy puppies to sell in order to partially fund our boys' college tuition. The puppies were not an overwhelming task, but an abundant blessing beyond what we dared to dream. I needed to change my perspective. The chorus, "The Lord is my strength and my salvation, whom shall I fear," came to mind. I had everything I needed because He is my strength. I needed to shift my focus from what I had to do to who He is. God, the power source living within me, does not get weary (v. 28). He gives power and increases strength (v. 29). The secret is in depending on Him rather than me.

My circumstances did not change, but my focus did. I was strengthened. I had little sleep, but adequate energy and abundant joy. I marveled at the miraculous growth of the puppies every day. I became eager to notice the details of how God was working around me, and to meditate on His character. Truly, the Lord is my strength.

Marriages will experience seasons of overwhelming tasks, discouragement, and inadequate sleep. In those times, remind yourself that God does not grow weary. Let Him be your strength.

WATERED DOWN WINE

Read 2 Corinthians 2:14–17

*P*aul explains that part of the triumphant celebration in Christ involves believers manifesting the fragrance of the knowledge of Him in every place (v. 14). To God, to other Christians, and to lost and confused people who want answers, the truth we display is a sweet, attractive aroma (v. 15). To some unbelievers, however, it will be a stench that smells like death because it convicts them and requires lifestyle changes they are not willing to make (v. 16). To unbelievers who are open to the gospel, the aroma will attract and lead them to experience new life in Christ. Since Christians cannot predict who will smell the stench of death or who will smell the fragrance of life, they must boldly live and speak the truth in every place.

Paul warns that there are those who do not speak the complete truth but instead corrupt the word of God (v. 17). The word "corrupt" is a marketing term referring to a peddler who sells wine after watering it down. In order to appeal to everyone, many Christians water down the word of God. Paul reminds us to speak in "sincerity." This is another marketing term referring to a craftsman who refuses to sell pottery that has flaws filled with wax, and deceptively covered with paint. Strong believers allow no cracks, but speak as God does, in complete truth.

In our culture, many activists are corrupting God's intent for marriage by attempting to redefine it to include two men, two women, or a group of any size or mix of sexes. It is vitally important that Christian couples refuse to dilute God's original design for marriage. We need to boldly manifest the fragrance of His knowledge in every place so that hurting activists can have the opportunity to smell the aroma of life. Don't water down God's plans for marriage. Make sure you market His full strength and flavor wherever you go.

THE PENETRATING QUESTION

Read Mark 5:25–34

*F*or twelve years, the woman described in today's passage suffers pain, stress, embarrassment, fear, and much disappointment. Her energy is drained. She exhausts all of her resources and all avenues of hope. When she hears about the power and ministry of Jesus, however, she takes action and works her way through the crowd to quietly touch His garment. She experiences immediate deliverance. What relief! What joy! Then Jesus asks the penetrating question, "Who touched Me?" The woman thought no one would notice. She trembles. She, an unclean woman, had touched a holy man. According to Jewish law, she had made Him and His garments unclean (Lev. 15:19–28).

When I re-live an experience I had in the 2nd grade, I have a sense of how this woman feels. On a rainy day, my class has recess inside. We are playing the eraser game. A really cute little guy is maneuvering around the classroom with the eraser balanced on his head, while someone else chases him. He rounds the corner and the eraser slips off his head. I am so focused that I shriek. The teacher immediately stops the game and asks, "Who screamed?" I am horrified. I have never been in trouble before, but I am absolutely guilty. I feel nauseated and fearful. I vividly remember trembling at the risk of admitting the truth.

The woman who touched Jesus without permission risks much more than I did when she falls down before Him and pours out the whole truth (v. 33). To her great surprise, Jesus expresses affirmation and acceptance as He responds by calling her "Daughter." He compliments and praises her (v. 34). The Truth sets her free.

In marriage, we will be faced with penetrating questions. The testimony of the woman in Mark chapter 5 challenges us to humbly admit what is true. We may risk rejection and disapproval from others, but the Lord Jesus will affirm and accept us. We, like this woman, can then proceed in peace.

THE MOST POWERFUL GIFT

Read Ephesians 1:15–21

I love my husband more than anyone or anything on this earth. With all my heart, I want him to experience the best life possible. I can care for him, cook, listen, support, and do many things, but I am limited. I do, however, possess an unlimited power source that is the key to ensuring he experiences the utmost in life. I can pray with great confidence, knowing that whatever I ask according to the will of the Father, He will grant. I know I am asking according to His will when I "pray" a Scripture.

Paul prayed Ephesians 1:15–21 for people he deeply cared about. I pray these same prayers for my husband, expanding on the thoughts to fit his current life. I begin by expressing gratitude for specific ways he has influenced and blessed me (v. 16). As I pray, I concentrate on and declare the greatness and faithfulness of God the Father (v. 17). I ask my Father to grant Sam the spirit of wisdom, that he would have God's perspective in everything. I pray God will increase Sam's intimate personal knowledge of Him and that He would reveal deep secrets and understanding. I ask the Lord to enlighten Sam's understanding, so he will be encouraged by the hope of His calling (v. 18). I pray Sam will realize he has an important purpose and that he is precious to Jesus. I pray he will know from personal experience the exceeding greatness of God's mighty power that is available to Him (v. 19). I ask that Sam will depend upon this power. I close my prayer by praising the majesty of Jesus Christ who makes my requests possible because of His greatness.

I consistently alternate praying today's passage and the prayer from Ephesians 3:14–21 for my husband. I marvel as God answers these prayers right before my eyes. Pray them daily for your spouse, both privately and out loud in their presence. Hearing you pray God's blessings for them is a gift they will cherish.

TAKE A BITE

Read Genesis 3:1–6 and 1 Timothy 2:14

My husband wants to make me happy. If he knows of anything I long for, he sacrifices to get it for me. If I desire to have him make a home improvement, he works it into his schedule. He will watch a chick flick, with a predictable happy ending, because he enjoys my companionship. If I prepare a new dish that looks questionable, I can convince him to take just one little bite. How blessed I am that my husband desires to please me!

When I reflect on the story of Adam and Eve, I recognize the responsibility that accompanies this blessing. The devil shifted Eve's focus away from the provision and character of God. He caused her to consider her own self interests. Step by step, he deceived her into eating the fruit. Eve did not stop with the pleasure of her snack, but turned and convinced Adam to take a bite also. The Bible says that Adam, unlike Eve, was not deceived, but her influence was so great that he ate the fruit anyway (1 Tim. 2:14). The Bible has other examples of wives who convince their husbands to make unwise decisions. Sarai pleads with Abram to have a child by Hagar and he listens to her. Delilah persuades Samson to reveal the secret of his strength. I can think back to different times when I talked my husband into changing travel plans or altering the way he planned to discipline our children. Sometimes my perspective was helpful, but other times I led him astray. Eve, Sarai, and Delilah influenced their men in harmful ways because their motives were self-centered rather than God-centered. It is vital that a wife seeks wisdom from the Lord before she voices her opinion. The Psalmist declares that he seeks the Lord wholeheartedly so he will not stray from God's commandments (Ps. 119:10). If I do not want to cause my husband to wander from the blessings of God, I must be cautious with my influence.

HOW INVIGORATING!

Read Psalm 119:17–40

Recently, a lady came for to us for prayer and counsel. Her husband did not understand her faith and desire for the Lord. At times, he treated her harshly and she was uncertain of how to respond (v. 23). Psalm 119:17 describes the condition of her heart. The Lord had stirred her with a desire to please Him by understanding and obeying His Word. She wanted to live in God's power and according to His ways. She was willing to set aside preconceived ideas and allow God to improve her spiritual eyesight (v. 18). Together, we looked up and read Scriptures specifically directed to wives. We reviewed verses about responding in unfair circumstances (vv. 27–28). We discussed how these principles applied directly to her situation. She became excited as God imparted His truth and hope (v. 24), and she marveled at the completeness of His Word. She was eager to live out these principles regardless of how her husband responded. In addition to helpful instruction and encouragement, the Scriptures revealed challenging personal adjustments she needed to make. In some instances, she needed to confess wrong attitudes and repent. Rather than dread the change, however, she was invigorated because God had proved that His word was living and relevant. Her controlling attitude was transformed into a reverent fear of the Lord (v. 38-39). This was evidenced by her delight in having the opportunity to obey Him (v. 35). She was revived by the Word, and ready to face the difficulties of life (vv. 37, 40).

The Bible is living, relevant, and powerful. Be invigorated as you search for wondrous things in God's Word and apply them specifically to your life and marriage. Rejoice in the power of the Holy Spirit because the conviction He brings magnifies not only the holiness of God, but His concern and love for you as an individual. Like the lady who came for counsel, you will be renewed as you seek His perspective and instructions for your life and marriage.

NEGLECT

Read Luke 7:36–50

I connect with the Pharisee described in today's passage. Like him, I was raised in an environment that stressed church attendance and living by the Ten Commandments. Being strict about outward behavior became a compulsion. Also, like the Pharisee, I want to spend time with Jesus. However, the account of this visit pierces me. Because I have consistently strived to outwardly control my behavior, I have often been commended for my lifestyle, but have overlooked the immensity of my debt to God. I may have avoided humiliating accusations of blatant sins like adultery, drunkenness, and robbery, but I have tended to be blind to hidden sins of pride and a critical spirit. As a result, my unworthiness has been minimized in my heart. Since the Pharisee was unaware of his haughtiness, Jesus exposed it.

God views such arrogance as an abomination. It diminishes our awe of Him, weakens our worship, and degrades fellow human beings, especially those closest to us. The Pharisee profaned the person of God by neglecting courtesies that are ordinarily extended to any guest. How often do I get so distracted in routine responsibilities that I fail to acknowledge the majesty of Jesus? It is common courtesy to focus intently on each person involved in a conversation, but how often does my mind wander from Him when I pray? How rude I am to God!

In contrast, the sinful woman was fascinated with the marvel of God's forgiveness. Oblivious to what anyone else thought, with all of her being, she expressed gratitude and love. She recognized that Jesus was worthy of undivided attention. There seems to be a direct correlation between worship and recognizing the depth of our personal wickedness. When we view sin from our own perspective, we not only distort its depravity, but we also diminish the glory of God.

How grateful I am that Jesus exposes the sin that I trivialize. After confession, I—like the sinful woman—can experience the freedom to unashamedly express myself in worship. This liberty releases me from the bondage of self-concern and self-exaltation to rightly view my spouse and loved ones. It empowers me to humbly and joyfully serve them.

NOURISH AND CHERISH HER

Read Ephesians 5:28–29 and 2 Samuel 12:1–3

Paul instructs husbands to love their wives as their own bodies (v. 28). When I am cold, I slip on a sweatshirt. When I am thirsty, I fix myself a glass of ice-cold tea. When I am hungry, I find something to munch on. When I'm tired, I rest. When I smash my finger, I automatically draw it close for comfort. When I am dirty and sweaty, I take a shower. I do not debate with myself about these simple acts, but perform them without hesitation. Just as a man attends to the needs of his physical body, he should not hesitate to nourish and cherish his wife (v. 29). To nourish means to "care for" (provide food, shelter, and other essential needs). To cherish means to exhibit tender loving care and to keep warm. I picture a husband gently tucking a blanket over his wife and kissing her on the forehead when she falls asleep.

The Old Testament story of the rich man who owns many sheep and the poor man who owns one little ewe lamb illustrates the dynamics of nourishing and cherishing (2 Sam 12:1–3). The poor man nourishes his lamb by spending time with it in his home. He sacrifices and shares his food. He demonstrates affection as he allows the lamb to drink from his own cup. He desires to be close and hugs the lamb to his chest while she sleeps. He treats her as a cherished possession. His provision is not a duty, but a display of loving devotion.

Husbands are to not only provide for the physical needs of their wives, but to also fill their "love" needs by tenderly displaying affection. Sensitive husbands look for opportunities to warm the hearts of their wives in the everyday routine of home life. Look for ways to nourish and cherish your wife today. Let her feel, hear, and experience your love.

THREE LITTLE PIGS

Read 1 Corinthians 3:9–15 and Proverbs 24:3–4

Our oldest son worked with two classmates on a building construction project for a nationwide competition. Unlike the childhood story of the three little pigs, they approached their structure with sound thinking. My son explained that although the foundation was the basis for the integrity of the entire building, the frame, roof, and inside features were also vitally important. The boys researched the strength of the materials and carefully chose the most efficient and dependable construction methods. Their team would be ashamed if a big bad wolf could blow their project into a haystack piled atop a solid, unmovable foundation.

In 1 Corinthians 3, Paul reminds church leaders that although the foundation of the church is crucial, they must take heed how they build upon that foundation. The same principle applies in marriages. The foundation is a husband and wife who by faith have experienced and applied the grace of God as the cornerstone of their life together. Without this foundation, the marriage is unstable. However, Christians tend to approach marriage with the idea that the only requirement for a fulfilling relationship is that both spouses are believers. Later, when their relationship is suffering, they complain, "We don't understand. We both are Christians and go to church."

Like the construction team, a couple chooses the materials for what they are building. The choices are gold, silver, and precious stones that will stand strong, or wood, hay, and stubble that will collapse (v. 12). Gold, silver, and precious stones may represent the building blocks of wisdom, understanding, and knowledge (Prov. 24:3–4). A couple must persistently research God's Word, know Him intimately, and apply His principles. Wood, hay, and stubble represent human reasoning, self effort, and manipulation. The quality of the structure is obvious (1 Cor. 3:13). Godly building blocks combine for a joyful lasting bond (v. 14). Human building blocks result in suffering and destruction (v. 15). What are you using to build your marriage?

IDLENESS

**Read Ecclesiastes 10:18, 2 Samuel 11:1–4,
and Ephesians 5:16-17**

*M*y home requires continual maintenance! Whether the roof leaks, a piece of siding blows off in a storm, or a doorknob breaks, there always seems to be something needing repair. I'm tempted to ignore the problem and let it lay idle, but I realize that if I don't repair it, the problem will only get worse. In Ecclesiastes 10:18, Solomon cautions that an inclination to be lazy results in a home that decays and even falls through.

Throughout Scripture, God warns us not to be idle (Rom. 12:11, Heb. 6:12). The fruits of idleness include poverty, hunger, bondage, tattling, meddling, disappointment, and ruin. Isaac Watts wrote, "The Romans said, 'By doing nothing, men learn to do evil. For Satan finds some mischief still, for idle hands to do.' The Jewish rabbis taught, 'He who does not teach his son a trade, teaches him to be a thief.'"[51] When I was a little boy, I often heard my mom or dad say that "Idleness is the devil's playground!" The virtuous woman of Proverbs 31 is commended by God for not eating the bread of idleness. While David's soldiers were in battle, he elected to stay behind and remain idle (2 Sam. 11:1). His idleness resulted in his lusting after Bathsheba. Even though he was forgiven by God, the consequences for his sin plagued David's family for generations. It all started with idleness—not appropriately redeeming the time according to God's calling upon his life.

In marriage, idleness manifests itself in different ways. Rather than communicating or working on projects together, many couples nightly melt in front of a television. Marriages are idle when spouses refuse to seek counsel for communication problems, sexual addictions, or other serious maladies. Some relationships are ruined by idleness in the management of finances. To prevent decay, we must avoid Satan's snare of idleness and redeem the time God has given us (Eph. 5:16–17). Has idleness crept into your life and marriage?

MOVING

Read Genesis 12:1–15

On the average, families in the United States relocate every three years. Other families consider their options and refuse the opportunity to move. In thirty-five years of marriage, we have transferred our family and belongings to six different cities. Much prayer and consideration went into every decision. Is the move helpful financially? How will the move affect our children? What will the new school system be like? Will we miss our family and friends? How will we adjust? Can we find a church that is right for us? Through it all, we have learned that there is only one consideration that matters. Does the Lord want us to move?

Abram faced the decision of moving his family. He had great possessions and many servants. The move would affect all of their lives. He would be leaving his relatives and familiar surroundings. He did not know exactly where he was going, so he could not even guess what the new location would be like. The only certain factor was that God had instructed him to move. He chose to go only for that reason (v. 4). God provided and blessed in every area of concern (v. 7). Another time, Abram decided to move to Egypt. The Scriptures list only one reason for his move. There was a famine in the land. Abram was looking for a more efficient way to feed his flocks and maintain his wealth (v. 10). As a result of the move, Abram faced a potential threat to his life that caused him to compromise his character and risk his wife's morality (v. 13). Later, Abram's nephew Lot was faced with the assessment of moving. He, too, considered only one factor. The potential for greater wealth and prosperity was the basis of his decision. The result of his move was loss of all possessions and the death of his wife.

When people face an opportunity to move, normally one concern will carry the most weight. Make sure God's leading is given top priority in the decision-making process for your family.

BETTER NOT BE BITTER

Read Colossians 3:19

*A*s a young boy, I remember inquisitively exploring a field on our newly acquired farm. I noticed a strange-looking tree with little orange fruit hanging all over it. My curiosity got the best of me. I went over, plucked off a piece, and plopped it into my mouth. Upon tasting it, I immediately spit it out. It was the bitterest thing I had ever tasted! I ran back to the house, washed my mouth out with water, and asked my mother what it was. Laughingly, she replied that I had tasted an orange persimmon. She told me they were good to eat only after they had turned dark and were ready to fall off the tree. The taste of the orange persimmon left such a lasting impression in my mind that whenever someone mentions something being bitter, I immediately think back to this experience.

Unfortunately, there are many men who are "orange persimmon" husbands, like bitter fruit to their wives. The word "bitter" means to be harsh, to exasperate, to irritate, or to be sour. In today's verse, God specifically commands every husband to avoid harsh or bitter treatment of his wife. One way a husband embitters his wife is by asserting tyrannical authority over her. Rather than leading her with love as Christ leads His church, he, like a dictator, demands blind and unquestioned obedience (Eph. 5:25). Some men embitter their wives by only giving affection when they have a sexual agenda in mind. A recent survey asked thousands of Christian women across America to define affection. Their answer was enlightening. They defined affection as "non-sexual, meaningful touch."[52] A husband must take time to caress, hug, hold, kiss, and whisper sweet words to his wife without any sexual motive. A husband who offers this kind of compassionate care to his wife leaves a sweet taste in her mouth. When she thinks of him, she does not think of a sour persimmon that repulses her, but rather a delicious and desirable piece of fruit she delights to taste.

WHAT DOES A WIFE DO?

Read Daniel 6:3–27 and Ephesians 5:33

A friend pulled me aside and questioned how she should respond to her husband. She explained that she felt her husband restricted their son for failure to do something that was beyond the boy's control. Her son had asked her why he was being disciplined. She could not explain, so she privately went to her husband who refused to discuss the matter. She wanted to know how to be fair to her son and respectful to her husband when she did not agree with his decision.

I encouraged my friend to read the story of Daniel with her son. Daniel faces a similar challenge because he does not agree with the discipline the king decrees. Daniel responds honorably by being faithful to both God and the king. In addition, there is no sin in his life that would wrongly influence his responses (v. 5). Throughout the misunderstanding, he depends on his God (v. 10). Daniel shows no contempt for the unfairness, and it is evident by his behavior that His only goal is to please God (v. 16). Instead of declaring that he had been right when the king was in error, Daniel emerges from the lion's den by declaring his loyalty to the king (v. 21). Daniel never displays rebellion or a bad attitude (v. 23). The secret of his forbearance is his intense trust in God (v. 24). His faith is so strong that the king is influenced to surrender to the Lord (vv. 26–27).

What a practical example for a wife to apply when she needs to maintain a submissive attitude in confusing circumstances. I encouraged my friend to pray and maintain a close walk with the Lord. Just as Daniel displayed respect for the king when he disagreed with his decree, I urged her to speak the truth, but in doing so to strive to convey honor and respect to her husband. (Eph. 5:33). A wife can trust the Lord to reveal truth to her husband through her respectful attitude.

I ONLY HAVE EYES FOR YOU

Read Job 31:1–12 and Matthew 5:28, 6:22–23

*I*n chapter 31, Job concludes a lengthy defense of his innocence before God by stating that he has made a covenant with his eyes. Job understands a profound truth; the eye is the window to the soul. Jesus elaborates by stating that a healthy eye is a source of light and a bad eye is a source of darkness that influences the whole body (Matt. 6:22–23).

Temptation often starts in the eye gate. In Genesis 3:6, Eve was drawn away when she "saw" that the tree was good for food and a delight to her eyes. Jesus states in Matthew 5:28 that adultery is initiated by first looking at a woman with lust. Job constructed a barrier of protection around his mind by resolving not to ponder the beauty of other women. Sexual thoughts about other women would never be entertained because he would never let a "snap shot" of them infiltrate his soul. He had no concubine or mistress. He only had eyes for his wife.

Every husband must guard against having eyes that gaze upon anything that could initiate adultery in his heart (Job 31:7, 9). Men today are bombarded by sexual images from all angles of view—commercials, billboards, and inappropriately dressed women including co-workers, waitresses, dental assistants, hairdressers, students, teachers, and even church members. It is impossible to avoid all of these visual intrusions, but like Job, a man can determine in advance to restrict his heart responses to them by planning to immediately shift his line of vision when they occur and by concentrating on pure thoughts. It is also vital for men to deny themselves access to any pornographic pictures or movies. A man should respond as the Flamingoes' singer who claims he is so captivated by his love that he only has eyes for her:

> *I don't know if we're in a garden*
> *Or on a crowded avenue*
> *You are here, so am I*
> *Maybe millions of people go by*
> *But they all disappear from view*
> *And I only have eyes for you.*[53]

GOD'S HIGHWAY

Read Proverbs 16:17 and Isaiah 35:8–9

I recently drove to Gatlinburg, Tennessee, from my home in Jamestown. During the three-hour journey, I passed through many different speed zones. On the first leg of my trip, I was on a two-lane road with a 55 mph speed limit. At one particular point the speed changed to 25 mph because of a school zone. Since I don't mind driving 55 mph, I may appear to be a safe driver who is outwardly obedient to the law. If my preference is to maintain that speed through the school zone, however, I become an immediate danger to any children who may be in the vicinity. I also risk getting a ticket with a stiff fine. My external compliance with the law can vanish if it conflicts with my inner desire to travel at a higher rate of speed. A highway that is meant to be safe for every traveler becomes treacherous if I take the law into my own hands.

Did you know that God has a highway? There are no speed limit signs, school zones, curves, or bumps. It is straight and unique. It is called the highway of holiness (Isa 35:8), and it leads to the very presence of God! Unfortunately, many couples journey through life at the speed of their own selfish desires, endangering both their marriage and their children. They foolishly assume that they merit travel on God's highway of blessings, but are detoured down another road that leads to destruction. His highway is reserved, however, only for the redeemed who have been ransomed by the blood of Jesus (Isaiah 35:9–10, John 14:6, Mark 10:45, Titus 2:14). Study the "map" outlined in the parentheses. Avoid the roadblocks of self-sufficiency, and make sure you and your family are traveling on God's highway of holiness.

THE CRABBY DAY

Read Genesis 4:2–8 and Philippians 4:8

I had a crabby day yesterday. It was evident in every glum response, in every frustrated sigh, and in every strained effort I initiated. I was so disappointed that my plans and schemes for the day were disrupted that I let aggravation and discouragement rule. Every person in my home and every acquaintance I spoke with probably detected an undeniable gloom. I even found myself controlled by expectations of more negative to come.

In today's passage, Cain experiences a similar despair. He plans to impress the Lord with his own manner of worship. He anticipates a warm welcome from God, but the Lord does not respect Cain and his offering. This aggravates Cain. It spoils his day. This is not according to his plan. The more he stews about his disappointment, the angrier he becomes. His irritation, like mine, is evident in his countenance (v. 5). But our merciful God gently speaks love to Cain. He challenges him to consider why he is so annoyed (v. 6). He offers him the same solution to crabbiness that is available to me. If I do well and respond to life according to God's purposes, He will accept my responses (v. 7). All I have to do is admit my self-centeredness and pride. I need to shift my focus back to trusting God's plans for the day. He promises me His acceptance. God's love is also evident in His warning that follows (v. 7). If I continue to view my life from my own perspective, if I refuse to change my views, I will not control my own destiny. Instead, sin will harass me and dominate my life. I will react to disappointments in shocking ways that I can't even predict (v. 8).

Obviously our crabby days will make life miserable for our spouses and anyone we come in contact with, but those same people will benefit from the change in attitude that results from the simple remedy (v. 7). Admit when we respond to life through our own perceptions. Repent and experience the refreshing presence of God (Acts 3:19). Allow Him to replace our views with His perspective (Phil. 4:8).

THE NAME OF THE LORD

Read Psalm 20:7–8, 2 Samuel 10:18, and Zechariah 4:6

I vividly remember the time when we were framing the roof of our home and I leaned on a truss that was not yet nailed into place. It quickly gave way to my weight and I nearly tumbled 40 feet to the ground below! I had faulty confidence in what appeared to be stable.

As King David pens Psalm 20:7–8, he is probably reflecting back to the battle when the Syrians fled before Israel (2 Sam. 10:18). In this conflict, David defeats an army of 700 chariots and 40,000 horsemen! God continually reminds His people to take no confidence in the bow, the sword, wealth, or personal effort (Zech. 4:6). David knows that the key to victory is continually remembering the name of the Lord, and who it represents.

Moses, when bowing before God at the burning bush, asked what name he should call the One who was sending him to the children of Israel. God instructed Moses to tell them that "I AM" sent him (Exod. 3:13-14). This name presented a new and special revelation to Israel. God was declaring, "I AM whatever my people need!" Seven times in the Old Testament, God offers further explanation of who He is by revealing His names that mean: I am thy banner, I am thy peace, I am thy righteousness, I am the One who provides, I am the One who heals, I am thy shepherd, and I am the One who is present. David confidently announces that victory is not won with horses or chariots, but by trusting His name (Ps. 20:7).

Likewise, I AM will deliver us from all our adversaries. The great I AM is all we need. When facing the instabilities of life—whether finances, health issues, marital disharmony, or family struggles—we can trust in the name of the Lord!

EXPOUNDING

Read Acts 18:24–28 and Ephesians 5:18

Recently, a friend I greatly respect drew some conclusions from examples in her life and used them to teach other people. I was saddened because I knew what she shared was incomplete. Last year, through some personal challenges and His Word, God had shown me an aspect of truth my friend was missing. Since then, I had experienced victory in areas of life where I was previously defeated. I longed for my friend to experience this same triumph over her challenge, but I wasn't sure how to communicate without offending her. I realized that married couples sometimes face the same dilemma. How do you correct someone that you respect and admire without insulting them, or appearing to be a know-it-all?

Apollos was very knowledgeable in the Old Testament scriptures (v. 24). He was an eloquent speaker with a deep commitment to the Lord's principles (v. 25). He passionately taught what he believed and was greatly respected. He understood the urgency of repentance as John the Baptist taught, but he had never heard of the divine enabling power of Jesus. When Aquila and Priscilla heard his powerful teaching, they realized he had never heard the complete truth (v. 26). Rather than approach him in front of his students, they invited him to their home where they could speak privately. The Bible reveals that they expounded the way of God to him. Translated, the word "expounded" carries the connotation of lovingly explaining. Their intent was to gently enlighten him for his benefit and joy. Aquila and Priscilla were not trying to prove they were wiser, but merely wanted to deepen Apollos' fellowship with them and the Lord. They achieved their intentions. Apollos was so excited about his enlightened understanding that his ministry greatly expanded (vv. 27–28).

Before approaching your spouse with a new insight that is corrective, confirm that the adjustment is significant and not merely a trivial detail. Make sure the intent of your communication is to benefit your mate. Speak with him or her privately, from your heart. Joyfully anticipate a closer bond.

Stiff-Necked

Read Deuteronomy 9:11–14, 10:12–17, Jeremiah 3:8,
Proverbs 29:1, and Acts 7:51–53

Has your neck ever been stiff? When the muscles tense up and become tight, it becomes painful to move your head up and down or from side to side. Your every thought revolves around the pain in your neck! You long for freedom from the discomfort that has taken your body captive. When I become physically stiff-necked, I first attempt to alleviate the pain by massaging my neck with my own hands. If it still hurts, I ask for Debbie's help. If the pain continues, I go to the doctor and seek relief!

In Scripture, God often refers to those who are stubborn and rebellious toward Him as stiff-necked. In Deuteronomy 9:13, He calls the children of Israel stubborn and stiff-necked because of their repeated idolatry. God is so provoked by their continual stubbornness that He threatens to destroy them and start over with a new people that will love and respect Him (v. 14). Their stubbornness and spiritual adultery continue until He eventually casts the Israelites aside to their enemies (Jer. 3:8). In Acts 7:51, Stephen describes the sin of being stiff-necked as repeatedly resisting the Holy Spirit. This stubbornness not only provokes God, but is extremely frustrating to our loved ones. Proverbs 29:1 warns that a person who is often reproved yet remains stiff-necked can expect to be broken beyond healing.

In marriage, one or both spouses often become stiff-necked. This condition results when either mate obstinately refuses to acknowledge their sinfulness to God and each other. Having been reproved repeatedly by the Holy Spirit, their spiritual necks remain tightened by pride. The only remedy is a spiritual massage, with the healing balm of repentance and obedience. Yielding to the hands of the Master will once again bring relaxation and peace to the relationship.

THE CURE

Read Philippians 1:9–11 and Ephesians 3:14-20

For several weeks, I had been battling a critical spirit toward someone. I repeatedly confessed my bad attitude. I kept vowing to change my way of thinking, but I found myself irritated that this person had not changed. I had been so consumed with justifying my frustration that my negative attitude invaded other areas of my life. I did not want to be controlled by this judgmental mindset, but I couldn't seem to shake it off.

As I continued to pray about it, God revealed that I was offended. I resented this person because he was not meeting my expectations. His failure deprived me of something extremely important to me. His behavior interfered with what I deserved. As a result, I felt trapped in a hopeless cycle of judging, justifying my attitude, and being ashamed of my self-centeredness. Once I realized my root problem was resentment and offense, God revealed the cure.

In today's passage, Paul prays the Philippians will be so overwhelmed with the amazing aspects of God's love that they will use it as the filter for all their decisions and responses (v. 9). As a result, the Philippians will concentrate on things that are excellent or worthy of attention (v. 10). If God's love prevails, they will be sincere and blameless before others and will not experience offense or resentment. The remedy for resentment is to let God's love overflow and be the judge rather than reasoning from a personal perspective. In order for His love to abound, an individual must personally experience its vastness. When concentrating on His love, a person will not be distracted by selfish attitudes.

When a critical attitude toward a spouse, friend, or employer surfaces, we should confess it and then pray for an expanded understanding of God's love (Eph. 3:14–20). We can apply this truth personally, and allow it to overwhelm our thinking. The cure for resentment is experiencing God's love to the extent that it becomes the basis of everything we think or do.

ONSTAR

Read Joshua 1:1–9

Several years ago, I purchased a new four-wheel drive vehicle that came with a GPS (Global Positioning System) navigation option called OnStar. At the time, the system was new and few people had it or were even familiar with it. Using satellite GPS, OnStar could pinpoint the exact location of my vehicle within a few hundred feet. If I was driving down the road and called OnStar, they could tell me exactly where I was, what exit was coming next, and what hotels and restaurants were located there. If I was involved in an accident where my airbags deployed, OnStar immediately dispatched emergency help to my location. One time I locked my keys in my car, called OnStar, and they remotely sent a signal to unlock it. I thought to myself, "This is amazing!" Having OnStar gave my wife and me a sense of security while traveling that we had never before experienced.

When Joshua stood at the Jordan River preparing to assume leadership of the Israelites, God promised to be an "OnStar" for him (v. 5). The anxiety of aggressively directing a nation to conquer a strange land had to be overwhelming, but God commanded him to be strong and bold for the task before him (v. 6). The Lord warned Joshua to be meticulous in obeying His commandments (v. 7). He connected the success of Joshua's campaign with obedience to the Law (v. 8). God assured him that he could fulfill the commandments and accomplish the tasks because like an OnStar system, the Lord would be with him wherever he went (v. 9).

Knowing God is ever present with us as His children, we can victoriously lead our families to obey the His commandments and achieve success. When we face difficult circumstances and become anxious, we can dismiss our fears and take confidence in our "Heavenly OnStar." What a comfort to know that the Lord watches over us, cares for us, and offers divine assistance in every situation!

A HOT IRON

Read 1 Timothy 4:1–3 and 1 John 4:1

Recently Debbie was pressing some clothes, and I haphazardly walked by and brushed my arm against the side of the hot iron. Immediately, the searing sensation burned into my flesh and my memory.

The Bible states that in later times, some will depart from the faith because they devote themselves to deceitful, seducing spirits and embrace the teachings of demons (1 Tim. 4:1). This will happen through false teachers who are hypocritical liars (v. 2). 1 John 4:1 stresses that the world is filled with such teachers. The result of adhering to the lies of these teachers is that the conscience becomes seared with a hot iron (1 Tim. 4:2). The word "seared" means to cauterize or brand. This searing has two effects. First, a person becomes numb and indifferent to the truth. Secondly, the devil's brand (stronghold) continually haunts, oppresses, and controls.

It is interesting that one of the distorted truths concerns marriage (v. 3). The first institution ordained by God is discouraged or even forbidden. What He declares holy and acceptable, Satan attempts to destroy. In today's world this does not happen overtly, but rather subtly through media and messages which interweave a spattering of truth with lies promoting self-centeredness and personal rights. Current trends ignore the principles of God and encourage individuals to cohabitate or dissolve a troubling marriage for the sake of personal happiness. Just as the physical healing of a burn is soothed by ointments applied to the skin, a seared conscience is healed by applying the eye salve of God so we can clearly see truth (Rev. 3:18). 1 John 4:1 warns us to test every spirit to determine whether it is from God. Make sure that the teaching and advice you apply to your marriage is based on His Word!

A LITTLE KINDNESS

Read 2 Chronicles 10:1–7

*I*t had been a very busy day. I had juggled household chores, school-work with the boys, and bookkeeping for the ministry. I was sitting at the computer plugging figures in as quickly as I could. I was unaware of any other activity when Sam quietly leaned over me, gently kissed my cheek, and set a cup of hot peach tea on the desk. He slipped out of the room and never said a word. I was so touched that I immediately wanted to return his kindness. I started thinking of things I could do for him.

The wise men who advised King Rehoboam, as described in today's passage, understood this principle. The people of his kingdom had not only experienced a stressful day, but had lived an oppressed life (vv. 4–5). They pled for mercy and understanding. Rehoboam sought the counsel of older men. They suggested that he show concern by lightening the load of the people. The men explained that kind acts and words would stir a desire in the citizens' hearts to please and serve the king (v. 7). When someone performs an act of kindness, the recipient of the good deed feels compelled by gratitude to serve in return.

The dictionary reveals that kindness is aroused by a sympathetic or helpful nature. In order for it to be kindled in one's heart, a person must first be aware of another's need. In my situation, Sam paid attention to what was happening in my life and noticed I was having a stressful, tiring day. He acted accordingly, with a kind act that showed he understood what I was going through. The desire to serve was then stirred in me.

Kind words and deeds in a marriage initiate a grateful cycle of benevolence in which the husband and wife concentrate on special ways to express love back and forth. A little kindness ends up going a long way. Show kindness to your spouse today.

A WOMAN'S INTUITION

Read Genesis 1:27 and Matthew 27:11–24

God distinctly created both male and female (v. 27). Researchers have noted interesting differences within the physiology of the male and female brain. It is believed that the left side of the brain controls logic skills while the right side controls emotions. The "corpus callosum" that connects the right and left hemispheres of the brain is proportionately larger in females. Information between the two sides of the brain is exchanged more quickly and less hindered in a woman than a man. Her logic, therefore, tends to incorporate more emotions. Scientists suggest this could explain a woman's intuition. A man tends to process most information on the left side of the brain without as much regard for emotions.

A husband can present a list of facts that indicates a certain decision. His wife may agree the facts point that way, but for some unexplainable reason, she feels uneasy about the decision. This could be woman's intuition, one of the specially designed features God created to distinguish male from female. It can be very frustrating to a man whose thought patterns are logical and precise.

Today's reading in Matthew 27 describes how Pilate experienced this frustration as he pondered the accusations concerning Jesus. The chief priests presented information. The elders explained their perspective (v. 12). The crowd shouted their opinions. Even Jesus, Himself, answered some of Pilate's questions (v. 11). Pilate logically concluded that envy was the reason Jesus had been delivered to him (v. 18). His wife, however, sent him a warning to have nothing to do with Jesus. Her intuition was so strong that she was having disturbing dreams (v. 19), yet Pilate washed his hands of it and let the crowd make the decision (v. 24).

As leader of the home, a husband must make decisions that impact the entire family (Eph. 5:23-24), but when his wife's intuition bears warning against the facts, he should not follow Pilate's example. Rather, he will be wise to consider her insights and invest extra effort to confirm his decision with the Lord. Husbands, be careful not to ignore your wife's intuition.

DECISIONS, DECISIONS

Read John 14:4–6 and Matthew 6:31–33

A high school senior pleaded with the youth group, "Please pray for me. I have to decide what college I should attend or if I'm even supposed to go to college. I don't know what to do." She was facing her first major adult decision, and she wanted clear direction from the Lord. I understand her anguish. We, too, are sometimes overwhelmed with urgent, stressful decisions. How do we effectively discipline our children? How do we pursue and choose the right jobs? How do we navigate the complexities of purchasing a home or vehicle? Discernment can be challenging.

In John 14 when Jesus announced he would be leaving, Thomas was troubled because he did not know where Jesus was going (v. 5). He wanted to know what to do and where to go. Jesus responded by explaining that He was the only way to get to the Father (v. 6).

When we ask the Lord to lead us in making decisions, we are asking for directions. His answer to Thomas applies to every request we submit to Him. He is the way; He is our direction. We can honestly inquire about what to do in a particular situation, and then we need not be overwhelmed with concern because He, Himself, is our way. I have learned to seek specific direction from the Lord and then rather than concentrate on finding the exact answer, I intently pursue His presence. Usually, He unexpectedly reveals His direction when I am engrossed in worship or Bible study. If we concentrate on His character, if we remind ourselves of His wisdom and faithfulness, if we give our attention to enjoying and honoring Him, He will lead us. Most of the major decisions we face concern our welfare and the welfare of our family. Jesus explained that if we focus on Him rather than being overwhelmed with concerns, all these things will be supplied to us (Matt. 6:31–33). He is the direction for every decision a husband and wife will face.

LET'S HAVE FUN

Read Matthew 16:13–23

*G*od created humans with varied temperaments. Recognizing the strengths and weaknesses of these personality types helps us to be both long-suffering and appreciative of our spouse, our children, and every one that touches our family. Devotions from the next five days explore ways to relate to the various types.

I was recently talking to Debbie about our friends who had launched a business together as husband and wife. I told her they were having a blast. She responded, "Anyone would have a great time with Sharon. She can make the most mundane task into a party. She is a typical sanguine personality who doesn't hesitate to talk vibrantly about anything and everything. Her energy is contagious, and she's never met a stranger. Her motto in life is, 'Let's have fun!' "

Most sanguine people can chat non-stop for hours. Some, however, struggle with forgetfulness. They talk so much that they forget to listen. Others are so eager to speak that they talk before they think. In the Bible, Peter demonstrates this temperament. He talked more than all of the other disciples put together! One minute, he boldly declared Jesus was the Christ, the Son of the living God (v. 16). Moments later when Jesus told His disciples He must suffer, be killed, and raised up on the third day, Peter, again, did not hesitate to speak. This time, however, he responded by rebuking Jesus (v. 21)! Even though Peter's goal may have been happiness for all, he often spoke before he thought (v. 23). Can you imagine a mortal man rebuking the Son of God? Peter meant well, but he did what many individuals with sanguine temperaments often do; he opened his mouth and inserted his foot. The stinging admonishment Jesus delivered to Peter is a warning that will save a sanguine from many thoughtless words (v. 23). Jesus chastised him for setting his mind on the things of man, rather than concentrating on the things of God. Later, when Peter was focused on the Lord, he delivered a powerful message and 3,000 people were saved (Acts 2:40–41). Maintaining a mindset for the things of God will not only eliminate some of the traps that a sanguine may fall into, but will free him or her to speak truth. If your spouse, your child, or family friends exhibit this temperament, delight in their love for life as you patiently help them maintain the correct focus.

LEAD, FOLLOW, OR GET OUT OF MY WAY

Read Acts 8:3, 9:1–2, 20:18–24, and 31

When our boys were little, I vividly remember pushing one of them through the mall in a stroller. As I approached an escalator, I read a sign prohibiting strollers. When I ignored the sign and proceeded to push the stroller onto the escalator, my wife shouted to me, "Didn't you see the sign?" I replied, "That's only for people who don't know how to operate a stroller on an escalator. Why should I walk all the way to the elevator when I can go straight up right here?" I had displayed the motto of the choleric temperament, "Lead, follow, or get out of my way!" Choleric people are driven and goal oriented. They get the job done, however they can easily become impatient and insensitive to the people around them.

Saul, later renamed Paul, had this kind of "driven" personality. Because he was intent in his goal to protect and defend the Jewish religion, he relentlessly persecuted Christians (v. 3, 9:1–2). Saul, like me, was naturally able to accomplish tasks quickly and efficiently. He permitted no one to get in his way. Although we may be born with a certain temperament or combination of inborn traits that affect our behavior, as Christians we are not limited to those characteristics. When Paul yielded his life to the Holy Spirit, the life change he experienced did not just impact his goal and message. It extended to his entire attitude and approach. Instead of being insensitive, his life was characterized by humility and tears (20:18–19). Instead of impatiently forging ahead with his agenda, he paused to meet the needs of others (20:20). Instead of relentlessly pursuing his goals, he was constrained by the Holy Spirit to wait on the Lord's leading (20:22). Although he continued to achieve much for the kingdom of God through the strengths of his personality, Paul's activities were effective because they were tempered by the Holy Spirit. This temperament will work hard to find success, but as with each of the personality types, he or she must be yielded to God in order to accomplish His purposes.

Individuals who are married to or work with cholerics will have opportunities to admire their efficiency and achievements, and have occasions to exercise grace when they are insensitive or impatient.

Paralysis of Analysis

Read Ecclesiastes 1:12–14 and 12:9–14

Have you ever met someone who was so detail oriented that it drove you crazy? The person with a melancholy personality brings home the groceries, and then carefully arranges the cans in alphabetical order on the shelves. His or her clothes are meticulously hung in the closet sorted by type, color, and texture. You often notice a melancholy stopping to adjust a vase or lamp back into perfect position, even though you felt it was okay where it was. If a melancholy makes a mistake on a piece of paper, he or she will not erase or mark it out, but will retrieve a clean sheet of paper and start all over. Individuals with this personality hate mistakes. When planning a trip, a melancholy will go to the Internet, research tourist attractions, print out detailed maps, plan rest stop and meal breaks, then estimate mileage and predict fuel costs. A melancholy often experiences the "paralysis of analysis." His or her motto is, "If you can't do it perfectly, don't do it at all." Melancholies expect perfection, not only from themselves, but from everyone around them. Since perfection is their goal and it is rarely achieved under their stringent standards, they are easily depressed and often moody.

Solomon, the wisest man who ever lived, seemed to have a melancholy temperament. His mind for detail was evident in the 3,000 proverbs he wrote and also in the architectural detail of the temple he built. As a gifted musician, he wrote 1,005 songs. As a meticulous scientist, he researched and analyzed everything from plants and animals to lifestyles and philosophies (1 Kings 4:32–34). Solomon became so engrossed with his analysis of pleasure that he forgot his relationship with God and allowed his many wives to intrigue him with their pagan religions. At the end of his life, the Lord caused Solomon to recognize the folly of a life so focused on analysis that obedience to Him was neglected (Eccl. 1:12–14).

Every individual who has the melancholy temperament must place devotion to God above the quest for personal perfection (Eccl. 12:13). His peace will override the obsessive tendencies and moodiness that frustrates family members. Those married to this personality type can encourage them by appreciating their attention to important details, and by reminding them to reverence the infinite perfection of God.

DON'T ROCK THE BOAT

Read Exodus 3:11–4:9

*H*ave you ever heard the statement, "Opposites attract?" We have found this to be generally true in marriages. More often than not, we find a husband and wife who are quite different in temperament. The opposite of my choleric temperament is the phlegmatic. Where the choleric is a born leader, achiever, and doer, the phlegmatic is patient, reluctant to lead, and avoids conflict at all costs. The phlegmatic's motto is, "Don't rock the boat." The term "phlegmatic" comes from the bodily fluid that Greek physician and philosopher Hippocrates thought produced a calm, slow, easygoing temperament.[54] People with this personality are normally the slowest drivers—the last ones to speed, to leave an intersection, or to take a chance passing another car. They make wonderful friends, however, since they usually express outward agreement, even if they disagree inwardly.

In the Bible, Moses exhibits this type of temperament. When God commanded him to go to Pharaoh to deliver the children of Israel out of bondage, he was reluctant (v. 11). Moses hesitated because he feared the reaction of the Israelites (vv. 13, 4:1), and he wanted to avoid conflict. He focused on his inabilities and the difficulties of the challenge. Obeying God's command would require Moses to function outside the comfort zone of his natural inclinations. The Lord will often ask us to do things or put us in situations that stretch us beyond our temperament, requiring us to depend totally upon Him. God was rocking the boat Moses had been floating in. He reminded him that the instruction was coming from the great I AM (v. 14), and repeatedly assured Moses that He would empower him for the task, even citing specific examples and promises (vv. 3:20–21, 4:4–8). A phlegmatic person who hesitates to lead or face potential conflict must first confirm through prayer and Bible study that an assignment is from God. Then, he or she must shift attention away from personal inabilities to the Lord's greatness and power. This practice will enable any individual, but particularly the phlegmatic to proceed, not in self confidence, but in God-confidence.

Spouses should be aware that mates with this personality will tend to hide their true feelings when they sense potential conflict. Inspiring them with conversations about the Lord will help them find the confidence to be transparent.

Putting It All Together

Read Romans 8:26–28, Ephesians 5:18, and 1 Peter 3:7

Not only does each person exhibit a primary temperament, but typically we also manifest a secondary temperament that coincides with the dominant one to make each of us distinct. While Debbie is phlegmatic-sanguine, I am choleric-melancholy. Knowing our mate's temperament allows us to have a better understanding of why he or she may respond or act a certain way (1 Pet. 3:7). Perceiving our spouse's temperament also helps us to be more appreciative of his or her uniqueness and ability to complement our weaknesses. For example, my impatience and drive is tempered by Debbie's longsuffering and sensitivity. God made the husband and wife distinctively different, not for the differences to become a point of division, but rather a source of celebration that works together for the benefit of their marriage and family.

Our love for God will motivate us to obey His command to be filled with the Holy Spirit (Eph. 5:18). As we allow the Spirit to control us, God can fortify the weaknesses associated with our temperament, while He accentuates and controls the strengths (Rom. 8:26). Oswald Chambers wisely states, "Unguarded strength is actually a double weakness, because that is where the least likely temptations will be effective in sapping strength. The Bible characters stumbled over their strong points, never their weak ones."[55] Placing our temperaments under the loving care of our Heavenly Father is crucial in maintaining harmony in marriage. Understanding that man and woman are not only physiologically and functionally different, but that individuals also vary in their God-given temperaments, enlightens spouses to enjoy and even celebrate their oneness in marriage! (Eccl. 9:9)

Take time now to do a fun project. Write down on separate pieces of paper what each of you believe are your primary and secondary temperaments. Switch papers and take time to discuss how God has allowed your temperaments to come together and work collectively for good in your marriage.

DR. JEKYLL AND MR. HYDE

Read Galatians 1:1–24

*I*n the movie, *Dr Jekyll and Mr. Hyde*, soft-spoken, even-tempered Dr. Jekyll drinks a concoction that turns him into the monster, Mr. Hyde. Sandy, a woman whose boys played ball on the team with our sons, noticed similar behavior in her husband Tom. Tom was attentive, loving, and kind whenever they were by themselves. In public, however, he changed into a totally different person. He no longer acknowledged or stood near her, or said nice things about her. Instead, he found pleasure in making jokes about wives and degrading women. Tom changed from the soft spoken Dr. Jekyll into the monster called Mr. Hyde. Although she never confronted Tom with his apparent metamorphosis, Sandy became inwardly bitter and resentful. It was apparent Tom was more interested in impressing his friends, at the expense of his wife, than in making her feel loved and cherished.

In today's passage, the apostle Paul addressed the problem of men who were preaching a different gospel depending upon who they were with (vv. 6–9). Paul was alarmed by this behavior, and said that these preachers were being men-pleasers instead of God-pleasers. He testified that his only concern was in pleasing God (v. 10).

In the Bible's instructions for marriage, men are commanded to love their wives in the same sacrificial way as Christ loved the church (Eph. 5:25). Because of a desire to impress other men, husbands like Tom practice a different lifestyle in public than they do at home. This behavior not only hurts the wives, but also openly denies the biblical example of marriage to other husbands who desperately need to see it. A wife who is the victim of such treatment needs to lovingly confront her husband. She should talk with him about the pain and embarrassment his actions have caused her. A loving husband will respond by asking forgiveness and by committing afresh to follow the example of Christ. There is no place in marriage for Dr. Jekyll and Mr. Hyde.

DUE SEASON

Read Galatians 6:7–10

Mary grew up in a Christian home and attended church regularly. David, however, was raised in a family where the Bible was never read and church was reserved for Easter and Christmas. David and Mary fell romantically in love. Going against her parents' wishes and resisting the conviction of the Holy Spirit, Mary wed an unbeliever. Eventually, while traveling for business, David began to drink and have affairs with other women. Mary claimed, "David was so shameless that he would bring other women into our home." Tearfully, Mary explained that she was reaping the consequences of her own disobedience to God (v. 7). Understanding this, she didn't yell at David or threaten him, but instead began to get up early in the morning, go to the privacy of their bathroom, and pray for David's salvation (v. 8)! Morning after morning, David could hear his wife crying out to God for his soul. As he continued in his immoral relationships, he couldn't believe that Mary never said a harsh word to him. One day, David took a woman from the bar to his motel room. He claimed, "When I got to the room, all I could see was Mary on her knees praying for me. I couldn't get this image out of my mind! I ordered the woman to leave and fell on my face before God and asked Him to save me!"

When I first heard their dramatic story, I immediately thought of God's promise in Galatians 6:9. If we do not grow weary or fainthearted, but continue to do good, in due season we will reap! Many times a husband or wife makes a fresh commitment to God concerning a troubled relationship, but in the back of his or her mind, there is a time limit set for the spouse to change. This restricts God to a certain amount of time to improve a relationship the couple has been messing up for years! But the Lord determines the due season. We, like Mary, must continue to do good, knowing the right timing will come when God determines.

EXERCISE

Read 1 Timothy 4:7–9

The Scriptures repeatedly exhort believers to be Spirit-filled and to walk in godliness. In today's passage, the apostle Paul describes this pursuit as exercise (v. 7). He instructs Timothy to train his spirit in the same way an athlete trains his body.

For example, a gymnast does not mount a balance beam and execute a routine perfectly in her first attempt. She breaks her routine into sections and masters one move at a time. Before a gymnast spins or flips on the beam, she chooses a focal point. She focuses on the point, spins her body around, and compels her head to stop quickly so her eyes can refocus on the point. This process enables her to avoid dizziness and maintain balance. She practices over and over. When she falls off the beam, she remounts, makes adjustments, and repeats the move until she achieves perfection. During this time of preparation, her coach notes the stunts she needs to modify. She then faces a choice. She can continue in her habitual, comfortable manner of execution, or she can fine-tune her routine according to his insights. The gymnast gradually adds different aspects of her routine until it flows together in a complete, graceful performance.

A Christian couple achieves a complete, graceful marriage through similar discipline and exercise. Each spouse might have to work on one element of the relationship at a time. In order to stay balanced when life turns and flips, each partner should intently seek God as the focal point of his or her life. Throughout the process, the Holy Spirit coach will use Scripture verses, challenges, and other Christians to reveal adjustments that need to be made in the relationship. Each partner is then faced with a choice – to listen to the coach and adjust to Holy Spirit promptings, or to continue in the lifestyle that is familiar and comfortable. When life jolts a spouse off the beam, he or she can admit weaknesses and follow the coach's advice. With consistent spiritual exercise and adherence to the Lord's guidance, the results will be a grace-filled relationship.

BE STILL

Read Psalm 46

I recently had my first MRI. As I lay on the flat bed, slowly being plunged into an opening barely large enough for my body to enter, I was filled with anxiety. The technician instructed me not to move an inch, but to remain quiet and very, very still. As I arrived inside the machine, I was forced to do something I had always found difficult—be still! Not for just a few seconds, but rather for about ten minutes. As I was becoming claustrophobic and somewhat stressed, the Lord whispered, "Be still and know that I am God (v. 10)." I responded, "But God, I am still!" It was then that He reminded me of the historical event that inspired today's Scriptures.

Enemy troops numbering 180,000 had surrounded Jerusalem to destroy it, but in the midst of this crisis, God manifested His presence. He wanted His people to understand that despite how strong Jerusalem was, even with its great protective walls, the city was not their refuge. God was! As the people focused on His presence, they realized the battle was not theirs. It was God's. He caused a plague to come down and destroy the enemy, and Jerusalem was saved.

In the Hebrew language, the words "be still" mean to "stop striving" or to "let go." The word "know" means to have an intimate understanding of someone. God is simply saying, "Quit striving in your own power, and have such an intimate understanding of Me that you will trust Me in every circumstance. It's only then that you will find true rest for your soul."

As the Holy Spirit ministered this truth to my heart in that tight MRI compartment, I was relieved of my anxiety and felt totally refreshed by His presence. There will be times in your marriage when you feel trapped by unfavorable circumstances and perhaps even enemies. In those times, stop fretting. Set aside the compulsion to force the matter under your control. Be still. Together reflect on the faithfulness and power of Sovereign God. Your marriage will be strengthened.

Falling for Flattery

Read Proverbs 7:1–27

A lady who had attended one of our marriage conferences called and asked me to meet her for lunch. She explained that she taught Bible studies and had a deep desire to inspire others to live according to the Word of God. During our conversation, she shared that she did not receive much attention from her husband. He rarely spent time with her, and was consumed by television whenever they were together. She longed to hear words of encouragement and approval, but he never expressed them. Her desire for affection was intense. One day, a friendly man at her church remarked on how nice she looked. She started making a point to chat with him. He always complimented her. She realized she was beginning to think a lot about this man during the day. She would recall the outfits he had commented on, because she wanted to dress to please him. Although there was no physical infidelity, this man was filling the emotional needs God intended for her husband to meet. This woman had come to me because, although she was deeply convicted, she could not let go of this new bond.

Proverbs 7 urgently warns that a woman's flattery can entice a man, and eventually start controlling the relationship (Prov. 7:5, 21). She will appeal to his fleshly lusts (vv. 16–18), and may even justify a relationship by exhibiting an outward compliance with God's commands (vv. 14–15). But, just as a man can be enticed by flattery, so can a woman! Even though the lady who told me her story had a strong faith, she was falling for flattery (v. 26). She was struggling with each of the traps mentioned in today's passage. Fortunately, she had an intense thirst to study and understand the Word of God. The truth she had stored in her heart caused her to be troubled and prompted her to seek godly counsel. Wisdom saved her from immorality (vv. 4–5). Whether we are male or female, we all need to be careful not to fall for flattery. What may seem innocent at first can easily lead to results we never intended. Our marriages and lives are at stake.

FRICTION

Read Proverbs 15:18 and Colossians 3:8–15

hen studying engineering in college, I took a course on friction. In this study, friction was defined as the tangential force that develops between two surfaces that move across each other. The magnitude of friction between the two surfaces is dependent upon how smooth or rough the surfaces are. To reduce the friction and, therefore, extend the life of the surface, different types of lubricant (oil, graphite, etc.) are applied. If a lubricant is not applied, the surface temperature will increase until some type of failure occurs!

The biblical equivalent of friction is called strife. Rather than two surfaces rubbing against each other, there are two people grinding against each other. Through my years in family ministry, I have observed many relationships filled with friction. When not corrected, the heat generated will eventually cause the marriage to burn out. God is so concerned about frictional relationships that He warns about the cause and effects of strife fourteen times in the book of Proverbs. He repeatedly declares that the cause of friction (strife) is wrath—a strong, vengeful anger or indignation (v. 18). Just as lubricant is needed to reduce friction between two objects, God's lubricant must be applied to the hearts of each partner in marriage to reduce friction in their relationship. The preventive oil of His grace can soothe hot tempers and hot words before they cause damage. Spouses must set aside the irritants of anger, slander, and harsh talk and put on the lubricant of their new nature in Christ. This is achieved by increasing in understanding of Him (vv. 8-10). Study His compassion, kindness, humility, gentleness and patience. The soothing ointment of God's love and forgiveness will turn a frictional relationship into one that is peaceful and without strife (v. 12-15). Do you need to reduce the friction in your marriage by applying an increased knowledge of Him?

TEARS OF JOY

Read Genesis 23:1–16

One of life's hardest experiences is attending the funeral of someone we love, especially an immediate family member. I have, with much grief and sorrow, attended the funerals of my father, mother, and a brother and sister. As we read today's passage, we see the great patriarch Abraham grieving over his dear wife Sarah, to whom he was married for 62 years.

I'm sure as Abraham stood beside his wife's lifeless body, he began to reflect back over their journey through life together. He probably remembered the time when Sarah was barren and she urged him to have sexual relations with Hagar, and he complied. Perhaps Abraham vividly remembered how he had lied to Pharaoh about Sarah being his wife; because of fear, he freely gave her to have sex with another man. Maybe he thought of how he and Sarah constantly lived on the move, holding onto a promise that God had given to them, yet having no real place to call home. I'm sure as Abraham grieved for Sarah, he may have shed many tears of regret. Because of the wonderful grace of God, however, I believe he also shed tears of joy and thanksgiving. Abraham and Sarah's marriage doesn't picture an ideal relationship that was free of trials or hardships, but rather portrays a couple whose life was marked by faith, who got through the tough times because of God's marvelous goodness.

In Abraham and Sarah's story, we see that the Lord's intention in marriage is not just happiness. Their lives reveal His purpose in the trials He allows, that we would exemplify faith and grow in holiness. Life is too brief to waste the opportunities God gives to exercise love and grace toward our mate. If you knew you only had one week left with your spouse, how would you live differently?

GOLDEN ANNIVERSARY

Read 1 Peter 1:6–8

*A*fter fifty years of marriage, my parents celebrated their golden anniversary when my siblings and I honored them with a dinner party. The guests viewed pictures and shared sweet memories that represented the events of their life together. However, it is not the achievements and prosperity of a couple that earn the description of golden. It is, instead, a reflection of the refinement process. Purified gold requires enough heat to melt the metal, causing the impurities and alloys to surface. Those elements are skimmed off, leaving gold which is soft, pliable, and free from corrosion. In today's passage, Peter compares this purification process to the fire of trials (v. 7). A couple can celebrate fifty years of marriage because they have proved their love is genuine as they have allowed the fire of trials to soften their hearts rather than harden them.

Peter explains that during certain seasons of life, Christians will suffer grief in all kinds of trials (v. 6). These tests could include tragedy, misunderstanding, persecution, or just the unrelenting, annoying habits of a spouse. Individuals tend to analyze an ordeal according to the inconveniences and pain it causes them. The fires of stress and pressure will cause impurity in character to surface when a person reacts selfishly to tribulation. Anger, bitterness, resentment, and greediness all tend to emerge during affliction and unfair situations. Writer John Bevere, explains, "Sin easily hides where there is no heat of trials. In times of prosperity and success, even a wicked man will seem kind and generous; however, under the heat of trials the impurities surface."[56] When, under the stress of a trial, a spouse who normally displays a kind, controlled temperament recognizes wrong attitudes or actions that have risen to the surface, he or she can repent and be cleansed by allowing God to skim the self-centeredness away. For a couple to remain happily married for fifty years requires that rude and harsh behavior be admitted, and that forgiveness be granted.

If you desire to one day celebrate your golden anniversary, allow the trials of life to soften your heart and purify your relationship.

LATE, LATE FOR A
VERY IMPORTANT DATE

Read Philippians 2:2–4

*T*he rabbit in Alice in Wonderland introduces confusion and nervousness to the routine of Wonderland as he scurries around declaring, "I'm late, I'm late, for a very important date!" Similarly, people who are consistently late disrupt unity.

In today's passage, Paul urges the Philippians to strive for unity by being of one accord and of one mind (v. 2). A disruption to unity occurs when all "minds" are not present because one person is tardy. The group is not in one accord because one member feels a different activity is significant enough to detain him or her. The late person considers his or her tasks more important than the group's plans. In Philippians 2:3, Paul continues by teaching that nothing should be done through selfish ambition or conceit, but that each believer should esteem others better than himself. A person whose life demonstrates a pattern of being late may be ambitious and feel that he or she can accomplish more than is humanly possible in the time frame allotted. A task may seem so important that he or she selfishly continues while delaying the next appointment. The habit of tardiness is especially frustrating to a spouse who continually waits for his or her mate. The routinely tardy spouse may be willing to immediately interrupt a personal schedule to meet another's need. In the process of being generous with personal time, however, he or she overlooks the time stolen from a waiting mate. In another scenario, a husband may allot adequate time to arrive promptly, but may become distracted by other activities on the way. He is esteeming his time more important than his wife's. A wife who is late may consistently and politely apologize for the inconvenience, but until she views it as selfish and conceited, she will justify the habit. Paul states that to achieve unity, one must be conscious not only of personal interests, but must consider the interests of others also (v. 4). If we desire to be prompt, we must regard the value of others' time as more important than our own. Do you often keep your spouse waiting? Adjust this habit by placing a higher value on his or her priorities. As a result, your marriage will become more unified (v.2).

SECURITY

Read Ephesians 5:25, Hebrews 13:5, and Romans 8:35–39

One night not long ago I woke to scratching at our back door. Thunder was crashing with lightning flashing all around! There stood Duke, our huge English mastiff, shaking like his life was in grave danger. He was frantic, and urgently wanted to come inside and be with us. I told him not to be such a sissy, but to go back in the garage and lie down. As I walked back into the house my wife asked me what was wrong. I explained that Duke was afraid and wanted to come inside. She responded, "You let him in the basement, didn't you?" I declared, "Absolutely not. He's a male dog. He needs to be a man!" I knew right away that Debbie did not agree. She pleaded, "Oh Sam, he's scared and he's just a dog. Poor thing! Why don't you let him in? When we let him in, he knows that we care about him." At that moment, I was reminded how God created men and women so differently.

One of a wife's greatest needs is security. From the beginning, God instructed man to provide for and protect his wife. In Ephesians, He commands husbands to love their wives in the same way Christ loves His bride, the church (v. 25). If Jesus reassures His bride by promising to never leave nor forsake her (Heb. 13:5), then in a society where divorce is rampant, a husband should also reassure his bride. She needs to regularly hear the words "I will always love you and never ever leave you. I am committed to you and our family!" Paul explains that Jesus will not allow any struggle, distress, problem, or tragedy to separate Him from His bride (Rom. 8:35–39). Jesus is committed to His bride, no matter what may happen. We are secure in His love. This same supernatural love is available to the Christian husband to convey to his wife. Voice your love to her. She needs to know she is secure in your love.

PREPARE THE TABLE

Read Psalm 23

*I*n the Middle East during Bible times, one shepherd from the group would proceed ahead of the flock and "prepare the table." He would scout the land and find a plateau that was flat and high enough to allow a protective view. The shepherd would comb the entire area, removing all poisonous plants. He would also be on the alert for adder holes since when the sheep grazed, the deadly snake would slip its head out of the hole and bite the unsuspecting sheep on its tender nose. When the shepherd discovered an adder hole, he would pour oil into it so the snake could not maintain enough traction to slither out. Although the shepherd did not capture or destroy the enemy, the shepherd prepared the table for safety, right there in the presence of the enemy (v. 5).

Likewise, as shepherd of the family, a husband should "prepare the table." He needs to position himself so he is aware of potential dangers to his wife and family. He needs to scout his city to find a neighborhood that is safe and a church that will provide spiritual food and reinforcement. He needs to study and know the Word of God so he can recognize false doctrine and remove sources of toxic ideas. He must recognize New Age or cultic thought in music and TV shows so he can eliminate them from his home. He must apply the oil of the Holy Spirit to every danger zone he encounters. The oil of the Holy Spirit provides discernment and power in spiritual battles that help prevent the enemy from slipping into the home undetected. When the table is prepared, the wife and family can live in peace and safety (v. 4). The family will recognize the goodness and love of their shepherd (v. 6). Is your table prepared?

REKINDLE

Read Revelation 2:1–5

*T*hink back to when you and your spouse fell in love. Were you concerned about his opinion of how you looked? Did you enjoy sneaking up to kiss her and making her jump? Did you gaze into his eyes and tell him how he fascinated you? Did you step ahead and open the car door for her whenever you went out? When you first got married, did you make a habit of preparing his favorite meal? Did you show concern and carry in the groceries for her? Did you rub her back? Did you turn the lamps down and light candles? Did you write love letters? Do you remember all the little signals you and your spouse once shared? Squeezing his hand three times meant "I love you." Winking at her across a crowd meant "I can't wait to leave and be alone with you." Do you still do these things, or are they long-forgotten memories?

The Scriptures teach that Christ's relationship to His bride, the church, is an example for the husband-wife relationship today. Therefore, the principles that Jesus points out in today's passage also apply to our marriages. He commends the church for a list of noteworthy attributes (vv. 2–3). The church has been competent to fulfill the mechanics of her purpose. She exhibits patience and perseverance. She labors diligently for the sake of her groom, but He sharply rebukes her. She is performing out of duty and obligation instead of love (v. 4). Her service is empty, without warmth and affection. The same is often true of our marriages. We may labor diligently to fulfill our marital duty, but the relationship is dreary without genuine affection and heartfelt love.

The solution for a boring relationship is to rekindle the romance. Remember what you used to do (v. 5). Send those private love signals again. Ponder the characteristics that first attracted you to your mate. Plan creative surprises. Daily take time from the duties of the relationship to enjoy each other's company. Dream together. Laugh together. Delight in each other.

REFLECTORS

Read 1 Corinthians 10:31

*R*ecently, we boarded a flight to travel to speak at a marriage conference in Florida. Being one of the last ones to get on the plane, Debbie and I ended up sitting several rows apart. At first I was very disturbed that I would not be able to sit by my wife, talk to her, snuggle up against her, and hold her hand. After all, this is part of our usual preparation before speaking to other couples about marriage. As I squeezed into my seat between two large men, one who was the former center for the University of Virginia (my arch rival when I attended Virginia Tech years ago), I could barely move. I began to think about how unfair my circumstances were, and how I had a right to sit by my wife. As I fumed and meditated on my rights, the Holy Spirit brought 1 Corinthians 10:31 to my attention.

Immediately, I began to wrestle with God about this truth. I reasoned, "Surely You understand my situation. God, You know that I don't drink, I don't smoke, and I don't chew tobacco (quite a testimony living in Tennessee)." In the midst of my silent protest, the Holy Spirit began to show me how I was reflecting self-centered, self-glorifying thoughts. Being made in God's image, my life should reflect His glory in every situation. I settled down in my seat and did the only thing I could—I prayed. I prayed for the men beside me, my wife, my sons, and the conference where we would be speaking.

Every day, we all have opportunities to reflect how Christ would handle the difficult circumstances we are facing. Each time we respond to a sales clerk, our boss, or the telemarketer on the phone, we mirror whatever we are holding as most precious at that moment. We should seek to glorify God in every thought and action, especially with our spouse and children. This will allow them to catch a glimpse of the character of God.

START AT HOME

Read John 4:7–30

*I*t's amazing how the testimony of Roy Hession, a British preacher who ministered in the 1940's, has impact for us today. At one point in his life, this man sensed that the power of God was not as strong in him as it had once been. He poured himself into deeper Bible study and prayer. He also set up a conference for revival and invited missionaries from East Africa to speak. In Africa, these men had been experiencing a great movement of God. Although the preacher was busy leading the conference and ministering to others' needs, the missionaries became concerned for *his* spiritual needs. They gently urged him to repent. He did not understand what area of his life needed repentance. The men from Africa told him they could not tell him where to repent, but they had noticed that his relationship with his wife was strained. He treated other ladies with more affection than he did his own wife. The men explained that for them personally, revival began in their most intimate relationship – the home. Forty years later in *The Calvary Road,* his book that has inspired millions (no exaggeration—also printed in 70 languages), Roy Hession describes the encounter, "That light came to show me sin where I hadn't seen it before, and I began on a path of repentance. Yes with my wife—my attitude toward her."[57]

In today's passage, Jesus used this same principle to stir the Samaritan woman to repentance. She, like the British preacher, did not realize her spiritual condition and need (v. 10). She was clueless until Jesus pointed to the sin in her family life (vv. 15–18). At first, the woman changed the subject. As Jesus continued to reveal truth, however, she realized He was using the turmoil in her family life to draw her into a relationship with Him (v. 29).

I have noticed that the Lord works this way in my life, also. He uses tension between my spouse and me, or between my children and me, to reveal my selfishness . . . Once I admit the truth and depend on Him, I experience the relief and refreshment of a deeper walk with the Lord. If your relationship with God seems distant, start at home by examining your relationships with your family. How you treat your loved ones is an indicator of the Lord's presence in your life.

STUDY

Read 2 Timothy 2:15 and Psalm 119:97–105

When our children were young, we took them to the pet store to buy a filter for their new aquarium. A teenage employee at the store assisted us as we looked through the choices. We asked her detailed questions about the differences of various filters. Our conversation expanded to types of fish and ways to care for them. We were impressed with her knowledgeable and enthusiastic responses. Her zeal was contagious. I complimented her on her refreshing attitude. I commented that she must really love her job. She responded, "My job requires hard work. I have to clean cages and scrub algae off aquariums, but every week, I make myself read a different book about the care of the animals. It is not a job requirement, but I do it so that I will have a better understanding." The secret to her excellence in service was study.

The same principle applies to married life. As we travel to speak at marriage conferences from church to church, we see that the husbands and wives who obviously enjoy the most fulfilling relationships are those who have chosen to read books about marriage, communication, and love, based on reliable Scripture. They eagerly browse our book table for titles they have not read. Their enthusiasm, like that of the pet store employee, is contagious.

Studying and meditating on what God teaches about marriage will cultivate love for His principles (Psalm 119:97). Wisdom in handling day to day family challenges will increase (vv. 98–100). The couple who meditates on God's truth will receive direction for decisions (vv. 101–102,105), and the sweetness of His character will flow into their relationship (v. 103). Prepare for excellence and fulfillment in family life by studying God's precepts. Studying Scripture and reading books about love is not a job requirement listed on your marriage certificate. Rather, it is a privilege and blessing. Yes, it will demand extra effort, but the results will be obvious, and worth it!

TAKE NOTE

Read Acts 4:5–14

One evening a few years ago, I was working in the kitchen as I observed an interaction between Sam and one of our teenage sons. I don't remember the issue they were addressing, or what was said, but I recall being very impressed with the manner Sam used in handling the situation. The combination of wisdom and love that was evident to me, as an observer, was astonishing. Later, I expressed my observations to Sam. He explained that he had been reading a new book, *Age of Opportunity,* by Paul Tripp. He told me the Lord had used the book to reveal truth and insight to him as a parent. My husband had spent time with the Lord, examining himself, and praying for our children.

Today's passage describes how the rulers, elders, and scribes experienced a similar observation during an interaction with Peter and John. The authorities considered the two fishermen to be ordinary and simple, but their confident, wise responses surprised and astonished the interrogators. Peter and John were not consciously trying to impress the group with their knowledge, but through traveling with, observing, and listening to Jesus, their way of thinking had conformed to His mindset. They were responding from their hearts, and did not realize the impact they were having. The observers, however, noted that in the midst of a crisis, there was something distinctively different about Peter and John. They linked the power of the men's responses to the fact that they had spent time with Jesus (v. 13).

Whenever I spend time seeking to understand the heart of Jesus, I recognize a difference in my perspective that influences my attitude and actions. I can sense the quiet control of the Holy Spirit. On the other hand, when, over a period of days, I get too busy and fail to spend time with Jesus, it is very evident to my family that I need to get alone with the Lord. Spending time with Him motivates and empowers me to respond with wisdom, love, and joy. My husband and children can take note that I, too, have been with Jesus.

AN ORNAMENT

Read Titus 2:9–10, Colossians 3:22–25, and 1 Peter 2:18–20

Are you a slave to your job, career, or business? Do the irritations caused by unreasonable requests follow you home? Do the pressures of your business steal your joy? The instruction in Titus 2:9–10 was addressed to slaves and servants, but offers direction to present day employees.

The slaves addressed in these verses are laboring at menial, dead end jobs. Masters and supervisors assign them tasks no one else wants. The jobs involve dirty, dangerous work that promises little hope for advancement, but God instructs the workers to be submissive to their supervisors. In today's world, this includes following instructions and complying with industrial standards. Both the Titus and Colossians passages urge employees to take pride in their tasks and perform with excellence. These passages teach that responses to fellow workers should not be defensive or disrespectful, but rather courteous, peaceful, and cooperative. The Scripture also warns workers not to steal time or supplies (Titus 2:10). This includes being honest in reporting work hours and expense accounts. A worker is to be loyal and dependable by keeping his word and striving to meet deadlines.

When a person endeavors to exemplify these principles in the workplace, the Lord considers this honorable behavior to be an ornament of His glory. Just as a Christmas tree ornament sparkles and delights observers, the attitude of a Christian who serves the Lord shines for the glory of God. This ornament will even continue to sparkle and delight the family as the worker returns home.

THE CURE FOR LONELINESS

Read John 12:24–28

At times, I withdraw from everyone to have a pity party. I build a protective shell around myself in order to justify my hurt feelings, or nurture my right to be resentful, or recite my frustrations with the world in general. All of life is narrowly viewed from my perspective. No one else can penetrate my protective shield unless he or she holds the key of my perspective. It is a safe, but solitary environment. Here, I find no joy in serving others. I find no comfort in another point of view. Loneliness consumes me.

God declares that it is not good that man should be alone (Gen. 2:18). As a solution, He lovingly provided my spouse. My outer protective shell can be so stubborn and strong, however, that it will prevents my mate from getting close enough to minister to me in my loneliness.

In today's passage, Jesus explains to His disciples that unless a person denies himself and dies to his self-centered desires, he will abide alone (v. 24). Just like the grain of wheat noted in Jesus' teaching, I have to shed my protective covering. My life and marriage will be lonely until I die to my futile attitudes and attempts to control my situations. When I let God take control, He will bring forth fruit instead of loneliness—His joy, peace, and love—instead of misery. As long as I am consumed with my own circumstances, I will waste energy and time, and lose the joy of life (v. 25). If I deny the self-centered influence of my world, I can experience the abundance God intends for me.

Jesus understands the emotional turmoil of dying to one's plans and personal desires, but He trusts God's purposes amid life's challenges (v. 27). My focus must shift from self concern and preservation to a desire for God the Father to be glorified—magnified and honored as supreme in my life (v. 28). To avoid loneliness, I have to face the death of my selfish ways. The result will be new life, purpose, and energy, enabling me to open up to the companionship my spouse can offer.

URGENT OR IMPORTANT?

Read Deuteronomy 6:1–12

I recently started using an iPod to replace my overfilled, well-used planner. When I tap on the tasks list, I am overwhelmed with deciding where to start. The register shows personal needs, ministry obligations, family responsibilities, and household chores. Each task seems so urgent, demanding immediate attention. The time required to complete the jobs always seems greater than the time allotted, and every category distracts from accomplishing the others. It is tempting to choose what is urgent above what is important, but to make that choice increases the likelihood that my marriage, family, and Lord would be repositioned to the back burner.

The Lord knew this dilemma would be a continual struggle for us today and for the Israelites in Bible times. He warned the Israelites that their homes and prosperous businesses would generate long lists of tasks that demanded attention (v. 10–11). The Lord expressed deep concern that in the midst of such busyness, His people would relegate Him to a lesser priority, and omit Him from their "to do" list (v. 12).

Our wise and concerned Father pleads with us to observe the instructions that will protect us from the trap of replacing what is important with tasks that are urgent (v. 3). He strongly emphasizes the main tenet of our faith: the Lord our God, the Lord is One (v. 4)! He is the One and only, the true and living God. He is almighty. He is our security. He is our life. The solution to the dilemma is to understand who God is and to love Him with every fiber of our being (v. 5). Loving Him with all our heart will generate a respect that acknowledges Him in every task we perform (v. 6–7). Every job will be centered on who He is. Instead of being an item on our list, He will become the power and direction behind every responsibility. God wants our relationship to be so intimate and dependent that our thoughts are on Him continually throughout the routine of our day. What is important will then control what appears urgent. The Lord, my marriage, and my family will align to the proper priority in my life.

WORD PICTURES

Read 2 Samuel 12:1–7 and Psalm 51

*J*esus was the master communicator of all time. His primary methods were parables and word pictures, conveying difficult messages in ways that would cause His hearers to intently consider what He was saying. This style of communication is seen in today's passage. After David had committed adultery and murder, God sent the prophet Nathan to confront him by using a word picture. Rather than bluntly saying, "You sinner, repent and get right with God," Nathan conveys an account of two men who both own sheep. One man is wealthy, owning many lambs, while the other is poor and owns only one little lamb (vv. 1–3). The poor man loves his lamb so much that he nourishes it as if it were his daughter (v. 3). When a traveler visits the rich man, instead of killing one of his own lambs and fixing a meal, the wealthy farmer takes the poor man's lamb and prepares it for his guest (v. 4). After David hears the story, he is angered and declares that the wealthy man deserves to die (v. 5). Nathan responds by telling David that *he* is the man (v. 7), and God uses the word picture to bring convicting realization of sin. As a result, David confesses and repents (Psalm 51).

Have you had times you needed to share something with your mate, but feared he or she might be offended if you stated it point blank? In these circumstances, word pictures can be effective communication tools. Carefully take time to pray and think about a word picture that illustrates how you feel or have been hurt. Painting word pictures does not come naturally for most people, but it can improve your communication and help you and your spouse develop a more transparent relationship. Take a few minutes, and practice sharing a word picture with your spouse.

THE WHISTLE OF THE REF

Read Colossians 3:12–17

To live in the continual power and presence of the Lord seems idealistic, but Colossians 3:15 incorporates it into the routine of life, "Let the peace of Christ rule in your hearts." Peace is defined as freedom from disturbance or oppression; a state of calm and security. In his book, *Calvary Road*, Roy Hession states, "Everything that disturbs the peace of God in our hearts is sin, no matter how little like sin it may at first appear to be."[58] Absence of peace reveals itself in daily life as grumbling, irritation, bossiness, carelessness, criticism, envy, oppression and anxiety. The Greek word for "rule" translates "to act as an umpire." The peace of God is to be the referee of our hearts. When that peace mutates to frustration, confusion, or irritation, the referee is blowing His whistle, alerting us to pause and listen to His warning.

Normally the "whistle" of the Holy Spirit convicts us of self-centered agendas or reactions that should be admitted as sins and released to Jesus Christ, the One who purifies and redeems. If the peace does not return, we probably are not really "broken," but have only dealt with the surface of the wrong, justified our actions, or even blamed another. Hession further explains, "We do not lose peace over another person's sin, but only our own."[59] In basketball, whenever a referee charges a specific player with an infraction, he or she must confess it, no matter what the other players have done. Protests result in additional penalties and delay of game. Likewise, protests of our innocence to God delay the return of peace in our routine of life. Colossians 3:15 calls us to be alert to the whistle and respond with a repentant heart so we can resume the pursuit of victory according to God's game plan. If we desire to maintain peace in any relationship, especially our marriages, we need to quickly recognize its absence and follow the divine plan for resuming the "game."

CONTRACTS

Read 1 Corinthians 13:4–8

After finding the truck I wanted to purchase, the salesman escorted me into his office to fill out the necessary paperwork. He immediately presented me with a credit application. The purpose was to verify that I was a reliable buyer who would faithfully pay the required payments. Once my credit was approved, the salesman handed me the actual contract which stated the terms of the agreement. I agreed to pay a certain monthly amount to keep possession of the vehicle. As long as I do my part as the borrower, the bank will let me keep the truck. If I fail to make payments, the bank will repossess it.

A contract is a legal agreement that requires both parties to do exactly what they have agreed to do. If either party fails, the contract is void. Many couples approach marriage in a contractual manner, "If you're nice to me, I'll be nice to you. If you love me, I'll love you, but if you don't, I won't." The list goes on and on. Although most couples may not compile a written list, they unconsciously accumulate a set of expectations that determine their acceptance of their mate. This is not what God intended. His steadfast, covenant love that should be exemplified by Christians is selfless, patient, and unending (vv. 4–8). Unlike a contract, a covenant says, "I'll love you, even when you don't love me. I'll be nice to you, even when aren't nice to me. I'll do my part, even when you don't do yours." You will never, in and of yourself, love your spouse in this way. This kind of love requires a relationship with God, with His grace flowing through you to your spouse. Take a few minutes and prayerfully do a mental inventory, asking God to reveal all of the contractual ways you are treating your mate. Repent of these, and ask Him to empower you afresh to love your spouse with His covenant love.

JUNK MAIL

Read Nehemiah 6:1–9

Every day I open my mailbox I am overwhelmed with a huge pile of mail that is stuffed so tight into the box that I wonder if I will need pliers to pull it out. To efficiently handle this never-ending accumulation, I have developed a sorting system with three categories: junk mail, essential mail, and surprise mail. Junk mail includes credit card promotions, marketing gimmicks, and sales flyers. Essential mail consists of bills, personal letters, and ministry correspondence. Surprise mail is unexpected correspondence that contains a donation to our ministry or encouragement from a conference participant or pastor. After dividing the mail, I process each category. Junk mail is discarded into a trash can while I'm still at the post office. The essential and surprise mail is taken back to my office for further investigation.

After thirty-five years of marriage, I have come to realize that communication between husband and wife can be like going to the mailbox and receiving junk mail, essential mail, and surprise mail. The happiness of the marriage relationship depends upon both how we handle the messages we receive from our spouse and the type of mail we send to them.

Through the prompting of God, Nehemiah embarked upon the great task of rebuilding the walls of Jerusalem. Two men named Sanballat and Tobiah, however, were disturbed by his actions. They ridiculed and scoffed at Nehemiah and when the walls were erected, Sanballat sent his servant to deliver some junk mail (vv. 4–5). The letter falsely accused Nehemiah of rebuilding the walls so he would gain enough support to be crowned king (v. 6). Nehemiah declared the accusations to be false, stating that they were drummed up in their imagination (v. 8). He recognized the letter as junk mail, discarded it, and stayed on task (v. 9)!

Marriage partners sometimes deliver junk mail to each other. For example, heated communication containing the words "never" or "always" normally signals an exaggerated accusation. ("You always forget … You never think about me.") Each spouse must avoid sending junk messages to their mate that distract or discourage them from building a God-glorifying relationship. And when junk mail comes our way, we—like Nehemiah—must continue in our tasks while responding with wisdom and grace.

ESSENTIAL MAIL

Read Nehemiah 2:5–9

*Y*esterday's devotional talked about how marriage can be like going to the mailbox and receiving junk mail, essential mail, and surprise mail from our spouse. We defined junk mail as communication that is disheartening, dishonest, and destructive, promoting isolation rather than intimacy. Essential mail, however, is vital to the function and health of a relationship.

After gaining approval to travel to Judah, Nehemiah asked the king to give him some essential mail to take with him on his journey. One letter was addressed to the governors beyond the river, requesting permission and protection for safe passage to his destination (v. 7). A second letter was addressed to Asaph the keeper of the king's forest (v. 8). It requested permission to retrieve timber from the forest to help in rebuilding the walls and constructing a home when Nehemiah arrived in Judah. Both of these letters were essential to the success of his quest to rebuild the walls of Jerusalem. One provided protection while traveling, the other, provision for completing the task.

Every day in marriage, we have the opportunity to send essential mail to our spouse. This correspondence communicates our willingness and even eagerness to provide, protect, and nourish the relationship through daily plans and schedules. Nehemiah successfully completed his task through specifically communicating his needs to the king, and his expectations of how the king could help him. A husband and wife must take time to share their daily schedules and expectations so that the essential needs of the marriage are met through planned, coordinated teamwork. This could include such things as who will pick up the kids, buy groceries, or pay particular bills. Even though this essential mail can be boring and burdensome at times, taking time to correspond is essential to maintaining harmony in the home. What essential communication do you need to send to your spouse today?

SURPRISE MAIL

Read Ezra 7:11–28

Approximately 15 years prior to the rebuilding of the walls, Ezra—a contemporary of Nehemiah—receives an exciting letter from King Artaxerxes. In this letter, Ezra is given the authority to take priests and valuable gifts from Persia to the temple in Jerusalem (vv. 15–16). He is also instructed to restore and teach the law of God to the people (v. 25). Elated by the letter, Ezra responds by blessing the Lord, who had put these desires in the king's heart (v. 27).

Even though the essential mail described in the previous devotion is necessary for coordinating daily tasks and responsibilities, marriage can become dull and listless without surprise mail! Even as Ezra received a letter from the king that thrilled his soul, marriage partners need to receive messages that ignite romantic sparks! Ezra noted that God had put this letter in the king's heart. Similarly, spouses need to be sensitive to the Holy Spirit as He prompts them to send surprise mail to each other. It can be in the form of spoken words, written notes, special deeds, and even gifts. The message should be designed to express affection, appreciation, acceptance, and affirmation.

When I am traveling alone, Debbie will often hide a note or an eatable goodie inside my suitcase to surprise and encourage me. I might buy her a small gift to show that I was thinking of her while I was away. Debbie frequently tells me how much she respects and admires me. I make it a point to express to her that she is beautiful and I love her, and will always be here for her. These expressions aren't the result of some ulterior motive. Rather, they are genuine letters from the heart, enclosed in the envelope of God's love, sealed with the gratitude of one who realizes a spouse is a gift from above. Surprise your mate with an unexpected love message today.

TUNE IN

Read Ephesians 4:21–32

Recently, when our family was traveling to a college football game, my son pulled out a list of radio stations he had compiled from the Internet. It included each city we would be driving through, with the corresponding local station number for sports news. I was very impressed! He realized that as we traveled, the signal would change, requiring an adjustment on the radio. He went to all this trouble so we would not miss any news about our favorite teams.

As I reflected on his diligence, I was reminded that good communication requires three components—a transmitter (the radio station), a receiver (the car radio), and the right frequency (the station number). To have effective communication in marriage, the same is true! There must be someone who is talking (transmitter), and someone who is willing to listen (receiver). Then, both communicators must be tuned to the same frequency regarding the situation being discussed. Omitting any of these elements will result in static and misunderstanding. Someone has aptly stated, "Communication is to marriage what blood is to the body; without it you will die." Many marriages die due to a lack of godly communication. To communicate effectively, both spouses must be willing to adjust their "dials" to God's frequency (v.23). They must turn the channel from pride and selfishness to self denial and humility (vv. 22–24), from exaggeration and deception to telling the truth (v. 25), and from anger to resolving conflict (vv. 26-27). Once this is done, a couple is ready to allow Jesus, the master communicator, to orchestrate their conversation. Grace is ministered to the hearer, and both the husband and wife are edified (v. 29). Peace and harmony are maintained in the relationship. Next time you turn on your radio and set it to your favorite station, remember that God wants you to be in tune with your mate, on His frequency of grace.

MAGNIFY THE LORD TOGETHER

Read 1 Samuel 21:10–14 and Psalm 34:1–6

Yesterday, Debbie and I strolled up the gravel road near our home to a nearby bluff line. As we walked along, we observed the splendor of the trees which had turned bright colors of orange, red, and yellow. We laughed at the playfulness of our dogs trotting along beside us. Once we arrived at the top of the cliff, we could not help but be overcome with the mountains and valleys covered with God's brilliant brush strokes. Our hearts were thrilled at the magnificence we observed. Immediately, I said to Debbie, "Our God is truly an awesome God!" In moments like these, all earthly thoughts and problems are forgotten in light of praising Him together!

Fleeing from King Saul, David found himself taking refuge with a Philistine king named Achish. Achish soon recognized who David was, and held him hostage. By pretending to be a crazy man, David escaped! He wrote Psalm 34, praising God for delivering him. David was so thrilled that he called the people to praise God with Him (Psalm 34:1, 3). This not only strengthened David, but inspired the entire nation to be filled with hope and joy.

One of the great privileges in marriage is being able to magnify and exalt the Lord together as husband and wife. When we do so, our minds and spirits are unified, and our relationship is strengthened by mutual trust in God. Fears, insecurities, and problems become increasingly insignificant, just as they did to David. Worry and anxiety are replaced with joy and gladness! Pain and suffering are replaced with healing and comfort. Make it a continual practice to magnify the Lord and exalt His name. Your marriage will be enriched and fortified as you enjoy the presence of God together.

ME-ISM IN MARRIAGE

Read 2 Corinthians 5:14–15

I have often been asked, "If you could put your finger on the number one problem that causes marriages to end in divorce, what would it be?" I confidently respond, "Me-ism is the number one problem in marriage." With a raised eyebrow, the questioner will often inquire "What is me-ism?" Me-ism is a word I coined to characterize the heart condition of an individual who is consumed with self. During the dating phase, people tend to hide their me-ism and present a pretense of selflessness so they can lure their partner into marriage. After they tie the knot, however, me-istic individuals who hid behind masks of good impressions definitely show up! It's like they morph into totally different persons. The bride quickly realizes she didn't marry Prince Charming, and the groom recognizes he didn't marry Cinderella. Instead, each of them married a me-istic sinner.

Although the symptoms are abundant and obvious—frustration, resentment, lack of communication, or a lack of intimacy—the root problem is always the same. Me-isim is a worship problem. Husbands, wives, or both are worshipping self instead of God. They are more in love with themselves than they are with God or their spouse. Their "me-ism" motivates them to unconsciously establish a mental list of expectations so their own perceived needs will be met. When their partner does not meet these needs, they reveal the condition of their heart through agitation and even indignation. Demanding their own way, they create distance between themselves and their spouse, which if not dealt with, will sever the relationship.

The way to eliminate me-ism is to die to ourselves by being so focused on the character and person of Jesus that His love actually controls us (v. 14). This is the reason He died, so that the confining worship of self would be replaced by the liberating life of worshipping Him (v. 15). When both spouses experience this freedom, His love will control their marriage.

OVERCOMING ME-ISM

Read 2 Corinthians 5:14–15 and Ephesians 3:14–19

To die to self, to submit to another person, to put our spouse's interest before our own, to give up our rights, is not instinctive. It is not something we will naturally do. Since me-ism (selfishness) is engrained within our sinful heart, there is no way that we, in and of ourselves, can put it to death without the supernatural work of the Holy Spirit. This depraved condition can only be resolved through the work of Jesus. Daily applying the gospel to our hearts causes us to recognize the unfathomable love Jesus has for us. Martyn Lloyd Jones explains, "There is only one way to get rid of self, and that is that you should become so absorbed in someone or something else that you have no time to think about yourself."[60] He goes on to say, "That someone or something needs to be Jesus Christ!" Scottish theologian Thomas Chalmers further elaborates, "The only way to dispossess it (the heart) of an old affection is by the expulsive power of a new one ... it is then that the heart, brought under the mastery of one great and predominate affection, is delivered from the tyranny of its former desires, and is the only way in which deliverance is possible.[61]

Only when we become immersed in the love of God will we be delivered from self-interest and self-love. Paul understood this when he passionately prayed that the Christians in Ephesus would be so overwhelmed with the love of Christ that they would be filled with all the fullness of God (vv. 14–19). The solution to overcoming "me-ism in marriage" is to be so passionately in love with Jesus that your life will be hidden in Him. Having found our identity and security in Christ, we can then unselfishly and freely give ourselves away to our spouse. Pray Paul's prayer (Eph 3:14–19) for each other today.

TAMING THE TYRANT: CORRECT MINDSET

Read Philippians 2:5–15

Bill and his wife Sarah never miss church. He is a deacon and she serves on the praise team. Their family is there every Sunday and Wednesday, and the children are active in all the youth functions. Everyone considers them a "backbone" of the congregation. The view from home, however, differs dramatically. Although not physically abusive, hot-tempered Bill dictatorially demands that his wife serve him unquestionably. He repeatedly reminds his family of his noble efforts to provide. He barks orders and is unwilling to listen. No one else suspects what is happening, but family life is miserable for Sarah and the children. When she suggests marriage counseling, Bill is insulted and angrily refuses to consider such a thing. Confused and hurt, Sarah does not know how much more she can take.

Tyrannical personalities are not confined to the male gender. Mean, domineering wives can also wear a husband down. Today's passage in God's Word provides principles for responding to tyrants, but before applying them, an individual must possess the mind of Christ (v. 5). The victim needs to think from Christ's perspective. Jesus, who as God deserved all respect, praise, and glory, was willing to subject Himself to ridicule, criticism, accusations, and betrayal in order to accomplish the will of the Father. He was not resentful and did not feel cheated of His rights (vv. 6–7). Likewise, it is important that an individual be so confident in God's sovereign wisdom (v. 13) that he or she is willing to temporarily set aside the emotional needs that should be met by the spouse. Replacing the resentment of unfair treatment with a mindset of obedience sourced in utmost reverence for God will clear the heart and countenance, allowing the glow of a selfless attitude to impact the spouse, the children, and the surrounding world (vv. 14–15). The mind of the individual will then possess the discernment of Christ that can direct him or her to respond as needed with patience, loving confrontation, or protective action.

TAMING THE TYRANT: CORRECT PRAYER

Read Job 42:1–10

*T*he Scriptures describe Job as a godly, upright man who feared God (Job 1:1). When his life was plagued with disasters, his well-meaning friends analyzed his life with respect to their understanding of God. Their analysis was critical and inaccurate during a time when Job desperately needed encouragement. He considered their remarks, but throughout his ordeal, he continued to seek God. Job declared the majesty and wisdom of God (Job 42:1–2). He then humbly admitted his personal sin (v. 6). Job's attitude was now acceptable to God and he was ready to pray. The Lord even encouraged Job's friends to go to him so he could pray for them (v. 8). The New Testament explains that the prayer of a righteous man taps into great power (James 5:16). Job's life bears witness to this truth because when he humbly prayed for his friends, God restored all he had lost (Job 42:10). Rather than a consuming desire for his own needs to be met, the intent of Job's prayer was the spiritual well-being and understanding of his friends.

A domineering, critical spouse can drag an individual through emotional experiences similar to the depressing, confusing ordeals Job experienced. When the criticized one has a correct understanding of God's righteousness (Job 42:1–2), however, and humbly acknowledges his or her own weaknesses (v. 6), his or her prayers will touch the heart of God. Along with declaring the power of prayer, as noted earlier, Scripture also warns against praying incorrectly (James 4:3). It is wrong to pray selfishly. Like Job, partners of individuals who act in harsh or critical ways are to pray for their spiritual awakening. The motive of an individual's prayer should be that his or her spouse will grow in an understanding and desire for God. When a person prays unselfishly, God blesses superabundantly, far above what we can imagine (Eph 3:14–21). In Job's case, the Lord returned double the amount of all he had lost (v. 10). Seek His wisdom as you pray for your mate.

TAMING THE TYRANT: CORRECT ENEMY

Read Matthew 16:21–23 and Ephesians 6:10–18

When Jesus unveiled God's plan for His suffering, death, and resurrection, Peter tried to convince Jesus there was a flaw in the plan. Peter's remarks and opinions were a distraction that made the purpose of Jesus more difficult to achieve. Jesus, however, acknowledged that Peter was not His enemy. Satan was the enemy. Likewise when a spouse makes life difficult for his or her partner, the partner needs to realize that the offending spouse is not the enemy. The devil is the true enemy.

Paul addresses husband-wife, parent-child, and employer-employee relationships in Ephesians 5:22-6:9. He concludes by reminding Christians to be empowered by and draw strength from the Lord because they are facing a spiritual battle, against a spiritual enemy (v. 10). When there is conflict and disagreement in relationships, people tend to view the other party as the enemy. Paul explains that Christians do not wrestle against mortals—their spouses, teenagers, or employers. The wrestling match is actually against the rulers of darkness (v. 12). The devil is the one that will try to destroy your marriage and steal your joy. His weapons are lies, resentment, and bitterness. Paul warns Christians not to manipulate and try to handle the situation by sheer will power. This is a spiritual battle that requires spiritual weapons. Paul lists the weapons that are effective against this enemy—truth, righteousness, peace, faith, salvation, the Word, and prayer. Paul instructs Christians to employ these weapons of protection and defense because this is what is effective against the strategies and deceits of the devil. It is vain to respond with defensive words and tactics. In marital or family conflict, the victim is to focus on and believe the truth, love, and righteousness of God. The battle plan is worship—continually rehearsing gospel truths in one's mind, remembering how Christ rescued from personal sin, praising Him for His righteousness and sovereignty. These weapons defeat the true enemy, and victoriously restore joy and harmony to marriage.

TAMING THE TYRANT: CORRECT ACTION

Read Romans 12:14–21

When an individual is faced with a harsh, unreasonable spouse, the natural first instinct is self defense—exposing the wrong or retaliating with equally sharp remarks. The Scriptures, however, warn against retaliation and encourage Christians to give a blessing when someone displays an antagonistic attitude (v. 14). Verse 16 promotes harmony by reminding believers not to be snobby in these situations, but to be willing to adjust to the disagreeable person by performing humble tasks. This response does not come naturally, but requires a person to give thought to what might be an honest, noble action (v. 17). Verse 20 elaborates on these kind deeds. If a person is hungry, feed him; if he is thirsty, give him something to drink. Likewise, we need to be alert to needs in our spouse's life and be willing to lovingly fill them. Our actions should be deeds of kindness that they do not expect. In biblical times, hearth fires had to be kept going constantly for cooking and warmth. If the fire went out, a person had to go to a neighbor's house for live coals. He would carry the coals home in a container balanced on his head. If the neighbor heaped coals on his head, he would be more likely to arrive back at his home with some coals that were still burning. This show of kindness went beyond what was expected, displaying genuine care and concern. The Bible is pointing out that un-expectantly meeting needs is like heaping coals on the head of someone who is opposing you. Ask God to fill your mind with specific, loving ways to demonstrate kindness to your spouse.

SEPTEMBER 12

INTERRUPTIONS

Read Mark 5:21–31

o you ever feel like your life is just a series of interruptions? We interrupt this regularly scheduled program with a weather bulletin. We interrupt this peaceful night sleep with a crying baby. We interrupt this meal with a telephone call. We interrupt this traffic flow with construction. We interrupt this marriage with a financial challenge. We interrupt this peaceful day with harsh, accusing words.

In today's passage, the disciples and the large crowd of people are determined to follow Jesus and observe the healing of Jairus's daughter. They greatly anticipate this significant event, but Jesus interrupts their mission with a question that makes no sense. In the midst of a huge, pressing crowd (vv. 21, 24, 30), He stops and asks who touched His clothes. To the people following Him, this question is absurd. In today's world, it would be like leaving the stadium following a college football game, when the fans are eager to return to the tail gate for a victory celebration. Along the way you get bumped and ask, "Who bumped me?" The disciples could not understand why Jesus would interrupt His important mission because of a trivial incident (v. 31).

Sometimes our lives will be interrupted by inconveniences or events that make no sense. We, like the disciples, may want to question God, but we must shift our attention from the disappointing interruption to the purposes Jesus reveals around us. The disciples wisely paused with Him and observed how He interacted with the woman. Through this experience, they grew in their understanding of God's purposes. Likewise, Jesus may use an interruption in your routine as husband and wife to reveal an unexpected, disguised blessing on the way to the anticipated completion of specific responsibilities. Rather than fretting over the inconvenience, prepare yourselves to recognize God's purposes hidden within an interruption. The halt in your schedule will become an opportunity for the two of you to acknowledge the sovereignty of God.

LEAN NOT

Read Proverbs 3:5–10

Chloe, our English mastiff, delivered ten adorable puppies. She was an excellent mother, with an intense drive to care for each one. I stayed with her and the puppies the first night they were born to make sure all ten of them were warm enough and no one was pushed out when they nursed. Since she weighs more than 100 pounds and had so many squirming pups, I did not allow Chloe to be alone with them. Rather, I tucked them into a large, blanket-lined bin under a heat lamp near Chloe's chain link kennel in the garage. Every three hours around the clock I brought the puppies and sat by her while she nursed them. This routine ensured that each one received adequate warmth and nourishment without being smothered. My plan, however, was not acceptable to Chloe. When I left the garage, instead of resting, she would tug at the chain link with her teeth. When she had a small opening she would strain to push herself through the hole even though the jagged edges sliced into her body. She wanted what she thought was best for her puppies, and nothing could stop her. She wounded herself and risked the life of her offspring by forging ahead in her own understanding. All she had to do was trust me to control the situation for her.

Similarly, couples will sometimes forge ahead in their own understanding, risking the welfare of their family. In an effort to provide luxury, a husband risks his health working too many hours. A wife justifies debt so she can buy her family the "extras" she thinks will make them happy.

The Scriptures warn not to lean on our understanding (v. 5). God sees dangers and opportunities that we cannot (v. 7). He can protect us and provide the best for us, but we have to trust Him to control our circumstances instead of forcing what we want (v. 6). When we release control to God, the result will be health, strength, and abundance (vv. 8–10). Trust Him today for every aspect of your life and marriage.

NO TIME

Read Luke 10:38–42

A common complaint that we hear from troubled couples is that they have no time together. Our son reminded us of a quote he heard, "If the devil can't succeed in making you bad, he will make you busy." If we apply this to marriage, we could reword the quote, "If the devil can't break up your marriage by luring you into adultery or dishonesty, he will lure you into such a hectic schedule that you will no longer have time for each other."

In today's passage, Jesus witnesses this temptation when he visits Mary and Martha. Martha feels she is nobly concentrating on her responsibilities, but is fretting because she has no time to spend with Jesus. Seeing Mary sitting with Jesus, she becomes irritated and complains about her sister's apparent laziness (v. 40). As a result, Martha feels lonely and uncared for.

The Bible describes Martha as distracted with much serving. These words perfectly describe the dilemma of many husbands and wives. They are distracted with jobs, church activities, care of children, children's activities, household chores, civic commitments, hobbies, and more. Jesus points out the fact that Mary chose to temporarily set distractions aside in order to spend quality time with Him. The same choice is available to us. We can be distracted by the urgency of non-family commitments, or we can temporarily set them aside to spend time with God and our spouses.

My husband just stopped by my desk and asked me to go for a short ride into town with him. I am tempted to say "no" because we are leaving for a few days tomorrow and I'm trying to get ready. I have to finish my ministry work, make appointments, iron clothes, prepare supper, help with homework, and bake a batch of brownies for an obligation on Saturday. But my husband is more important that my "to do" list. The clothes can remain wrinkled for one more day and supper can be simplified. I choose to spend time with the man I love.

OUR GUIDE

Read Galatians 5:13–26

*R*ecently, my son and I went white water rafting down the Ocoee River in the majestic Cherokee National Forest in Tennessee. After registering, we were assigned a guide. He instructed us that when he said "forward," we were to row forward, when he said "rear," we were to row backwards. When he said "rest," we were to take our oars out of the water and hold them in our lap. But the last instruction was perhaps the most important! He told us that when he said "down," we were to immediately slide into the bottom of the boat so we would not be thrown out. Our guide knew the river and how to handle all potential obstacles. We just had to trust and obey his instructions.

As we navigated the river, even through class-four rapids, I was amazed at how smoothly the trip went. As long as we listened to our guide's instructions, our boat proceeded safely through the white water. As we drove home, God began to say to me, "Sam I have given you a guide to empower you and lead you safely down the river of life. If you listen to your guide and obey His instructions, you will not fulfill the lust of the flesh (vv. 19–21), but will exercise the fruit of the Spirit (vv. 22–23). You must never resist My control, but trust My directions. Otherwise you will provoke one another, envy each other, and promote yourself over others (v. 26)."

Husbands and wives are in a boat paddling themselves and their children through the rough rapids of life. If they ignore their guide, the boat will capsize and the family could drown. Both spouses must daily submit to the guide, the Holy Spirit, so they will walk in love, joy, peace, longsuffering, gentleness, goodness, faith, meekness, and temperance. The result will be a strong marriage and a family who enjoys life's journey together! Don't ignore your guide.

JOY

Read Philippians 4:4, Luke 10:20, and Psalm 51:1–12

Several years ago one of my sons attended World View Academy (a teen summer camp that teaches apologetics). When he called home, we asked him if he was having fun. His response was profound. He said, "We have been instructed to tell our parents that we are not having fun. We're having JOY!"

God commands His children to have joy (Phil. 4:4). Jesus told the disciples they should rejoice because their names were written in heaven (Luke 10:20). True joy is found only by having a relationship with God. The world can experience the fleeting emotions of happiness, but only a Christian has inner joy! John W. Sanderson states that a lack of joy "is practical atheism, for it ignores God and His attributes."[62]

What robs joy from God's children? First, sin destroys our joy since it interrupts our intimate communion with God. After committing the sins of adultery and murder, David begged the Lord to restore the joy of his salvation (Ps. 51:12). Confession and repentance stirred God to renew his joy (vv. 3–4).

Our source of joy is not in our accomplishments, our possessions, or our pleasure, but in our position and relationship with the Lord (Phil. 4:4). Joy dissipates when we seek it anywhere except our relationship with God. If we base our joy on our circumstances, life will be like riding on a roller coaster. Circumstances change, but our standing in Christ will never waver. We have a tendency to lose our joy when we suffer trials and tribulations, but James 1:2-4 says the lessons we learn from them have such value that we can find joy even then.

The Bible talks very specifically about joy in marriage. Ecclesiastes 9:9 commands the husband to live joyfully with his wife. A married couple can experience joy no matter what they face if they walk in holiness, and keep their eyes on their loving Savior.

SHOCK TREATMENT

Read Ephesians 5:8-13 and 4:15

veryone who knew Gary and Melissa described their marriage as ideal. They had two happy, well-adjusted boys. They were active in their church. Gary enjoyed life and Melissa worked hard to run an efficient home. Gary and everyone else were shocked when Melissa announced she was unhappy with their marriage. But even though all appeared well on the surface, underlying problems had been eating away at the relationship for years. Gary provided income for his family through his job, but did nothing to help around the house. Even when he temporarily lost his job, he never assisted Melissa with the children or their home. Over time, she allowed unexpressed resentment to build until she was deeply disgusted and bitter. Gary had been insensitive and lazy, but he was totally clueless. Melissa had hidden the truth and lived in a pretense that fooled her husband and closest relatives until she finally exploded with the shocking revelation. By this time, the disgust was so great that she had no desire to resolve the problem.

Ephesians 5:8 explains that as non-Christians, we were full of darkness, void of truth and virtue, but now we are different because we have the light of Christ. We should live accordingly. Melissa had presented the impression that she was walking in the light, living righteously (v. 9), even though she had no peace and was harboring growing resentment toward her husband. Her fellowship with Gary was broken because she had erected a wall of bitterness. If we walk in the light, we will not only have fellowship with God, but also with other people. A person who is walking in the light allows God to expose His truth to them in every area of their life. When one spouse is insensitive, unreasonable, or involved in sin, the other should shine the light (v. 13) by speaking the truth in love so the mate can adjust and grow spiritually (Eph. 4:15). Speaking the truth in love gently exposes attitudes or actions that harm the spouse or others. A couple that walks in the light avoids resentment by eliminating pretense and maintaining transparency before God and each other.

THE DANGER OF DISGUST

Read Numbers 20:2–13

Moses cares greatly for the children of Israel. He desires what is best for them and sacrifices greatly on their behalf, but their behavior is unreasonable. Moses is baffled. He falls on his face before God. God reveals His glory to Moses and gives him clear directions to respond to the Hebrew nation. He wants Moses to demonstrate His grace, power, and majesty before the children of Israel. He desires to graciously remind them that He is their faithful provider, so they will develop a lifestyle of trust in Him. Moses is disgusted, however, with their childish complaints and feels he should reprimand the people and prove that their behavior is ridiculous. He reasons that these self-centered people need more than just witnessing the goodness of God. His irritation is so intense that he adds harsh emphasis to the gentle, gracious instructions of the all-wise God. Moses allows his disgust to dominate his actions rather than trusting God's plan.

Family life frequently presents a similar scenario. A spouse or child will exhibit unreasonable behavior that is baffling. The behavior can be so obviously wrong that we are filled with disgust. We become consumed with a desire to produce repentance and avoid future irritation. We can become so disgusted with the inconveniences that have disrupted our lives that we determine to prove our point instead of trusting the plan God reveals to us. In the Israelites' situation, the Lord had poured out his glory on Moses in the midst of the challenge, but the power of disgust prevailed. Beware of the danger of disgust. Trust the grace-filled direction of God when you respond to unreasonable behavior within your family.

THE GIFT OF GENTLE TOUCH

Read 2 Samuel 12:19–24

When we attended the funeral for Sam's sister, my heart was especially moved for her three grown children. They deeply loved their mother, and she had played an active, esteemed role in their lives. Their loss was obviously great. As I watched them and prayed for them throughout the service and family time that followed, I noticed our nieces occasionally leaning over and gently kissing their husbands on the cheek. They also periodically reached out to hold the hand of their mate. These small, tender acts caused strength to flow through their inner most beings so they could continue to deal with their tragedy.

David experienced similar grief in the heartbreaking death of his baby son. The Bible records that he had been so overcome with the child's illness that the servants feared he would lose control and harm himself when he heard the news of his son's death (v. 18). David shocked them all when he demonstrated amazing emotional stability. He immediately dressed himself and went to worship the Lord (v. 20). He chose to concentrate on the unchanging goodness and faithfulness of God. After fortifying his trust in the Lord through worship, he was able to accept what the Lord had allowed to happen (v. 23). David then turned his attention to his hurting wife. He comforted her with his gentle touch (v. 24).

Through the wondrous gift of touch, God has endowed spouses with the ability to transfer strength and comfort to one another during tragedy. When your spouse hurts emotionally, fortify yourself through worship, then give the gift of gentle touch.

BELIEVE IN HIM

Read 1 Peter 3: 1–5 and Ephesians 5:33

Do you remember the lyrics to Kenny Rogers's song, "She Believes in Me"? The man in that song receives motivation to face the world and fulfill his responsibilities because he is certain his wife believes in who he is. Today's passage from 1 Peter points out that Sara expressed belief in Abraham by addressing him as lord (v. 5). Back then, this conveyed her respect for his position as husband. Sara was declaring to Abraham that she had faith in him and wholeheartedly supported him.

Secular surveys reveal that a man's number one need is respect. When Shaunti Feldhahn surveyed men about things they wished women understood about men, a major consensus was, "Men had rather feel alone and unloved, than inadequate and disrespected."[63] Since one of God's purposes for a wife is to complete her husband, a godly wife should be attentive to his deep longing for respect. The language of Ephesians 5:33 conveys an urgency or a sense of utmost importance related to a wife showing respect to her husband. Peter reminds wives that husbands are profoundly influenced by godly behavior displayed with reverence. In the Amplified Bible, the wording is "to feel for him all that reverence includes: to respect, defer to, revere him—to honor, esteem, appreciate, prize, and in the human sense, to adore him, that is to admire, praise, be devoted to, deeply love, and enjoy your husband."[64] What a definition! When a husband feels discouraged, worried, or defeated, a wife can inspire him to live up to or surpass his potential. A husband is a prized gift from God that belongs solely to his wife. She does not share him as a husband with any other woman. She should enjoy that privilege and honor—laugh with him, go on dates with him, plan surprises for him, be proud that he is hers—and let him know she is his number one fan!

THE HANDWRITING IS ON THE WALL

Read Daniel 5:1–31 and Proverbs 29:1

Have you ever heard the old saying, "The handwriting is on the wall"? Normally this statement refers to something that has happened that could easily have been foretold. It comes from the story of King Belshazzar, son of King Nebuchadnezzar. King Belshazzar and his concubines took the golden vessels which his father had stolen out of the God's temple in Jerusalem and drank from them, therefore defiling what God considered holy (vv. 1–4). God had previously dealt with Nebuchadnezzar's sins by taking away his throne and all his glory. Nebuchadnezzar ended up dwelling in the wilderness as an animal (vv. 18–21). Daniel admonishes Belshazzar because even though he knew all that had happened to his father, he had not humbled himself. Rather, he had insulted the holiness of God (vv. 22–23). The finger of God wrote on the wall, spelling out His judgment on Belshazzar (vv. 25–28).

Over the years, Debbie and I have observed marriages fail and afterward sadly acknowledged to each other, "The handwriting was on the wall." These couples had been warned by a friend, relative, or Christian counselor to correct their hearts and behavior and to turn to God for help. Ignoring this admonition, they succumbed to their pride. Proverbs 29:1 teaches that someone who has been warned but remains hard hearted will be destroyed without hope of recovery. Just as King Belshazzar suffered when he ignored the warning of God's judgment against his father, a marriage will fail when the couple continually disregards God's truth about their unholy behavior.

Lack of prayer, Bible reading, communication, sexual intimacy, and other telltale signs indicating distance in a marriage serve as handwriting on the wall. Unless a husband and wife repent and turn their relationship back to God, suffering will follow. How blessed we are to have a God that sends warnings and opportunity for behavioral adjustments before it is too late. Are there warning signs you need to address in your life and marriage?

HOPE FOR THE BETRAYED

Read Hosea 1:1–11

One of the most excruciatingly painful challenges of marriage occurs when a spouse is unfaithful. Betrayal pierces deeply, but God offers hope and practical insight about responding to unfaithfulness through one of the most beautiful love stories in the Bible. The drama begins when God makes an unusual request of the prophet Hosea. He commands him to marry Gomer, a woman God knew would sin against Hosea through adulterous relationships (v. 2).

As in most marriages, the couple initially appears worry free. Problems become apparent, however, when the children start arriving. God requests that Hosea and Gomer give each child a specific name. The first child (boy) is named Jezreel, which means "God's judgment is coming." The next child is named Loruhamah, which means "not loved." The third child is named Loammi, which means "not my people." The names of the first two children describe the marriage as Gomer becomes distant from Hosea and her affections drift to other lovers. As Hosea ponders the names God assigned to the first two children, he realizes that Gomer no longer loves him. When God instructs Hosea to name their third child Loammi, Hosea understands that Gomer has been unfaithful!

The Lord knows that marriage partners will selfishly hurt each other. He begins the healing process before the problem is apparent by revealing truth. He exposes the problem so He can work through the betrayed partner. Awareness of the difficulty is God's first step to a stronger, more fulfilling marriage. When the one-flesh relationship is broken, how should the betrayed mate respond? As God directs Hosea to respond to Gomer's unfaithfulness in chapter two, He gives every marriage a pattern for reconciliation. Just as God did not give up in His relationship with Israel, He desires that spouses not give up on a wounded marriage. Tomorrow we will see how Hosea responds according to the grace of God.

LOVE THAT ALLOWS PAIN

Read Hosea 2 and 3:1

How should a spouse who has been betrayed by the sin of unfaithfulness respond? God directs Hosea to respond to his adulterous wife in the same way that He responds to the unfaithfulness of Israel. Hosea sends his children to where their mother is living with another man. He instructs them to plead with her to stop committing adultery so that judgment will not come upon her (v. 2). Can you imagine three children knocking on the door of the house where their mother is living in sin, worried sick that she will reap devastating consequences, begging her to forsake her wrong doing and return home to them?

Gomer assumes that her lovers are the ones who are providing her comfortable lifestyle. However, Hosea is the one who had supplied her food and clothing, along with silver and gold, which her lovers were offering up to Baal (v. 8). Hosea demonstrates that unconditional love never forsakes the spouse, but also shows how true love confronts him or her with the sin, and offers both help and forgiveness. Gomer ignores the reproof and judgment follows. Notice that Hosea does not protect her from judgment, but allows the consequences to speak God's message. It can be tempting to step in and prematurely ease the pain before it has the opportunity to break the spouse's heart. Once Hosea has warned and pleaded for Gomer's return, however, he gives her space to learn sin's lessons. Sin eventually wears her down, and her lovers sell her into slavery. At this point, many would say Gomer deserved the cruel bondage of sin.

Once Gomer is broken, God instructs Hosea to again shower unconditional love on his undeserving wife, modeling His love toward His children who commit spiritual adultery (v. 3:1). True brokenness opens the heart for complete reconciliation. Waiting for this brokenness will require the betrayed spouse, like Hosea, to depend upon the Lord for patience and strength to both help and forgive. God expects you to do what is best for your mate.

THE SLAVE BLOCK

Read Hosea 3:1–5

*H*ave you ever been to an auction where the auctioneer is rattling off so fast that you can hardly understand what he's saying? You have to be careful not to accidentally move your hand, or you'll be the new owner of an item you have no desire for. Imagine an auctioneer calling for the top price to sell someone you dearly love.

The setting in chapter three finds Gomer on the slave block being auctioned off to the highest bidder. As was the custom, her clothes are stripped off, and she is standing in public, naked, in total humiliation. Exposure is the cost of her adulterous lifestyle. When Gomer sees Hosea approaching, she probably thinks to herself, "He's come to say I told you so, to laugh at me and scorn me like everyone else." She is startled when she hears him actually begin to bid for her (v. 2). As the auctioneer opens the bidding, Hosea unashamedly shouts, "I'll give fifteen pieces of silver and one and a half homers of barley. I love my wife and I want her back!" The observers are thinking to themselves, "What are you doing, why do you want her, she's nothing but a slut." Hosea has purchased a white robe from a nearby merchant and carefully drapes it around his wife to cover her nakedness and shame. He then takes her by the hand and escorts her back home. What a picture of a loving God who with mercy and grace pays the ultimate price, the death of His only son to rescue man from his slavery to sin. This is the picture of love that God wants every married couple to continually hold in their minds. Marriage partners must follow God's example by offering unconditional love to a partner who has sinned against them, providing an atmosphere of forgiveness and reconciliation. Be ready to love as He loved, to forgive as He forgave, and to wrap a white robe of reconciliation around the one who belongs to you.

YOUR OWN HUSBAND

Read Colossians 3:17–19

*I*t is interesting that each time the Bible directs wives to submit to their husbands, the little word "own," modifies the word "husband." God emphasizes that wives are to submit to their own husbands. The word "submit" means to voluntarily align with and be loyal to, to cooperate with, to help, and to adapt to. In order to effectively coordinate and be a helper and companion, a wife must consider the specific, individual needs of her own husband. Submitting will vary for every wife according to the needs of her husband.

My husband is a preacher. His needs are different than those of a physician or a farmer. I relieve pressure in his life when I help with his correspondence and scheduling. I support him by traveling with him and attending his meetings. When he was an engineer, I adapted to his work schedule. I expressed an interest in his projects and admiration for his accomplishments. When God first called Sam into full-time ministry, we started a Christian theater outreach. At that time, I adjusted to his needs by manning the ticket booth, popping popcorn, and selling concessions.

Support for an individual husband not only varies according to his career, but also according to his physical and personality differences. My husband functions better when he eats regular, hot meals. He watches his weight, so I adjust the menu according to the diet he chooses. Other men desire sandwiches or fast food. During the day, my husband works at an intense pace. At night, he wants to relax, so I try to avoid a busy schedule after 8 o'clock. Other men may sit at a desk all day and want to go out at night. Some men are frustrated if an item is out of place. Others prefer a more relaxed atmosphere. Godly submission is not a mechanical routine, but rather a creative endeavor employing the skills and sensitivity of one who understands the unique requirements of her husband. Lovingly responding to these specialized needs promotes the smooth operation of a marriage.

HOT WATER

Read 1 Corinthians 2:1–5

On a chilly evening, when I am weary, I enjoy sipping a soothing cup of hot tea, especially loose leaf tea with dried fruit or spices in the mix. The aroma of the dried mixture is tantalizing, but it is essentially potpourri without two significant additions—hot water and a filter. The hot water infuses the flavor while the strainer removes the unnecessary, soggy leftovers.

The apostle Paul had a habit of getting into hot water (arrested, stoned, shipwrecked). He repeatedly faced trials. When he was in hot water, the true character of the people around him would surface. Some were intent on causing him problems. Others were searching for godly direction. Responding to differing needs in a high-risk environment gets complicated, even baffling. God directed Paul to an approach that simplified his responses.

We see in today's reading that the challenges were extremely intimidating (v. 3), but Paul chose to avoid the temptation of using personal skill to dominate the outcome. He elected to set aside the use of intellect, flattery, and manipulative or convincing arguments that might give him an advantage (v. 1). Paul determined to filter every situation and every person through the gospel—Christ, and Christ crucified (v. 2). This ensured that he humbly offered wise responses that did not compromise or minimize the person of God. He would always be passionate for righteousness and truth, yet humble and sensitive to the difficulties and struggles of others. The longing of his heart was that the listeners be influenced by the Spirit of God (v.4). He focused on the goal of creating a thirst for intimacy with Christ. He was so enraptured with Christ personally that he naturally inspired others to keep reverential thoughts of God prominent in their daily routine (v. 5).

Milton Vincent states, "I have also found that when I am absorbed in the gospel, everything else I am supposed to be toward God and others seems to flow out of me more naturally and passionately."[65] If we are focused on Christ and what He has done, we can filter the hot water of marital challenges through Him and release the soothing flavor of humility and forgiveness to our spouse.

A SALTY MARRIAGE

Read Matthew 5:13 and John 13:34–35

*T*oday, salt is inexpensive and common. Salt shakers are found on most tables, and in the winter, salt is seen in huge piles beside icy roads. Salt seems somewhat insignificant. In the days of Jesus, however, it was considered extremely valuable. Salt was not only needed to maintain proper metabolism in the body, but was also used as a preservative, a seasoning, and a medication to promote healing. More importantly, it was required by God in all sacrifices (Lev. 2:13).

Jesus uses the metaphor of salt to describe how a Christian should influence others (v. 13). We are to be so salty that we season the world around us, creating a great thirst for Christ! Jesus adds that if salt loses its taste, it is good for nothing, but to be cast out and stomped under foot. When salt was no longer useful for seasoning, it became an agent of destruction. After conquering a city, the armies of the Old Testament would sow salt through the fields. It would be trampled into the ground, steal the life from the soil, and cause utter desolation where nothing would grow. Christians who have lost their saltiness hinder spiritual growth. Rather than inspire those around them to live according to the goodness and greatness of God, they are so preoccupied with personal challenges and commitments that they portray a disinterest or boredom that destroys respect for His kingdom.

For example, Christian husbands and wives should be affectionate and caring toward one another. When others see this kind of marriage, they will be "salted." That is, they will develop a thirst to have for themselves what makes this marriage so vibrant and alive—Jesus! When two spouses who claim to know Christ have a marriage that looks nothing like the picture of Christ and His bride, the world is repulsed and Christian marriage becomes a mockery (Matt. 5:13). A salty marriage is an essential part of the foundation of a healthy community. As you seek to honor the Lord, your relationship with your spouse can be the seasoning that attracts those around you to Christ.

ASCRIBE TO THE LORD

Read Psalm 29:1–11

Brother Lawrence was a 14th century monk known for abiding in the presence of God. I usually picture a monk as a man who lived in totally quiet seclusion, with no responsibilities other than to meditate and pray. However, the monks divided care-taking chores and responsibilities of the monastery between themselves. These included lawn care, household cleaning, kitchen duties, shopping, writing, and bookkeeping. Brother Lawrence was assigned kitchen duty and food preparation for the entire monastery. Even though this was an overwhelming and consuming task, Brother Lawrence was described as being more united to God when he was performing his kitchen assignments than when he was concentrated in devotions.

This godly man explained the thought process he had trained himself to practice, "We should feed and nourish our souls with high notions of God which would yield us great joy in being devoted to Him."[66] In his daily routine, whenever he realized that his thoughts had strayed, he did not condemn himself or become weighed down with guilt; he simply shifted his thoughts to the attributes of God. At first, he only occasionally thought about God, but over time, he became more and more sensitive to Him. After a while, his thoughts of God were so continual that they dominated his life.

Psalm 29 says to ascribe to the Lord the glory due His name. We are to credit the Lord with His attributes by considering and then marveling at what each characteristic means, and how it impacts us and the world around us, especially our marriage. When, as a husband or wife, we are involved in a task requiring design or organization, we can think on Him as Creator. When marriage requires us to deal with relational challenges, we can consider His grace and justice. When we sense danger, we can encourage our mate by remembering His protection. This simple exercise of shifting our thoughts to God's attributes whenever we realize we are not thinking on Him will progress from a hobby to a habit, then to a lifestyle that will strengthen our marriages with His presence.

BAD HABITS

Read 2 Corinthians 10:1–6

A friend of mine recently attended a PMA (Positive Mental Attitude) conference that emphasized getting your life under control. One of the techniques the speaker explained involves ridding yourself of undesirable habits such as smoking, overeating, or an explosive temper. The motivator challenged participants to associate bad habits with something negative or repulsive. Every time a person considers the undesirable habit, he must immediately shift his thoughts to the predetermined repulsive thought. As a result, he will instinctively want to steer away from the bad habit. The plan is somewhat effective, but different than the biblical principle Paul explains in today's passage.

Christians face the same tempting challenges of bad habits as non-Christians, but they possess a much more powerful weapon to overcome them (v. 3–4). Motivated non-Christians depend on human-powered mind schemes such as negative association. Christians can depend upon the power of Almighty God. Scripture challenges believers to view all habits with Christ's perspective. Every time a Christian considers a thought, he should shift to and then embrace God's point of view on the matter (v. 5). If a habit is pleasing to God, the believer can depend upon the Holy Spirit to empower him to continue it. If it is sinful, the believer should admit the wrong, ask forgiveness, and then consciously depend upon the Holy Spirit to deliver him from its power. Continuing the wrong attitude or action expresses a desire to please self that is greater than the desire to please God. Although human mind control may have some effectiveness, the divine weapons are much more powerful (v. 4). The key to employing them is recognizing that bad habits demonstrate disobedience to God (v. 6). If a husband and wife each possess a passion to obey God in their thinking, the bad habits that can harm their marriage can be overcome.

BURN YOUR SHIPS

Read Genesis 2:24 and James 1:2–8

In 1519, Spanish explorer Fernando Cortez set out to conquer Mexico. He landed on the shores at a place called Veracruz. As his men trudged up a nearby mountain, they looked back and discovered all their ships were ablaze. Cortez explained to his men that he had burned the ships so there would be no possibility of turning back! He knew if things got tough and there remained a way of escape, his men would want to head back to the ships and sail home to the comfort and security of the life they once had. Because the ships were destroyed, they had no choice but to band together and work toward their goal of victory.

When a man and woman leave their father and mother and enter into the marriage covenant, they are burning the ships of singleness they once knew. When they look back, they no longer see the safe harbor of their former home to which they can retreat. Instead, they must brave the mysterious frontier of becoming one with the partner they have covenanted to remain with till death. This new journey—with its twists, turns, and even potholes—becomes one of committed love where the couple's faith in God keeps them going. With this "burn the ships" attitude, divorce is never considered as an option. When problems come, the response is proactive rather than reactive. Together as a committed team, the marriage partners look for a solution that will help them to not only resolve their conflict, but better understand how to develop deeper intimacy in the face of trials. By also "burning the ships" of selfish attitudes and bad habits, God's grace becomes the compass by which we find our way to a peaceful, fulfilling marriage. Excuses for sin are replaced by true repentance and an open, unashamed relationship results. Burn your ships!

A SPECIAL GIFT

Read Genesis 2:22–23 and Ephesians 5:26

*A*t the conclusion of most wedding ceremonies, the presiding minister will introduce the couple as one. The bride, who bore her maiden name just a few minutes ago, now takes on the name of her husband. The two become one, and are recognized by the same last name.

God gave Adam the authority in the Garden of Eden to name both the animals and his wife. Recognizing that God had created from his side someone who was bone of his bone and flesh of his flesh, Adam gave her a very special gift, a derivative of his own name! Naming her woman ("ishah") when he was a man ("ish") showed he had an understanding of the helper God had given to him. This name positioned her (sanctified her) in the relationship as his wife, as part of his own flesh. Bearing his name symbolized to all observers that she was part of him, united to him, identified with him. Adam was given both the privilege of his wife bearing his name, and the responsibility of maintaining a respectable name she could be proud to share.

Similarly, when individuals accept Christ as Savior, they become His bride and are positioned (sanctified) in Christ (Eph 5:26). They bear the very special new name of "Christian." As the bride of Christ, we have the privilege of bearing a name of utmost integrity, character, and honor! His name is one we can proudly wear and must be careful not to mar. In marriage, the husband must ensure that his name can be proudly worn by his wife. She should never be ashamed to be called by his name. Therefore, to emulate the example of Christ, the husband must live a life of integrity, purity, and character. His name then becomes a special gift of honor to his wife!

HAPPY FOOTWORK

Read John 13:3–17

We know pastors of large churches with enormous responsibilities. Because of their faithful leadership, the message of Christ is broadcast and ministry is extended to many people. We know evangelists whose travel schedules are intense and fast paced. Through their efforts, churches are encouraged and challenged, and the lost are exposed to the gospel. These men daily impact our country with truth. The tasks they perform are important to the kingdom of God. The significance of their work and the urgency of their schedules dictate that they use their time and resources wisely.

The disciples viewed the ministry of Jesus in the same way. They were protective of His time and energy. Once, they even reprimanded parents who allowed their children to distract Him. In the passage today, Peter attempted to stop Jesus from wasting time and surrendering His dignity with the menial task of foot washing (vv. 6–8). Jesus realized the urgency of His calling and time (v. 3), but He also knew how to be happy (v. 17). Taking the time to individually serve and show concern for the people who were dearest to Him brought Him deep satisfaction. Washing the disciples' feet met their need for that moment. Jesus proved that their well being mattered to Him and as a result, He found joy in serving them. This chore was not His duty. It was His delight.

Jesus was concerned that the people who gave their lives to serve Him might miss this path to happiness. He realized they could become so overwhelmed by the urgency of serving the world that they would not take time to individually serve the ones they love most, so He asked if they understood what He had done for them (v. 12). This concern can especially apply to spouses who have demanding responsibilities outside of their home. The Lord deeply desires that we understand the significance of carving out time to serve our mates and the people closest to us. He wants us to be happy and blessed (v. 17).

ALWAYS THE SAME

Read James 1:17 and Hebrews 13:8

One of my favorite attributes of God is that He never changes. I can read about how He related to Abraham as a "covenant" God and have confidence that He will keep His covenants with me. I can read of His faithfulness to lead and deliver Moses or David, and know that God will do the same for me. When I study the tenderness of Jesus as he dealt with sinners, I know that He views me in the same, loving manner. His immutability gives me the confidence to trust Him for my future.

On a recent Sunday at church, we sang the hymn, "Jesus is the sweetest name I know, and He's just the same, as His lovely name." As soon as I recited those words, Hebrews 13:8 came to my mind and confirmed what I was singing. The character trait that I held so dear seemed to expand to much more than the fact that Jesus is able to perform the same powerful and kind acts that He did in history. No matter what I do or what I face, I can trust Him moment by moment to always be the same—loving, truthful, patient, faithful, holy, and full of peace. I thought about my mood swings and how circumstances or people irritate and annoy me. Other times I have great patience. One day, my attitude is positive, no matter what I face. The next day, the most trivial situation will depress me. I can be extremely critical or very encouraging. My responses and my countenance fluctuate. No one knows this better than my family because they witness my varying moods. James 1:17, however, explains that God does not vary; He does not shift like shadows. He is consistently good. Therefore, when I look to Him and let Him control me, my moods fluctuate less. My responses become consistently peaceful. My family can trust and respect my attitudes and actions. If I am yielded to the Lord, my wife and children can depend upon me to be the same yesterday, today, and tomorrow.

ANTICIPATION OF THE CALL

Read Jeremiah 29:11–14

When Sam travels out of town overnight, I feel lonely, but I am confident that before I go to bed, he will give me a call. Knowing I'll get to hear his voice fills me with anticipation. As I wait to hear from him, I consider the importance of his trip. I think about how I want him to be safe, successful, and happy. I am anxious to hear the details of his day because I deeply care about him. I want to express my love and encouragement. I long for him to know I'm proud of him and I miss him. I want the phone call to be a source of joy to him, so I keep the phone near me.

The Lord understands my anticipation because He intently awaits my calls to Him. He knows all of the encouraging thoughts He has for me, and He longs to express them to me. He desires that I realize He can grant me peace and hope when my life is confused by turmoil. The Lord wants to reassure me that He is in control and has plans for my future. Just like I am eager for Sam to call me, the Lord is eager for me to call Him (v. 12). He is ready to listen.

Sometimes when Sam calls, instead of hearing my voice, he hears a recorded message telling him the circuits are all busy and he is unable to get through. He must wait to secure a signal that is free from distractions so his call will reach me. Likewise, the Lord explains that I cannot be distracted when I call Him. I have to seek Him with all of my being—with my whole heart (v. 13). If other concerns interfere, my prayers will be hindered.

Communication with the Lord not only strengthens me, but prepares my heart to minister more effectively to my mate. It fills me with love and truth that I can pass on. My spouse benefits every time I call on my Heavenly Father.

The Lord is eagerly awaiting your call. He desires to encourage and reassure you so that you can bless your loved ones. Set aside anything that could short-circuit your connection, and seek Him with your whole heart.

AVOIDING AN IGNORANT SPOUSE

Read 2 Corinthians 1:8–11

When Sam worked as an engineer, he faced different stresses that come with high pressure jobs. He would come home and I could tell he was frustrated, but when I questioned him about it, he would shrug it off and say it was nothing. I had been married to him long enough, however, to know something was wrong. I would start to analyze our relationship and try to figure out what I had done to upset him. He was actually trying to protect me from negative aspects of his job, but I started drowning in anxiety, wondering if I had done something to irritate him. Over time, he came to understand that I need to be aware of his struggles.

In today's passage, Paul explained to his friends, the Corinthians, that it was important they not be ignorant about his troubles (v. 8). The trials he faced were so heavy that he felt crushed. He was drained of all strength, to the point he felt he couldn't face life and might die. Paul trusted the Lord and He was faithful to deliver him (vv. 9–10), but God used his friends as part of the process. The Corinthians had diligently prayed when they heard about Paul's struggles (v. 11). Now they could join him in joyous, meaningful thanksgiving because they understood the depth of the struggles from which he had been rescued.

This principle is the same for husbands and wives. When we understand the difficulties our spouse is facing, we can pray more effectively. A deep bond will result when we pray diligently for one another. It will be strong because, as Paul explained, we will be trusting in Almighty God rather than our own efforts. Our relationship will deepen when we join together in thanksgiving and rejoice in the specific answers God sends. Don't keep your mate ignorant of your struggles. Allow him or her to bond with you in prayer, trust, and thanksgiving.

October 6

Seasons

Read Genesis 8:22 and Ecclesiastes 3:1-8

*T*his morning, I awoke to a slight chill in our bedroom. I wrapped the covers tightly around myself and snuggled up to my wife. The cool temperature made me want to linger and enjoy just a few more minutes of warmth and relaxation. Later, I walked outside on the deck to witness a deep blue sky, a slight breeze, and the invigorating feeling of the sun as it touched my face.

Fall, one of my favorite times of year, is in the air! The leaves turn bright colors and to my delight, the weekly chore of cutting grass gradually disappears. Fall is the season to enjoy the thrill of college football. The chill in the air makes that cup of coffee taste even better than it did in the summer. Fall also presents the opportunity for Debbie and me to take a late afternoon stroll to the bluff line and behold the brilliant colors of the trees accented by the beauty of an autumn sunset. This season constrains me to glorify God by taking pleasure in His magnificent creation.

In the mighty sovereign work of our great God, He has given us seasons, or divisions of time. He regulates them for our good and His glory! Ecclesiastes 3:1 tells us there is a specific season or time for every matter or purpose under heaven. Writer Stephen Olford states, "The two words 'under heaven' are not only a reference to this earth, they are also a reminder that everything that happens on this planet is under the eye of God, and therefore, to be done to the glory of God."[67]

Just as there are climatic seasons, our marriages experience seasons of change that are regulated by God. There are seasons of laughing, dancing, mourning, healing, enjoying the birth of a child, and experiencing the loss of someone we love (vv. 2-8). Each of these is a unique opportunity to unite as a couple and look to, trust, and glorify Him. What season is your marriage currently experiencing? In what ways can you approach this period so that God will be honored?

BEYOND FORGIVENESS

Read 2 Corinthians 2:5–11

Have you ever forgiven someone for a wrong they committed against you, but then noticed that even after granting forgiveness, tension remains in the relationship? In today's passage, Paul counsels the Corinthians concerning the danger of this situation. A man had caused trouble and grief in the church (v. 5). The believers had followed Paul's instructions to confront the offender and appropriately deal with the problem (v. 6). Paul now instructs them to forgive the man, and not hold the offense against him any longer. In addition, Paul states that forgiving the man is not enough. Although the church members may continue their lives without hard feelings, the relationship could still be strained because the offender is overwhelmed with guilt (v. 7). Paul urges the congregation to not only forgive, but to comfort the offender. The word "comfort" means with strength. The people need to strengthen the man's spirit with their kind words. They can emphasize the joy of his repentance. They need to remind him of God's love and promises. Next, Paul challenges the believers to reaffirm their love to the hurting man (v. 8). He wants them to convince the man that they still care about him. They should point out his value and benefit to them personally. He wants them to include him in their activities and conversations. Paul instructs them to go out of their way to show love for this man.

The same principles apply after exercising forgiveness in our marriages. Speaking words of strength and comfort can relieve a tense atmosphere. Cards, flowers, or a special date can reach miles beyond forgiveness. When you experience awkwardness in this situation, ask God to fill your mind with expressions of kindness you can use to reach out in love to the one who has offended you.

BROKEN

Read Psalm 34

*W*hen I was a little boy I loved to take things apart to see how they worked. I'll never forget my first experience of disassembling a broken watch. I carefully took a screwdriver and pried off the back. When I looked inside, I saw what seemed to be thousands of tiny parts. Having confidence that I could replace them correctly, I carefully started to take out each piece and lay it on the table beside me. Before I knew it, all that was left was an empty watch shell. As I started to reassemble everything, I quickly became confused. I wasn't exactly sure how to put it back together. I tried over and over again to reassemble the watch, only to miserably fail in each attempt. My pride kept me from asking someone else for help. I thought that eventually I could complete the task all by myself.

The struggles and trials of life often leave us like this broken watch. Many things can disassemble our lives. As a child, it could be an abusive parent. As a teenager, it could be our peers. As a married couple, finances, children, health problems, and other difficulties can leave us clueless as to how to put a broken relationship back together. Because of our pride, we unsuccessfully attempt to reassemble our lives by ourselves. After failing time and time again, it is easy to become frustrated and give up.

Since God created us and knows our inner-workings, he knows and understands our hurts, fears, and insecurities. He knows what makes us tick! Therefore, He knows exactly how to put us back together when we are broken and crushed. According to Psalm 34, if we will humble ourselves and cry out in dependence upon the Lord, He will comfort us, heal our hurts, and give us the directions needed to reassemble our lives (vv. 4, 6, 8, 9, 10, 17). What is broken or dismantled in your life or marriage that you need to trust God to repair? Don't let pride deter you from seeking His help.

A DIVINE DESIGN

Read Genesis 1:26–28 and Proverbs 31:10-31

One of the arguments expressed by supporters of the homosexual lifestyle concludes that except for the sexual organs, men and women are basically the same. This viewpoint leads to the assertion that there is not much difference between homosexual and heterosexual couples. Today's passage, however, proves otherwise. Instead of using a general statement about creating humans, God distinctly differentiates between the two sexes as male and female (v. 27). The physical and emotional differences were designed so man and woman could mutually complete each other. As a team, they would fulfill God's purposes for the family (v. 28). God assigned the husband the role of protector and provider (Gen 2:15). In order to equip man to fulfill this assignment, He designed him with 40 percent muscle. He made his skin tougher, and his bones and lung capacity larger than those of a woman. By God's neurological design, a man tends to function more from the left hemisphere of his brain where logic predominates. Adam immediately recognized and delighted in the differences between him and Eve. He gave his wife a derivative of his own name (woman) indicating that she was of him, but not exactly like him. God designed Eve to be a nurturer and caregiver (Gen 3:20, Prov. 31:10-31). To fulfill this role, He gave her softer skin and a smaller frame with less muscle. Unlike a man, a woman thinks more bi-laterally, which adapts her to multitasking and gives her greater ability to consider emotions with her logic. Physically, a man can enjoy the softness of his wife while a wife can receive a sense of security from the stronger, more muscular frame of her husband. Emotionally and psychologically, male and female bring different perspectives to life, benefitting the marriage in many ways. Take time to talk with your spouse about how God made you different from each other, and how that specifically enhances your relationship. Pray together thanking God for the differences.

DISTURBING THE PEACE

**Read John 16:33, Matthew 10:29–31,
and Philippians 4:6–7**

Have you ever been intensely concentrating on a matter only to be interrupted by your spouse? As I was engrossed in studying, my wife came into my office and asked me a question about one of our sons. I reacted immediately by giving her a quick, "Why did you disturb me?" look. This interruption, if I let it, would create anxiety and disturb my peace of mind.

In this world there are numerous disturbers of the peace. Most come from one major source, a change in circumstances. It might be a financial reversal, a medical diagnosis, mistreatment by our spouse, or as mentioned, unexpected needs of our children. Life is full of uncertainty. John 16:33 describes how on the eve of His betrayal, Jesus informed His disciples they would have tribulation in this world, but He wanted them to experience peace in the midst of these difficult circumstances. The secret to peace and even joy was contained in one fact: He had overcome the world. Nothing comes our way that escapes His attention. Why then should we let worry rob our peace? The only answer we can offer is that we do not believe Christ's promise. When we fret over missing a flight, unfair treatment, or lack of finances, we are not convinced that He cares enough to help us through these changing circumstances. We fail to acknowledge that He will work everything together for our good.

One thing is constant in marriage—change. We are not to worry or be anxious over interruptions or changing circumstances, but rather take everything to the Father in prayer with thanksgiving (Phil. 4:6–7). Next time your spouse or unexpected circumstances interrupt or disturb you, look to the Lord and thank Him that He is in control. The peace you receive will calm your life and marriage.

OCTOBER 11

FILLING THE BARNS

Read Genesis 41:29–49

Our family is healthy. Each of our boys is growing in their relationship and understanding of the Lord. New doors are opening for our ministry. It is tempting to become satisfied and lazy. At times like these, the urgency to pray and seek God seems to fade since most areas of our life are prosperous. We don't need anything right now. I read a wise challenge written by Corrie ten Boom. She stated, "Gather the riches of God's promises which can strengthen you in the time when there will be no freedom. Nobody can take away from you those texts from the Bible which you have learned by heart."[68]

Today's passage takes us to the story of Joseph. In it, we see that he didn't calculate and store just the amount of grain he predicted he would need. Instead, he stored huge quantities that were beyond measure (v. 49). His zeal probably seemed like overkill, but the Bible explains that during the severe famine, there was no food to be found in Egypt or Canaan (Gen. 47:13). The people were desperate and begged for help so that their land would not become desolate (Gen. 47:19). Because Joseph had diligently obeyed God during the season of abundance, he not only fulfilled his job responsibilities to Egypt, but he was able to minister to his own needy family (Gen. 45:7).

During the smooth seasons of life when stress is less and the victories are encouraging, a married couple needs to zealously seek the Lord. They need to study the promises and character of God and store truth in their hearts and minds until they cannot contain their joy. Then, when devastating, uncontrollable pressures drain life from their family, those truths and promises will be readily available. Like Joseph, a spiritually prepared couple will not panic during famine, but will nourish their desperate family and friends with the hope and stability of God's Word.

LIFTING THE DEPRESSED

Read Ruth 1 and 2

*H*ow frustrating to deal with a spouse, a relative, or a close friend who is depressed to the point of utter despair and hopelessness. No amount of reasoning or cheerfulness can dispel the cynicism. Ruth overcame this dilemma with her mother-in-law, through consistent covenant love. The principles that drew Naomi out of her depression are worth analyzing.

Naomi had abandoned hope to the point she convinced herself that even God was against her (vv. 13, 20). Ruth firmly declared two commitments that were the source of Naomi's eventual recovery (v. 16). First Ruth vowed that she would never leave Naomi—that she would not give up, but that she would always be there for her. This was not a lofty intention, but a deliberate promise that Ruth proved true through her daily actions when she accompanied Naomi to Bethlehem and took care of her. Ruth also vowed that she was surrendering in complete dependence and trust to Naomi's God, the God of Israel (v. 16). This declaration reminded Naomi of their true source of security.

Ruth strengthened Naomi through her consistent dependability. Every day, Ruth gleaned in the field and brought food to Naomi (vv. 2:2, 17–18). The routine and care stabilized Naomi's shaky life. Ruth daily reported her work activities to Naomi (v. 2:21). She repeated conversations, and described her tasks and the people she worked with. This reporting linked Naomi with society again. Naomi and Ruth were both challenged to ponder the goodness of God because they had surrounded themselves with other believers who spoke freely of His ways during everyday life (vv 2:4, 11–12). Ruth revitalized a sense of significance in Naomi's life by showing respect for her advice (v. 3:6). Ruth loved her mother-in-law out of depression with her positive attitudes, consistent deeds, and dependence upon God.

In this stressful society, any spouse could unconsciously succumb to depression. Be prepared to help. Pray that the Holy Spirit will bring these truths to your mind and allow you to minister effectively to your loved one.

OCTOBER 13

THE INVITATION

Read 2 Kings 4:8–10

Elisha was God's prophet to the northern kingdom, and he traveled from town to town ministering as God directed him. He relied on the Lord to feed him and supply his needs, often through someone's hospitality. Today's passage tells about how his travels took him to the small town of Shunem, where a prominent woman of the community constrained him to eat meals with her and her husband. The word "constrain" means to compel, strongly urge, or even beg someone to do something. This woman whose name is withheld, but is described in Scripture as wealthy, desperately wants Elisha to eat with her family. We might ask, why?

Verse nine offers insight into her desperation to have the prophet of God in her home. She told her husband she could sense or perceive that this man was a genuine man of God. Unlike our day, where believers have access to God through the Holy Spirit within them, people in that time had to rely on prophets such as Elisha to hear from God. She wanted His prophet in her home so she could experience His presence. In verse ten, she asks her husband to construct a room where God's prophet, hence God's presence, would reside as often as possible. It's no wonder that the Lord includes this woman in Scripture since she had such a perceptive and discerning heart for Him.

Since Pentecost, Jesus sends the Holy Spirit to live within all who trust in Him as Savior (Rom. 8:9). We no longer need a prophet in order to hear from God. We can now listen to the voice of the Holy Spirit. But we must, even as demonstrated by this Shunammite woman, consciously make room for God in our homes. He must continually be invited to dine and daily abide with us, so His presence can invade every crack and crevice in our family relationships. Does God have a place in your life, your marriage, your home? If not, invite Him to take up residence today.

GOD CARES

Read 2 Kings 4:8–17 and Psalm 37:4

While enjoying a peaceful rest in the room added onto the home of the caring Shunammite woman, Elisha meditated upon what he could do to show his appreciation for her gracious hospitality. He instructed his servant Gehazi to ask her what he could do to express his gratitude (v. 13).

Elisha first suggested that he could talk to the king or the commander of the army on her behalf to help her with any need her family might have. The woman replied that she lived among her own people. She wanted Elisha to know that her motive for taking care of him and his servant was not for position, power, or possessions, but rather because of her genuine love for God.

Realizing her godly contentment, Elisha probed deeper to search for anything she might desire, but perhaps deemed impossible. Having often stayed and eaten in her home, he knew of one important thing that was missing—a child. One of the greatest gifts a Jewish woman could give to her husband was a son who would pass on the heritage of the father. Since the Shunammite's husband was old, this dream had long dissipated (v. 14). When God revealed to Elisha the inner desire of the woman's heart, he promised her a child. Upon hearing this promise, she was so shaken that she wanted Elisha to confirm that he was not making small talk or a joke. After nine months passed, she delivered a baby boy. God had given her the desire of her heart.

The Lord finds great pleasure in doing what we cannot do, especially what we believe to be utterly impossible. This woman loved serving Him and was content to receive nothing in return. However, God takes notice when we take great pleasure in Him (Ps 37:4). Even when it appears that our spouse does not recognize a particular hurt or desire, He knows the recesses of each heart and cares about every hurt, every inward pain, and every dream we may have abandoned. Whatever we face personally or in our marriage relationship, God cares!

OCTOBER 15

I MELT

**Read Song of Solomon 1:15, 4:1, 4:9, 6:5, 7:4,
Proverbs 31:30, and Matthew 6:22–23**

Solomon declares to his bride that he is overcome when he gazes into her eyes (6:5). One penetrating glance causes his heart to melt. Earlier in the Song, he tells his bride that she captivates his heart with merely a glance (4:9). I'm reminded of the song lyrics from "I Melt," by Rascal Flatts, "I melt every time you look at me that way." What is it about looking into her eyes that causes him to melt and be overcome with passion?

Twice in the Song of Solomon (v. 1:15, 4:1), Solomon declares that his wife has eyes like doves. A dove is the traditional symbol of purity, innocence, and beauty. Solomon is saying that when he looks into his bride's eyes, he sees a pure virgin of great beauty. He values this woman who reflects reverence for God and therefore captivates and causes him to praise her (Prov. 31:30). Eyes that have an undistorted view of the Lord cause the whole body and personality to be filled with His light (Matt. 6:22–23). Solomon could see the light of God's holiness within his wife by merely glancing into her eyes.

Along with comparing them to doves, Solomon also says his wife's eyes are like fish pools by the gate of Bathrabbin (v. 7:4). What does that mean? Bathrabbin was noted for its quiet and beautiful pools of water. Gazing at them was soothing and peaceful to the viewer. When Solomon looked into his wife's eyes, he was not only overcome by her purity, but he was quieted by her peace. Looking into her eyes brought tranquility to his inner being. It's no wonder that he melted with passion when he looked into her eyes. A wife whose eyes reflect the rest and stability of the Lord can stir her husband to great passion by a single glance.

INTERCESSION

Read Romans 15:30–33

A few weeks ago, an evangelist we have known for several years preached at our church. He had always spoken practical truth that was relevant to his audience, but this time, there was a new power to his preaching that had never been evident before. Several months earlier, he and his wife had traveled to the island of St. Thomas to minister at a church. Upon their arrival, leaders from the congregation ushered them to a private place and announced they were going to pray for them. The group surrounded the couple and began to pour their hearts out to the Lord. The preacher admitted he was tired, but he had not realized how drained he was. He described the intercessory experience as revitalizing beyond his greatest expectations. His life was forever changed as he recognized the power that was infused into his being by this display of love. He explained how the simple, unselfish action of this group prompted him and his wife to sincerely commit to intercede for each other daily. The result has been a divine power in their ministry and an increased joy in their personal relationship.

In today's passage, we see that Paul understood the urgency and potential of intercessory prayer (v. 30). He admitted he was struggling, and urged his friends to pray for him. He appealed for much more than a casual routine request of God's blessings. He implored these people to focus on the character of the Lord Jesus and to pray for him with recognition of the love of the Spirit. He was confident that the result would be refreshing to his soul and to their relationship (v. 32).

Like the apostle Paul and our evangelist friend, your spouse experiences struggles, and needs more than a casual mention before God. Pray for him or her with the love and discernment of the Spirit. Through this consistent exercise, your relationship will also be refreshed.

BUT

Read James 1:5–9

As a result of our family ministry, we steadily receive emails, phone calls, and requests for appointments from people who want to know what to do in their particular marital dilemma. In response to them, we ask questions in order to gather as many relevant facts as we can. We pray over the information and compare it to principles from God's Word. We then share precepts and Scriptures that apply to their situation. We pray they will trust God by wholeheartedly responding to His truth. Sometimes, however, we receive swift acknowledgment of our answer that includes more personal scenarios preceded by "but" or "what if," implying they would like us to send an alternative idea or Scripture. Occasionally the additional information clarifies the problem and leads to further enlightenment from the Bible, but many times when the dialogue continues with repeated "buts," we conclude that the inquirers are not seeking wisdom from God. Rather, they are relying on their own wisdom in seeking various options from which to choose.

Today's passage from James discloses an incredible promise—abundant wisdom from God—just for the asking. It applies, however, to someone who genuinely admits his or her reasoning is inadequate and is ready to receive truth from the Lord. Verse six explains that the one who asks should be prepared to accept the answer in faith without hesitating, doubting, or considering alternatives. Someone who desires to contemplate the biblical answer along with other possibilities is exercising his own wisdom. Such a person is unqualified to receive the Lord's answer because he is still clinging to his own mindset, and will not embrace what God has for him (v.7). He is double-minded and unstable, flip-flopping from one perspective to the next (v. 8).

The Lord's abundant wisdom is available to the person who sets aside his personal will and determines to wholeheartedly trust God and receive what He reveals. Are you facing a marriage issue which requires divine wisdom? Confidently ask in faith, not doubting His answer as He graciously and generously directs those who sincerely seek His wisdom (5-6).

LET'S PARTY

Read Ecclesiastes 9:7–10

*F*all brings activity—ball games, after school activities, financial planning for the holiday season, and job deadlines. With all of this comes stress that can take the fun out of life! I can be so overwhelmed with problems and agendas that I forget to savor the juicy crunch of a Winesap apple on a crisp autumn day. Instead of drowning in the pressures, Ecclesiastes is telling me to sip on the hot apple cider. God desires that we enjoy the fruits of our labor (v 7). He has blessed us with food and drink, and He does not want us to lose sight of His generosity because of stress. He invites us to celebrate His gifts. On His party invitation, God describes how we are to dress (v. 8). He discourages drab apparel and requests that we be clothed in white, reflecting a fresh, clean, vibrant life. While we are dressing for the festivity, we should smell good, too. On all special occasions, the Jewish people anointed themselves with sweet smelling spices and oils. As we enjoy the blessings of this life, we should not only attract others by wearing fragrances, but by exuding the aroma of Jesus (v. 8). God's invitation specifically includes our spouse (v. 9). Enjoy your sweetheart now, while you can. Husbands, love your wife with every fiber of your being. Surprise her. Laugh with her. Dance. Wrap your arms around her and plant a big kiss on her, now. Wives, look into his eyes. Remind him of the reasons you love him. Meet him for lunch. Plan a candlelight dinner or a picnic. Life is fleeting. God warns us to enjoy our family while we can. This life will include hard work (v. 9), but we are to live every aspect with full strength and energy (v. 10). This lifetime is our chance to live with gusto. Let's party with God! Invite your mate to join you, and celebrate God's great goodness!

PEACE BE STILL

Read Mark 4:35–41

No one would sign up for a cruise if they knew that a fierce storm was brewing. Although the disciples are clueless, the omniscient Jesus is fully aware of the impending danger. But, exhausted from teaching all day, He decides to take a nap. Everything is fine until the storm suddenly hits and waves crash over the sides of the boat. The disciples' possessions, future, and finances are all sinking. As they focus their full attention on the storm, terror strikes the hearts of Jesus' followers. Like all of us, when we zone in on our difficulties and the apparent hopelessness of our situation, the disciples convince themselves that the Lord is not concerned about their trials. He is right there with them, but they accuse Him of abandoning them, of not caring. But Jesus is always in complete control. He does care. He stands, rebukes the wind, and commands peace and quiet.

We might ask, "Did Jesus know the storm was coming?" Yes. He is God! Could He have kept the storm from coming? Yes. He is God! Then why did He allow the raging waves to nearly swamp the boat? We find the answer when He questions the disciples about their fear and their faith (v. 40). Jesus allowed this storm to test their belief in Him. They had previously seen the miraculous works of the Savior, but still continued to doubt.

We might ask, "How could the disciples forget the miracles they had seen Jesus perform? How could they so easily doubt?" These are easy questions to ask until we examine our own lives and marriages and honestly admit how little faith we often demonstrate when we experience a storm. Like the disciples, we often forget it was just last week or last month when Jesus rescued us in the midst of a significant challenge. Reflect on the difficulties from which He has delivered you, both in everyday life and in your marriage. As you reflect, God is asking "Have you still no faith"? Whatever you face personally or as a family, Jesus is in the boat with you. He is in complete control, "Peace! Be still."

OCTOBER 20

REPEAT

Read Ephesians 5:25, 28, 33, and Colossians 3:19

I recently opened my email and noticed I had received the same online devotional twice. I thought, "Oh, that's odd." The next morning I received the same article in my email nine more times. I contacted the local server and website host that processes our bulk emails to find out why the repeats happened.

Sometimes God repeats messages in Scripture. When He tells us something once, it is important, but if He reiterates the same message, He is emphasizing its urgency. If He repeats the exact instruction multiple times, we desperately need to heed its contents.

One of God's recurring messages is addressed to husbands. He directly repeats it four times in the New Testament, and indirectly infers it numerous times in the Old Testament. The repetition is God's way of emphatically calling husbands to love their wives. In order for His plan for marriage to function, a wife needs to know that her husband loves her. He may habitually and regularly voice the words to her, but she can sense whether the message is a recorded duty from the brain or an expression of genuine delight from the heart.

God understands this dilemma because our praise to Him also takes the form of either duty or delight. When we sing a praise chorus or familiar hymn from memory without considering the wonder of His character that validates the words, the message is noisy static in His ears. When our hearts ponder His goodness and greatness as we sing, He receives our adoration, commitment, and true love. When a husband considers one of his wife's qualities—like her selfless service, her ability to make him laugh, or her commitment to believe in him— the words "I love you" convey a sincere and intense message from his heart. His beloved hears spontaneous delight rather than catalogued duty.

Take a few minutes to consider specific, admirable qualities in your mate and then express heartfelt messages of love to one another. Thank God for loving you and allowing you to be husband and wife.

R-RATED

Read Genesis 19:1–29

When our son Josh was in the second grade, he came home one day and told us about a classmate who bragged about the R-rated movies his dad allowed him to watch. I explained that exposure to such filth would eventually affect the boy's behavior. Josh confirmed my warning by telling us his friend used very foul language. Most parents understand this danger and restrict young children from exposure to ungodliness. Many of these same Christian parents, however, are not concerned about exposing themselves. They explain that they have an adult awareness and can tune out inappropriate language or behavior. They assert that they have enough self-control and respect for God to keep them from adopting such ungodly behavior themselves.

In today's passage, we see how Lot prospered in the midst of R-rated wickedness. He controlled his behavior enough that God sent angels to deliver him before the destruction of the city where he lived. He remained sensitive enough to God's ways that he recognized the angels that came as servants of God (v. 1). Lot stood firmly against the corrupt townsmen and bravely protected God's servants (v. 6). He was able to maintain his righteousness while surrounded with ungodliness, but his choice to live under the influence of sin cost him dearly. In a panic, when he was desperate to safeguard God's servants, he offered his own daughters to be molested in their place (v. 8). Eventually, he was forced to leave all his possessions to be destroyed (v. 25). In the process, Lot was strong enough to resist temptation himself, but he was not able to protect his wife from the temptation to glance back at the home he had given to her (v. 26). Finally his daughters—after giving him much wine—tricked him into committing incest with them (vv. 31–33). Lot's R-rated choices put his family at risk in ways that he never imagined.

God warns believers not to become entangled with the world and its influences. Heed this warning. The risks of an R-rated environment will cost our marriage and family in greater ways than we would ever want to pay.

SEASONING SOUP

Read Colossians 4:2–6

Today is damp and cloudy. The weather motivates me to reach to the back of my cabinet and pull out my large stock pot. Homemade vegetable soup warms my family up on a day like this. I start with large cans of tomatoes. I peel and chop potatoes, carrots, onions, and green peppers. Next I add several cans of green beans, lima beans, and corn. My pot is almost full when I add a tiny bay leaf, a small clove of garlic, a teaspoon of pepper, and a couple teaspoons of salt. The quantity of seasonings compared to the amount of vegetables is miniscule, but their potency brings vitality to the flavor.

Similarly, when a loved one makes ungodly choices or elects to participate in a sinful lifestyle, our outlook for their life becomes as dismal as a cloudy day. Verse five in today's passage reminds us to walk wisely in relation to people who are living outside of God's will. We need to be aware, however, of any opportunity to add warmth to their gray, confused life. The recipe for this encouragement is much like homemade soup. Verse six urges us to always speak with grace. Just like my pot of soup is filled with fresh vegetables, my conversations with struggling loved ones should be filled with the warmth, hope, and strength of the Lord. My confidence and peace with God should be the loving basis of every comment I make to them. This will only be possible if I am prepared with the required ingredients of prayer and thanksgiving (v. 2). In addition, God's recipe calls for our conversation to be seasoned with salt. Salt represents pure, penetrating, convicting truth that preserves life and halts corruption. The main thrust of our words should be grace, but sprinklings of convicting truth spoken in care and concern will help make the most of the time we invest in a loved one's life. Warm your marriage and family with conversation filled grace, but also seasoned with salt.

SOLO

Read Hebrews 13:5

The day had finally arrived. I had taken flying lessons and prepared the best I possibly could for months. When my instructor stepped out of the plane and said, "She's all yours," my heart began to beat furiously as I anticipated flying the J4 drag wheel airplane. I was only 16 years old. This was my solo day! It was totally up to me to take off, fly around the airfield, and land the aircraft by myself. Or was I really alone?

I nervously taxied down the runway and prepared to take off. I began to pray, "God please help me to make it back safe, I need You." At that moment, the Holy Spirit reminded me of God's wonderful promise to never leave me or forsake me. Comforted by that truth, I completed my solo flight. When I landed and headed back to the hangar, my father inquired, "Son, were you scared?" I answered, "Dad, I was a little afraid at first, but God gave me a promise. He said that He would be right there with me." Over the years, this verse and others like it have echoed in my mind when I faced a potentially fearful situation. God does not promise that everything will turn out the way we want it to, but He will be with us and will never leave His children in the midst of any tribulation or trial that we face.

In marriage, this promise is particularly comforting. Many husbands and wives go through times in their relationship when they feel rejected, lonely, and even sometimes unloved. They feel they are flying solo in their marriage. In these moments, however, they can rest assured that that they are not alone. Christians have the power of God resident within them. They have a Father who will hear their prayers, and can touch the heart of their mate to bring them back into the oneness they once experienced. Whatever you may be facing today, you are not flying solo!

THE FRAGRANCE OF A DELIGHTFUL WOMAN

Read Esther 2:3–4 and 8–12

A few years ago, one of my sons gave me a bottle of bath gel for Christmas. One night after I had enjoyed a leisurely bath using my gift, he breathed deeply and commented, "I can tell when Mama takes a bath because the whole house smells good." Even though he was only twelve years old, the fresh, penetrating scent made an impression on him.

God emphasizes the importance of fragrance in chapter two of Esther. Virgins from all over Persia had been gathered together in the palace at Shushan so that King Ahasuerus could choose a queen (vv. 3–4). Every maiden was taken through twelve months of intense beauty treatments. For the first six months, her body was continually bathed, rubbed, and polished. Oil of myrrh treatments were steamed into her skin as a natural astringent. By the end of that time, all impurities had been removed and her skin was completely fresh and soft. Over the next six months, cosmetic burners filled with sweet smelling spices were used to steam gentle fragrance into her body. By the end of the entire twelve months, the baby soft skin of the maidens was permeated with sweet delicate fragrance. The purpose of this lengthy regimen was to prepare each young lady for one night with the king. Obviously, smooth, lightly scented skin was very pleasing to the king and to any man. When Adam named Eve, he called her woman, which translates as "soft man." The difference between her smooth skin and his rugged skin attracted him. Today's Scriptures remind us of one of the little things that delight our husbands. Exercise the femininity that God designed for women by taking the time to be fresh, soft, and fragrant.

THE SECRET OF BECOMING QUEEN

Read Esther 2:12–17

Throughout time, women have pondered the best way to win the heart of the man of their dreams. Yesterday's devotion pointed out that men are delighted with soft, fragrant skin. The virgins who were competing to be selected as queen invested a full year in intense beauty treatment to prepare them for one night with the king (v. 12). Historians tell us that Esther was in competition with anywhere from 400 to 1,460 other young ladies who were each taking advantage of every luxury imaginable in order to make themselves the most attractive of them all (v. 13). They were presented with the finest fabrics and latest fashions in the kingdom. Each of them was concentrating on selecting their dream wardrobe, with an unlimited expense account. Each one of the maidens was "drop dead gorgeous," so what was it that influenced the king to love Esther above all the other women? What gave her the edge?

Verse 15 reveals that when it was time for Esther to choose her attire, she did not become consumed with the beautiful fashions or with fulfilling a desire for the "chance of a lifetime" wardrobe. Instead, but she consulted with the man who best understood the king. Whatever he felt would please the king the most is what Esther selected. Rather than concentrating on what she liked, she exhibited a humble, teachable spirit that was totally unselfish. She was more concerned about the king than she was about herself. This character trait granted her favor with everyone, including her competitors.

As husbands and wives, we can also delight and gratify our spouses as we seek to study their individual preferences. As we set aside our demands and find fulfillment in pleasing our mates, we will find favor and approval in their eyes.

WINNING FAVOR

Read Esther 2:9, 15, 17, 4:10–5:3, 7:1–5, and 8:7–8

Scripture teaches that Esther's husband—the king—is demanding, prideful, and impulsive. He kills people who irritate him! Esther has the task of telling him he has made a mistake and decreed an unjust law. Through this risky challenge, she gains her husband's favor. It is evident that she had a pleasing disposition because the Bible repeatedly explains how she wins the favor of not only those in authority over her (2:9), but also of her peers (2:15). God's word reveals aspects of Esther's character that win the favor of her husband. These traits are virtues that can help any person win the approval of their spouse, whether godly or ungodly.

Esther respects the advice of people who have wisdom. She complies with her uncle's admonition not to reveal her nationality (2:10). Also, rather than request attire and jewelry to increase her personal wealth, she seeks the advice of Hegai, the man who best understood the king's preferences (2:15). In addition, Esther yields to the integrity of her uncle's reasoning even though his instructions require her to risk her life (4:12–16).

As we observe Esther's actions, we see that she does not plot, scheme, or manipulate in order to get her way. Instead, she humbles herself before the Lord in a three day fast (4:16). She honors her husband by following the protocol for approaching royalty. When she approaches him, she does not lose control or panic. She does not rush or appear frantic. She prepares a banquet to show honor to him, then explains that she respects his time too much to bother him with trivial matters (7:4). She speaks the truth without accusing or criticizing her husband (7:3–4).

It is tempting to rush in and demand our rights as a spouse. Sharp, convincing arguments may technically prove that a mate foolishly made an unjust decision, but the outcome resulting from our "win" would not promote unity. In the story of Esther, we see the example God would have us follow. He uses humble, respectful, calm integrity to win the favor of a spouse (8:7–8).

THE TROAS MOMENT

Read 2 Corinthians 2:12–14

*A*rriving in Troas, Paul acknowledges that the Lord has opened a great door of opportunity for him to minister there (v. 12). He is ready to fulfill God's purpose in his life. He should be eager to settle into the work God has for him, but he declares he has no rest in his spirit (v. 13). He is so heavy with concern over the struggling believers in Corinth, and so anxious to hear the news Titus has about them, that he cannot give his attention to the ministry. Rather than waste time and energy going through the motions, Paul leaves for Macedonia to try to find Titus (v. 13).

Once Paul takes a leave of absence, he is able to shift his attention to God. Instead of remaining overwhelmed by the unknown status of his loved ones, he concentrates on God, who always, no matter what the situation, leads to triumph in Christ (v. 14). The "triumph" he refers to is a prestigious Roman ceremony in which a victorious general—with elaborate and festive celebration—displays the spoils of war. Paul uses this imagery to remind himself that God will be triumphantly victorious in the Corinth matter also. No matter what the situation is now, the final outcome will be victory. Jesus Christ is the victorious general with a powerful battle plan. He will always emerge with great displays of His sovereignty.

There may be a time when we, too, experience deep anxiety concerning the welfare of our spouse or family. It can be so great that we are unable to function effectively in the routine of life. I have a friend that labels this a "Troas moment." During such a time, we should follow Paul's example, temporarily setting our routine aside and focusing on the triumph of Jesus Christ. Our distress will be replaced with peace and confidence. We will be able to return to our responsibilities with renewed strength.

THE TRUTH ABOUT HATE

Read 1 Corinthians 13:4–8 and 1 John 2:9–11

I eagerly anticipated an appointment at a medical office that employed a friend whom I had not seen in several years. As we chatted, she mentioned that she had defended me when the receptionist described me as hateful. I was shocked and horrified because hate is such a strong word. When I prayed and considered the only time I had talked with the receptionist, I remembered that I had been consumed with worry about the health of my child. Medical records that were critical to his care had been misplaced, and I was irritated, impatient, and sharp in my conversation.

If hate is the opposite of love, an inversion of 1 Corinthians 13 expounds its definition. Hate is impatient and mean. Hate is jealous, boastful, and arrogant (v. 4). It is conceited, rude, and brash. Hate demands its rights, and is touchy, irritable, and resentful. Hate remembers mistakes and unfair, wrong treatment (v. 5). It is eager to hear about the failure of others (v. 6). Hate is negative and assumes the worst (v. 7). Relationships built around hate disintegrate under pressure (v. 8). I had to admit that varying shades of hate are alive within me, and affect my relationships.

In today's passage, the apostle John teaches that those who hate their brother as a pattern of life are not true believers walking in the light, but rather nonbelievers walking in darkness. When Christians manifest hateful attitudes toward someone else, they act like unbelievers living in the darkness of sin (vv. 9-10). How convicting! The message the receptionist conveyed about the lost records was actually an instrument God used to expose what was hidden in my heart. I was unaware that hate was the actual source of my rude reaction and I was behaving like an unbeliever.

Often, variations of hate surface in family relationships. We claim to love our spouse, but we express emotions in a hateful way. I am grateful God exposes sin in my life so that I can confess it and walk as a child of God should. Have your reactions conveyed arrogant or unloving communication toward your spouse?

WHAT IF?

Read Genesis 24:1–9

*A*braham completely trusted his servant's ability and loyalty. He was in charge of everything that Abraham owned (v. 2). Abraham stressed the urgency of his request (v. 3), but the responsibility was so heavy that the servant could only cite reasons not to enthusiastically obey. The excuses, however, were not facts about the difficulty or danger of the journey. They were not details that proved a conflict in schedule. They were speculations, "what if's," that overwhelmed his sense of judgment (v. 5). I have found that when I am faced with an urgent and difficult task, in which success is dependent upon another person's response, I am also flooded with convincing "what if's" that overpower my desire to obey. I find it heartrending to speak the truth in love when I fear rejection, ridicule, or failure. The risk of an irrational response from someone I care about can quickly quench my zeal to reach out and help.

Abraham's response to the draining power of speculations offers me strength to move forward in difficult realms. He set a boundary on the assignment by warning the servant not to take Isaac back to the old country (v. 6). He reminded the servant of a specific but similar instance in the past when God proved He was in control (v. 7). The servant would not be scheming and planning in his own power, but would be dependent upon the sovereignty and faithfulness of Almighty God. Abraham relieved the pressure of the urgent task by releasing his servant from the oath if the young woman failed to comply with God's plan (v. 8). The servant was responsible for his own obedience before his master, not the response of someone else. In light of these principles, we, like the servant, can proceed in complete dependence upon the Lord (vv. 9, 12–14). Are there "what if's" you are facing in regard to a request your spouse has given? Abraham relieved some pressure by setting boundaries on his expectations. Discuss possible parameters for your challenge and, like Abraham, trust God for the outcome.

WORDS IN THE WIND

Read Job 6:1–3, 14, 25–26

ob was devastated. He hated what was happening to him and he desperately needed an emotional release. When he was with his friends, he poured out the hopeless confusion that was within his heart and cursed the day he was born. His speech expressed everything as negative and depressing. His friends felt it was their responsibility to help him by correcting what he said. They each presented arguments to prove how wrong he was (v. 25). This was not what Job needed. He needed someone who would comfort rather than correct his explosive words. Deep down, Job knew his words were ridiculous. He even described his speech as nothing but wind (v. 26). He explained that what a despairing man needs is kindness. Kindness will steer a hurting person toward the Lord, whereas a lack of it will cause an upset person to forsake his fear of God (v. 14). If Job's friends really wanted to help, they would have ignored the rash words and empathized with his pain.

When our spouse is faced with crushing, hard to handle circumstances, he or she may react like Job and explode with unreasonable, rash remarks (v. 3). We should view their speech as the wind and let it sweep right by us. At this point, it does no good to refute angry or hopeless words as wrong. The despairing mate needs understanding and compassion. The Bible tells us that when Mary and Martha were heartbroken over the death of Lazarus, Jesus did not respond with immediate theological explanations. Rather, He acknowledged their pain and wept with them (John 11:35). During times of devastation, a husband or wife needs the freedom to release emotions to a partner who unconditionally accepts and desires to comfort them. Remember to be empathetic when your spouse fills the wind with emotionally charged words. Rather than pointing out their faulty logic, choose to lovingly respond to their pain.

GOOD LUCK CHARM

Read 1 Samuel 4:1–11

*I*t was only after they had been overwhelmingly defeated by the Philistines that the Israelites woke up and realized they had overlooked their most important ally, God. They immediately fetched the ark of the covenant—which represented the presence of God—to come to their rescue.

Israel, like the majority of American families, acknowledged God. Their lives, however, were not centered on Him. Most Americans would admit that God exists, claim that we are one nation under Him, acknowledge that God has some control over things, and that He is bigger than we are. But most Americans run their own lives, do their own thing, and plunge forward to solve their own problems without acknowledging God. Yet when tragedy strikes—such as a financial reversal, life threatening health condition, a child on drugs, or national catastrophe like 9/11—we recognize our desperate need for God. Church attendance and prayer increased dramatically following the tragedy of 9/11, but within a few years, God was once again overlooked in everyday life. Like the Israelites, many Christians treat Him like a good luck charm. When the Israelites found themselves in trouble and needed increased power, they performed the ritual of retrieving the ark (v. 3). Similarly, when we seek the benefits of God only when we are in the midst of a crisis, we are treating Him as our good luck charm. But God is not fooled. He knows the intent of our hearts. He knew the Israelites did not care about Him; they only cared about gaining victory over their circumstances. When the ark of the covenant was brought into their camp, they cheered enthusiastically (v. 5). They assumed God's presence had returned, and their victory would now be won. How wrong they were! The defeat was disastrous (v. 10-11).

Don't wait for a crisis or a breakdown in your marriage to call upon God. Seek His face today. Show reverence by daily seeking Him and not just His benefits. God is not a good luck charm. He is God Almighty!

INTO THE MIND OF JESUS

Read Philippians 2:2–8

The defensive coordinator for our favorite college football team is regarded as one of the best in the nation. Year after year, he consistently produces a defense that ranks in the top ten. During the final four minutes of a nationally televised game, the opposing offense, which had been stopped all night, hit a few plays and scored twice to win the game. Media replayed those particular plays repeatedly as they analyzed and criticized the decisions of the defensive coordinator. They explained what he did, and why he did it. The audience and fans responded by attacking the coach for his "faulty" decision making. The plays he had called were not what they appeared to the public. He had correctly adapted to complications and alignments in the offense that outsiders overlooked. The offense, however, had executed with superior athleticism. Yet he, the expert, was mercilessly bombarded with criticism for something he had handled wisely.

Sometimes, like the media or passionate fans, a spouse can react based on surface information. The typical human reaction is to be defensive, but as Christians, we are urged to respond with the mind of Christ. Jesus, more than just an expert in His field, is equal with God Himself. He set aside the glory of God in heaven, where He was worshipped for who He truly was (v. 6), in order to submit to the misunderstanding and repeated false accusations of sinful people. Paul reveals the secret that enabled Jesus to deal graciously with the gross misunderstandings. Christ adopted the mind of a bond servant (v. 7). By definition, a bond servant completely assigns all personal rights to the authority and will of another person. In this permanent relationship of servitude, the slave's will is absolutely surrendered to the will of another. The mindset of Jesus and the basis of His decisions was, "It's not about me, it's about the Father." To handle criticism and false accusations, we need to think "It's not about me, it's about Jesus." When falsely accused by an irritated spouse, pause and remind yourself to adopt the Christ-like attitude, "It's not about me, it's about honoring God in our marriage."

OUT OF MY MIND

Read Philippians 2:3–5

We are acquainted with a woman who incessantly gripes either at her husband or about him. No matter what he does, she is irritated and she grumbles about it to the people around her. Even a kind gesture from him can evoke harsh criticism because she views any minor interruption as a major, unreasonable inconvenience. She feels her complaints are justified because she can back them with specific reasoning. Even though her arguments are logical, however, the premise they stem from is her own self-centeredness. Her perspectives focus on how everything affects her. As a result, she makes her loved ones miserable. In return, they make every effort to steer clear of her.

This extreme behavior emphasizes the significance and need for verses three and four of today's passage. They not only instruct us to avoid concentrating on our own interests, but call us to shift our concern to others' interests, to the point that we consider them more significant than our own. This is the attitude of humility. This is the mind of Christ. Verse three specifically implores each person to regard others as more significant in every activity. I am challenged to consider the premises on which I base my own reasoning and decisions. If my attitude is humility, then the motivation for every decision I make will be based on the character of Jesus. I will concentrate on the truth of Jesus, and respond not to the situation, but to who He is. Tim Keller says, "The essence of gospel humility is not thinking more of myself or thinking less of myself, it is thinking of myself less. Gospel humility is not needing to think about myself." [69] Humility requires stepping out of my mind, and into the mind of Christ. Are your complaints about marriage based on how trivial annoyances inconvenience you? Relieve the misery by delighting in truths about Jesus Christ.

POUR OUT YOUR HEART

Read 1 Samuel 1:1–18

Hannah faced a dilemma common to many Christian women today. She was harassed by "the other woman." The "other woman" could be an ex-wife, a mother-in-law, a neighbor, a teacher, a boss, or any female rival that endeavors to torment you. Hannah's "other woman," Peninnah, was her husband's other wife. In an attempt to prove her superiority, Peninnah mercilessly degraded Hannah for her inability to conceive. This vindictive woman repeatedly frustrated Hannah until she was so consumed with feelings of disgrace, inadequacy, and worthlessness that she could not eat. She felt so defeated that all she could do was cry. Hannah's husband, Elkanah, responded by showing her double affection and attention. He could not understand why she was stressed to such an overwhelming degree. Her agony was beyond Elkanah's comprehension, and she could not explain it to him.

In Hannah's case, she could not avoid Peninnah, nor could she reason with her. And, her hurt was so deep that she could not find comfort in her husband's love. Finally, after years of torment, Hannah removed herself from the presence of her family and poured her heart out to the Lord at the temple (v. 9-10, 15). She allowed herself to freely express her emotions and wept uncontrollably. She was real. She did not hide any of her feelings. She told Eli, the priest, that she cried to the Lord out of her deep pain and anguish. Once Hannah completely released her problem to God, she experienced relief and was able to eat, worship, and proceed with everyday life (v 18).

Jesus understands our agony, even when our loved ones cannot relate. He is ever ready to receive our problems and work them out for our good. He came to set us free from the captivity of emotional torment and stress. Are there feelings of despair, either individually or as a couple, that you need to release to the Lord?

FORGOTTEN PRAYERS

Read 1 Samuel 1:10–20

I recently heard a pastor glorifying God by detailing major ministry accomplishments directly linked to church members' specific prayers. As I listened, I recounted the times my prayer partner and I earnestly cried out to God for what we considered "impossible" requests in the lives of our children. The Lord has answered so many of those prayers—not in the way I would have devised—but according to His sovereign grace and wisdom. Those memories inspired me to increase the intensity of my prayers for difficult, God-given tasks that are before me right now.

In today's passage, Hannah was uncontrollably crying out to the Lord (v. 10). For years she had prayed for a son, but now the prayers had reached a point of such intensity that she was consumed by them. After Eli spoke to her, she surrendered her burden to God in complete trust. She left with a different attitude. When she gave birth to her son, Hannah named him Samuel to acknowledge that, "I asked the Lord for him" (v. 20).

As I've studied these verses, God has used them to remind me of prayers I brought to Him many years ago, when I was clueless about His power. As a youth, I attended a Christian camp where the counselors taught that it was important to pray for your future husband. I thought that was a great idea, so I prayed for a godly guy who would love the Lord. I also asked if he could be a football player, so my dad would be enthusiastic about him. When I was a junior in high school, Sam asked me to the football banquet. My dad was excited, and I was stepping into the blessed, unknown future adventure of marrying a preacher. God has reminded me that I asked Him for my own Samuel, even though I didn't know it at the time. The power of my request was in the One prayed to, not in the elegance of the one praying. Although I had forgotten about the prayer, Jehovah God was faithful to answer. Discuss any forgotten prayers that God has answered in your life and marriage. Praise Him for His faithfulness.

Surrendering Your Children

Read 1 Samuel 1:24–2:11

We now officially have an "empty nest." Adam and Josh are married and have started their own families. Philip graduated from college and lives in Lexington, Kentucky. Daniel is the IT director at a company in Lynchburg, Virginia. We really miss our sons, and I have this longing to be where they are so I can make sure everything is okay.

I can recall other times I had to "let go" of the boys. I remember the first time Sam and I went out for a couple of hours and left Josh, our first baby, with his grandparents. All I could think about was, "What if he needs me and I'm not there?" Leaving him in the church nursery was difficult, although not quite as traumatic because I knew someone would come and get me if he needed me.

One of the toughest experiences was watching the nurses wheel one-year-old Philip down the hospital corridor into emergency surgery. That day, it felt like our hearts as parents underwent surgery without anesthesia. Then there was the time when Adam was on a mission trip in India, and we received the call telling us he was very sick and in the hospital. We, just like Hannah, had to once again release our child into the sovereign hands of the Lord. Also, I remember when we took Adam to freshman orientation at college and he muttered, "Don't you dare cry, Mom. I have to have my picture taken as soon as you leave." I wondered how Hannah could take her very young son and leave him at the temple with Eli, knowing she would only see him occasionally. As I read her prayer in chapter two of today's reading, I realized afresh that the only peaceful way to surrender our children in the different phases and events of life is through worshipping the Lord and wholeheartedly acknowledging His sovereignty. Our nest is empty, but by rejoicing in the goodness of God, we are enjoying this new phase of life.

A DOUBLE SCOOP

Read Isaiah 26:3 and Romans 8:28

When I was a small boy, I considered myself privileged when my dad took me to High's ice cream shop. Our family did not have a lot of money, so this was a special treat. As we walked across town to the ice cream shop, my imagination soared. I would envision the different flavors of ice cream lined up in the paper barrels located behind the glass counter. When we finally arrived, I immediately ran over to select my favorite flavor. The sales clerk promptly asked, "Do you want a single or double scoop?" I looked up at my dad with hope in my eyes, and he said, "Why don't you get a double." This was rare and unexpected. My taste buds began to anticipate the creamy goodness as I thought about choosing not just one flavor, but two.

Our heavenly Father offers us not just one scoop of peace, but a double! In Isaiah 26:3, He promises to give His children "perfect peace," which translated in Hebrew is "Shalom, Shalom" or "Peace, Peace." To receive this peace, however, there are several things we must do. First, our minds must be "stayed" on God. The word "stay" means to lean or meditate on. We must continually think about God and depend on Him. Second, we must trust Him in whatever circumstance we are facing. God wants us to understand that even when we experience unexplained trials, He is still in control and will work out everything for our good (Rom. 8:28). If this isn't enough, God also promises to "keep" us in this state of double peace. The word "keep" refers to a garrison of soldiers who continually guard something or someone. God will continually protect our peace if we focus our minds on Him and trust Him. What a wonderful promise He offers to each of His children. Is something in your marriage causing you to fret? Are you worried about the future of your marriage and family? Order up a double scoop of peace today.

LISTENING AND LOVE

Read Psalm 116:1–2

One of the reasons I love the Lord so much is because I know He always listens to me. No matter how extreme or trivial, distressed or excited, senseless or logical my communication is, He listens. And, He not only listens, but bends forward to intently listen, proving that what I have to say matters to Him. When my children were little and I was busy in an activity, they would press my cheeks between their small hands and turn my face toward them to insure they had my undivided attention. The Lord understands that I need His undivided attention also.

In the realm of counseling, much of the time spent by psychologists and psychiatrists amounts to listening to their patients unwind and bear their innermost feelings. The patients are grateful, and like the psalmist, continue to call upon the one who listens. In marriage, many affairs slowly develop when an unhappy or worried spouse expresses frustration to a co-worker who is willing to listen. The spouse finds relief and comfort, and often becomes emotionally attached to the listener. In these situations, the spouse may gradually fall in love with the co-worker, simply because he or she took time to give full attention to their concerns.

It is very important that you listen to your mate because he or she will grow in love for you as you offer your undivided attention. When you focus on your husband or wife by listening with both your eyes and ears, you show interest, concern, and support, proving that your spouse is a priority. Just as I continue to call upon the Lord because He listens with an understanding ear, your mate will continue to share his or her heart with you and love you because you listen.

CHOSEN

Read 1 Peter 2:9

I vividly remember playing dodge ball in elementary school. Two students were chosen as captains of teams that would frantically throw a big rubber ball at each other until only one person was left untouched by the ball. The skills required to succeed in the game were speed, good reflexes, and a strong arm to throw the ball. As the captains selected their teams, the students who met those qualifications were chosen first. The rest watched helplessly, desperately hoping they would be picked next! As the choices of players dwindled, you could see that neither captain desired any of those who remained. Unfortunately, the memory of an event such as this becomes deeply engraved in many people's minds. The thought of not being chosen haunts them for the rest of their life!

In his book *Classic Christianity*, Bob George states, "The most destructive force in the human experience is living under conditional love and acceptance."[70] The pain of this relationship dynamic lingers in the hearts of many individuals, and the ache continues to throb in their souls. One experience that will erase the hurt and vindicate the life of a person who feels rejected is the deliberate decision by someone else who says, "I choose you." God made a purposeful choice to select Israel as His chosen people (Isa. 43:20). Today's passage reminds us that the phrase "chosen people," which at one time only applied to Israel, is now used by God to describe all believers! How exciting to be chosen to be His bride, to be unconditionally loved and accepted by Him forever! Marriage brings with it the wonderful experience of being specifically selected by another person. Our mates see us as so special that they make a conscious decision to spend the rest of their life with us. Look at your spouse and say, "I chose you!"

CLIMB A TREE

Read James 1:5

When I was a young boy, there was a huge pecan tree beside our house that seemed to be two hundred feet tall. Since it was too big around to climb, I would slide out of my second story window, scoot across the tin roof, and scramble onto a large branch. I would carefully crawl across it to the tree trunk, and vertically ascend up to the highest point. From there, I could see all across town.

In J.R.R. Tolkien's classic fantasy, *The Hobbit*, a hobbit and some dwarves are lost in an ancient forest called "Mirkwood." It is so dense that they can't see the blue sky. Desperate to find their way out, the dwarves send Bilbo (the hobbit) up the trunk of a massive old tree to the top. From there, he could look for a reference point to see which way they should go. When he gets there, Bilbo is dazzled by the brilliant blue sky and the sunlight, but he remembers his purpose. He gets his bearings, shimmies back down the tree, and leads the group to safety.

Many husbands feel like Bilbo and the dwarves. They are lost in the woods and can't see which way to go. To get their bearings and obtain God's perspective, they need to climb the tree of wisdom. The Lord graciously promises wisdom to all those who ask. Seeing life from His viewpoint clears up any distortion we may face in our marriage, our finances, or other aspects of life. When we take God up on His offer, we begin to see the blue sky and feel the fresh breezes of His discernment. If you sense that you are lost in the forest of life—confused about which direction to proceed—climb the tree of God's wisdom and receive His fresh vision.

CLOGGED UP

Read Ephesians 4:29–32

*D*ebbie frequently comes to me and says these dreaded words, "Sam, I hate to tell you this, but the toilet is clogged up." I know that it's my unpleasant duty to retrieve the plunger, follow the stench to the clogged commode, and attempt to plunge until all debris flushes down the drain. When plunging doesn't work, the next step is to go to the store, purchase a drain cleaner, pour it in the toilet, wait several hours or even a day, and then plunge again. The job is nasty, but if we want to eliminate odor and keep things flowing smoothly, it must be done.

Unfortunately, some marriages are like a clogged toilet. For days, weeks, or even years, the garbage and debris of corrupt words (bitterness, slander, anger, and clamor) have been dumped into the relationship (v. 29). As a result, the Holy Spirit is stifled and clogged, and communication no longer flows smoothly (v. 30). The marriage begins to decay and stink. If ignored, the stench intensifies. Something has to be done. Every Christian couple has access to plungers and drain cleaners that can clear the air and pipes, but they must be purposefully retrieved and appropriated. Words that build up or encourage the hearer minister grace to the flow of communication. The speaker—the spouse who decides to remedy the problem—must purposefully retrieve kind, forgiving words of hope and affirmation from his or her heart, and then deliver them to their troubled mate (v. 32). Once the words are spoken, the speaker may have to back off and allow the cleansing grace to take effect before plunging in with additional kindness and affirmation. Unleash the power of the Holy Spirit. Let your forgiving words reflect a heart that is in love with God. His grace cleanses, heals, and comforts. Communication can flow smoothly again.

WINNING THE ARGUMENT

Read 1 Corinthians 1:10–11 and 2:1–5

I heard on the news today about a Hollywood couple who filed for divorce after 10 years of marriage. Apparently, they had differences in religious views and they disagreed on vacation spots. Their differences grew to contentions, eventually leading to separation and divorce. Today's passage talks about a similar scenario concerning a group of Christians (1:11). These believers were divided by differences of opinions. Proving their perspective was superior had become the intense goal. Winning the argument was more important than rejoicing in the victory of Jesus Christ their Lord.

Sometimes, I catch myself being extremely intent on proving I am right about the most trivial fact. I waste precious energy and delve into elaborate detail, just because I want my husband to recognize that I am right and he is mistaken. For example, I might want to prove that we received a phone call on Wednesday instead of Thursday, or that I was the one who picked up the dry cleaning last time. I may be right, or I may be forgetting the detail that proves me wrong, but winning a trivial argument is not worth the cost of division. Paul urges the contentious believers to refocus and join together in thoughts of the truth (1:10). He reminds them that when he is with them, he does not concentrate on their differences, but he determines to know Christ and His sacrifice (2:2). He does not argue using human reasoning and persuasive techniques, but allows the Spirit of God to control him (2:4). He encourages all believers not to place our faith in our own reasoning and theatrical abilities, but in the power of God. If there are contentions in your marriage, follow Paul's admonition and shift your attention and purpose back to the person of Jesus Christ. Determine to know Him, and the personal benefits of His death on the cross.

DEALING WITH DEPRESSION – PHYSICAL EXHAUSTION

Read 1 Kings 19:1–18

epression is recognized as one of the greatest problems in our culture. Almost one in ten people struggle with it, and fifteen percent of depressed individuals will commit suicide. Everyone, at some point in their life, will be affected by depression.[71]

Winston Churchill called depression a "black dog" that followed him all of his life. Abraham Lincoln described his depression, "I am now the most miserable man living. If what I feel were equally distributed to the whole human family, there would not be one cheerful face on the earth. Whether I shall ever be better I cannot tell; I awfully forebode I shall not. To remain as I am is impossible; I must die or be better, it appears to me."[72] Even one of the greatest preachers who ever lived, Charles Spurgeon said, "I find myself frequently depressed, perhaps more so than any other person here."[73]

We see in today's passage that Elijah had just won a great victory over the prophets of Baal, when fire fell from heaven and consumed the burnt sacrifice on Mount Carmel. When he returned to Jezreel, however, he received a death threat from Jezebel (v. 2). Elijah became so depressed that he went into the wilderness to hide, sat under a juniper tree, and asked God to take his life (v. 4). What was God's cure for Elijah's depression?

The Lord sent an angel to Elijah to refresh him with some food, water, and needed rest (vv. 5-8). Simply put, God knew that Elijah needed some R &R ... rest and relaxation. While there are situations where professional help is needed, many times the remedy for depression can be as simple as getting a good night's sleep and eating a nutritious meal. Does depression cause you to withdraw from your spouse and family? Does it zap energy that you could otherwise devote to your loved ones? Do you need to be refreshed with some R & R?

Dealing with Depression – Loneliness

Read 1 Kings 18:7, 13, 19:1–18; Psalm 46:10

One reason for Elijah's depression was physical exhaustion. God's cure was to provide him with some needed R&R. Depression can also be caused, however, by upsetting circumstances that lead to emotional loneliness. Sometimes, when a spouse just doesn't understand, we can be left feeling all alone. A spiritual high followed by a seemingly drastic turn of events can cause the heart and emotions to follow, which in turn can affect our ability to reason. It was the alarming news of Jezebel threatening to kill Elijah that led him into despair (v. 2). Instead of reflecting on the recent victories that God had wrought, he immediately withdrew and had a pity party. Elijah's emotions were twisted in knots! He was unable to minister to anyone. He felt so alone that he complained to God that he was the only prophet left and they (Jezebel and Ahab) were seeking to take his life (v. 10). Of course, this was not true because Elijah had just conferred with Obadiah, who had taken 100 prophets and hidden them in caves (18:7, 13).

What is God's solution? He instructs Elijah to go out and stand on the mountain before Him (vv. 11–12). As Elijah does so, he experiences fierce wind, an earthquake, and fire. These are all dramatic signs announcing that the presence of God is imminent. It is like hearing a siren before the fire truck arrives. Yet it is not until Elijah hears a faint whisper—quiet and soft—that he knows he is in God's presence. This is a fresh revelation of the Lord! As God directly ministers to Elijah's soul, He restores within him a peace that passes all understanding.

When you are emotionally spent and feel there is no one who is sympathetic with your plight, you, like Elijah, will be unable to effectively minister to your spouse or loved ones. Separate from activity and stand before the Lord and wait (Ps. 46:10). Know that He controls all of nature, all of the world. Allow Him to speak refreshment into your soul. He will exchange the darkness of depression for the light of His peace! You will be fortified to once again lovingly serve your family.

DEALING WITH DEPRESSION – FOCUS

Read 1 Kings 19:1–18

*I*n order to overcome depression that had been intensified by physical exhaustion and emotional loneliness, God provides Elijah with some R & R and a fresh revelation of His presence (see Nov. 12 and 13). But Elijah also faces spiritual depression. The devil, a master strategist and tactician, knows how to attack us, where to attack us, and when to attack. Even though Elijah had just experienced a great victory over the prophets of Baal, he allowed the devil to minimize his faith and maximize his foe (Jezebel). The enemy used the fear of what might happen to overwhelm him. The devil sometimes maximizes obstacles in a spouse's life that bring him or her, like Elijah, to a point of debilitating despair. The defeated partner has a tendency to withdraw and become consumed with hopelessness.

The devotion from November 13 describes how God uses a fresh revelation of Himself to lift depression. The Lord, however, does not stop there. Once Elijah refocuses on Him and his faith is restored, God continues to shift the prophet's focus away from Jezebel's threat by assigning a new task. He asks him to go into the wilderness and anoint Hazael as king over Syria. Someone once asked the famous psychiatrist Carl Menninger what to tell a person who is experiencing deep depression. To many people's surprise he stated, "Lock the door behind you, go across the street, find somebody that's in need, and do something to help them."[74] This is great advice. When we get our eyes off of ourselves and onto someone else in need, we are then carrying out the great command to love our neighbor as our self. It is then that the debilitating fear of what might happen is replaced with love!

Has a threat or obstacle consumed you with worry to the point that you have emotionally withdrawn from your spouse? Look to the Scriptures and remind yourself of the sovereign love of God, then use your renewed energy to display an act of kindness to your mate or someone in need.

AVOID A RELAPSE

Read Luke 11:24-26

ornography is a rampant problem that severely damages marriages. Spouses are devastated when they discover their mates regularly find sexual stimulation from Internet sites, phone sex, or videos. Many began the practice at a young age and assumed marital relations would override the urge. Wrong! This sinful habit is addictive. The chains of this bondage are extremely difficult to break, but Christ—who has conquered the power of sin—sets captives free. The one who genuinely wants help can incorporate practical biblical principles to defeat the demonic influence, but the path to freedom requires genuine repentance, accountability, and consistent, determined effort. One resource we like to suggest is a website that offers a variety of extensive Bible studies, each geared for whatever addictive behavior an individual is struggling to overcome. We receive emails notifying us each time he or she completes a lesson. We are thrilled because the daily reports are filled with gratitude and awe for the Lord. When the notifications become inconsistent or stop completely, we become alarmed. The danger of relapse is imminent.

The principles from today's Scripture apply to the precariousness of the situation. Although perverted sexual habits are not evidences of demonic possession, the devil efficiently utilizes them in his war to destroy marriages. Some individuals on the path to recovery become accustomed to the freedom and let their guard down. Other activities gradually overshadow daily worship and Bible study. They pray less for protection and cease to diligently follow biblical guidelines that brought them strength. The enemy strategically tempts them in their weakened state with an innocent glance at a provocative billboard or scene in a movie, and the door for re-entry is open, only this time the attack is even stronger, leading to deeper bondage than before. The setback inevitably re-opens marital wounds.

Have you applied biblical principles to a detrimental habit and seen the power of Christ rescue your marriage? Never cease to praise Him for His power to overcome sin. Be careful to avoid a relapse by continuing to fervently exercise the spiritual disciplines He used to deliver you.

LIGHT THE APPROACH

Read 1 Corinthians 1:1–10

Dealing with people who know nothing of the grace and goodness of the Lord can be a stressful ordeal because their perspective is distorted. Their hope is limited without Christ; they trust only themselves. As a result, they often feel compelled to control and manipulate for their own advantage. Loving and respecting them can be a complicated challenge. However, dealing with Christians who are divisive and selfish is much more frustrating because they should know better. For example, a number of our acquaintances and friends are employed by the same locally owned business. We are amazed at how many of them continually feel harassed by a Christian co-worker who happens to be a leader in her church. This woman pressures herself to prove her value by demeaning fellow employees. She nitpicks and blames others for problems, but refuses to help with the solution. Her attitude is decidedly un-Christ like, but those who confront her end up working in increased tension. They eventually transfer or accept another job.

In today's passage, we see the apostle Paul facing a similar challenge. The believers in Corinth were striving with each other, even suing each other. They were rationalizing their wrongs. He had to confront them, but before he urged them to repent, he determined to see them from God's perspective. He took time to remind himself and the erring people of their position in Christ (v. 2). He expressed joy in what God had done for them (v. 4). He reinforced his declarations by reminding them of the riches and power of Christ and the spiritual blessings that belonged to them as Christians (vv. 4–7). He reminded them that God would strengthen them to live a blameless, victorious life (vv. 8–9). Only after he confirmed that he believed in them and their future did he urge them to consider their errors and to pursue God's ways (v. 10). The key to influencing straying Christians is not in the delivery of the confrontation, but in the tone and focus. We would do well to follow Paul's example, approaching struggling believers by shining the light of the glorious truth of God's undeserved blessings. Is someone who claims to be a Christian exhibiting ungodly behavior that makes your life difficult? Talk with your spouse about ways you can respond by applying today's passage.

GRACE AND PEACE

Read Philippians 1:2 and Acts 22:6–10

While writing his letter to the Philippian church, the apostle Paul is sitting in a jail cell, possibly awaiting death. He hasn't seen the people at Philippi for four long years. As he begins to pen his letter, he opens with the words, "Grace to you and peace." As you read his writings, it becomes obvious that Paul never tires of using this greeting. He had never gotten over his conversion on the Damascus road where Jesus came to him and gloriously redeemed him through His marvelous grace (Acts 22:6–10). Remembering that he is unworthy of salvation, Paul often describes himself as the worst of all sinners (1 Tim. 1:15.) Grace is one of his favorite words to meditate upon, to write about, and to use in writing to his brothers and sisters in Christ.

Interestingly, Paul links peace with grace. These words seem to be inseparable in his vocabulary. Peace always follows grace! He wanted all the churches to understand that God's peace could only come after first experiencing God's grace. No matter what sins have been committed, peace is the birthright of the child of God who has experienced His grace.

Like the relationship between Jesus and His bride, marriage requires grace before there can be true peace. Spouses must first experience the saving grace of Jesus Christ before they can have true peace with God and manifest those qualities to one another. Through the empowering grace of God, each marriage partner is enabled to continually enrich the relationship with love, forgiveness, and reconciliation. Have you experienced the saving grace of Jesus which brings empowering grace into your marriage? If so, peace with God and your spouse is the wonderful result that you, like Paul, will never grow weary of talking about!

THE BIT AND DRILL

Read 2 Corinthians 1:1–9

As I got out of my truck to enter the church where I was preaching, a strong wind slammed the door shut on my left index finger. I immediately opened the door and saw my fingernail turning black and blue as my finger throbbed intensely. Having only fifteen minutes before preaching, I began to pray and ask God for relief. Thankfully I felt no pain while I preached in all four services, but as soon as I finished speaking, my hand began to ache unbearably. Before going to the doctor the next morning, I told my son how my dad would take an electric drill with a very fine bit and make a hole in the smashed nail to relieve the pressure. He laughed and said, "You had better check that out with the doctor." When the doctor looked at my finger, he instructed his nurse to bring him a Bunsen burner and a paper clip! He heated the end of the paper clip until it glowed red and then applied the hot, sterile wire onto my fingernail, burning a hole through it! As the wire penetrated my nail, I winced in agony. But the pressure was immediately relieved, and the pain and throbbing subsided.

In today's passage, the apostle Paul told the Corinthian church that he was stressed beyond measure (v. 8). He was under such strain and tension that he despaired for his life! How could Paul survive under this weight? He did not worry or trust in himself, rather he trusted God (v. 9). God was his bit and drill!

The pressures of marriage and family can cause intense stress. How we deal with it will determine whether our relationship remains peaceful or throbbing. Relief from the trials and tribulations of life comes from trusting the drill bit of God (v. 4). His methods can appear alarming at first, but His results offer relief (v. 9). Take the daily strain and tension of your marriage to God, our great pressure reliever!

Turn the Light On!

Read John 3:20–21 and 1 John 1:5–10

When I sort laundry and load the washing machine I need a bright, well-lit room so I can detect stains and apply pre-wash. When I sweep and mop the floor, I open the blinds and turn the lights on so I can spot dirt hidden in the corners. John 3:20 describes evil-doers or unbelievers by explaining that they hate and avoid light because it exposes the "dirt" of their deeds.

Roy Hession explains that John 3:21 describes the opposite of someone who practices evil, not as someone who practices *good*, but someone who practices *truth*, someone who acknowledges truth about his or her depraved condition.[75] Rather than avoiding light, this person comes to light so that his deeds may be exposed. Jesus, the light of the world, exposes the dirt in our lives so we can be cleansed.

If Christians act as though they are enjoying fellowship with God when they are actually defeated by discouragement or controlled by secret sin, they are not practicing truth, but are acting as unbelievers, walking in darkness (I John 1:6). When the light of Jesus exposes error in the life of a believer and that person denies it by making excuses, he is deceiving himself and not practicing the truth. When a Christian justifies sin as "not that bad," he, like an unbeliever, calls God a liar (v. 10). However, a Christian who practices truth brings his life before the light of Jesus and agrees with God concerning his sin (vv. 7, 9).

None of us will be a perfect spouse. We will at times fail to exhibit the love of Christ to our mate. In those times, when sin is exposed, avoid the pretense of denial and excuses. If you are a child of light (a believer), walk as a child of light by practicing truth. Be transparent and freely admit the wrong. Is there any bad attitude or action you need to admit to God or your mate?

HUMPTY DUMPTY

Read Psalm 42

"Humpty Dumpty sat on the wall, Humpty Dumpty had a great fall, all the king's horses and all the king's men, couldn't put Humpty together again." In Psalm 42, King David is crushed in spirit. He has fallen off the wall, and he passionately longs to be made whole once again.

According to the nursery rhyme, a valiant effort is made to put Humpty back together. The king's horses, a symbol of strength and power, are summoned first. Some people look to power as the healing balm of a distraught life, but they discover that achievement, wealth, and the world's success offer only brief relief, but not lasting comfort. The king's men are called upon next, but they are powerless to heal. The nursery rhyme ends without hope.

The enemy rejoices and taunts us when we are broken (vv. 9–10). David fights the enemy of his soul, however, by reminding himself of specific examples of God's steadfast love. He compares His lovingkindness, which in the original language is "hesed," (v. 8) with the reproaches of the enemy (vv 9–10). The meaning of "hesed," is rich and multi-faceted. Breshears and Driscoll say it refers to "the consistent, ever-faithful, relentless, constantly pursuing, lavish, extravagant, unrestrained, one-way love of God. It is often translated as covenant love, lovingkindness, mercy, steadfast love, loyal love, devotion, commitment, or reliability … In the Hebrew Scriptures, *hesed* refers to a sort of love that has been promised and is owed—covenant love … Covenant love is the love God promised to give to his covenant people, and which they in turn were to respond in kind, loving God with all their hearts, minds, and strength."[76]

The conclusion to David's comparison is confidence that God's "hesed" love will prevail and mend the broken spirit. "Hesed" is the covenant love you promised on your wedding day. When your spouse has been crushed by the enemy of the soul, display this love so that his or her countenance can be mended to emerge as smooth as an egg shell (v. 11).

BLINDED BY LOVE

Read Ephesians 4:1–3 and 1 Peter 4:8

Perhaps you have heard the cliché, "Love is blind." If love is blind, then marriage appears to remove the blinders. Habits that were ignored or thought to be cute before marriage can become extremely irritating after the wedding. Someone has said that marriage is like buying a CD. You buy it for a few songs you love, only to find out that it has a lot of songs that you don't want.

Whether the habit is tapping fingers, leaving the toilet seat up, throwing dirty clothes on the floor, expelling odorous gases, belching, or being consistently late, the aggravating acts require forbearance for the relationship to survive.

The word "bear" or "forbear" literally means "to put up with." God states that we are to put up with or tolerate others in love (v. 2). We are to be patient. The result of forbearing one another in love is that we keep the unity of the spirit in the bond of peace (v. 3). That is, when we graciously bear the annoying faults of a loved one, peace is maintained in the home. 1 Peter 4:8 says that love covers a multitude of sins. Love for our spouse will help us to overlook and tolerate their shortcomings.

I can remember many times waiting for Debbie in the car, thinking we would be late for an appointment if she didn't hurry up. Unfortunately, my reaction at times was disgust and anger. At other times, I used the extra minutes to concentrate on my love for her and how she was a special gift to me from God. The results were longsuffering in the midst of the circumstance and marital peace when she arrived in the car. Maintaining peace is far more beneficial than the relief of expressing petty irritations about the habits of our spouse. Love is the answer! What irritating habits do you need to overlook or tolerate for the sake of your marriage? Let true love blind you.

KNOWING YOUR SPOUSE

Read Genesis 4:1 and Hosea 4:6

I remember the first time I laid eyes on my wife in a tenth grade biology class. Since she was beautiful and I learned that she had good character, I wanted to meet and get to know her. It was only when we started dating and I spent time with her that I really began to know her. Having now spent more than thirty-five years together in marriage, I know her and she knows me like no one else could possibly fathom. As our knowledge of each other continues to escalate, we daily enjoy the benefits of increased intimacy.

The Bible uses interesting language to describe the sexual relations between Adam and Eve. It says that he "knew" her. Obviously this word does picture the sexual act between Adam and Eve, but "know" in Scripture has a much deeper meaning. It describes an immeasurable intimacy that cannot be gained from just an intellectual knowledge of someone. Rather, it comes only through spending time and conversing with the person you desire to know. It's interesting that we often refer to physical intimacy between a husband and wife as "sexual intercourse." The dictionary defines intercourse not only as sexual contact, but also as the exchange of thoughts and feelings between two people. God states in Hosea 4:6 that His people are destroyed because of a lack of knowledge. He is not simply saying that the children of Israel did not know about Him, but that they refused to have an intimate knowledge of Him that would result in a loving, responsive relationship.

Similarly, God never intended for sexual relations between husband and wife to be the mere fulfillment of physical desire. Rather, it is to be the culmination of the couple knowing each other intimately, the climax of shared hearts joined together in covenant love. Take time to learn your spouse's heart. Your sexual intimacy will be taken to new levels of gratification!

THANKSGIVING

Read Psalm 100

After many delays and complications in arranging transportation, Pilgrim husbands and wives joined hearts to start a new life together in America. 102 Pilgrims were forced to live between the decks of the Mayflower for seven weeks. The ceilings were low; the room was dark and overcrowded. The windows were closed because of bad weather, so there was no fresh air and no circulation. Bathroom facilities were crude with little privacy. Vomiting was frequent because of seasickness. Babies screamed and the crew harassed them continually. The group landed in America during the cruel winter of December 1620. Six people died that month. Eight died in January. Seventeen passed away in February. Thirteen died in March. Many fought sickness through the winter. They lost much of their clothing during a fire. With help from Squanto, they planted and harvested enough corn for winter. With thankful hearts, they invited the Indian chief to join them at a celebration feast. He showed up with ninety other Indians, forcing the Pilgrims to dig deeply into their supplies.

How could these husbands and wives remain thankful following a year of such crushing challenges? Psalm 100 details the prerequisites for genuine thanksgiving. Joy, singing, and celebration should be enthusiastically expressed as we concentrate on the Lord (vv. 1–2). We have to possess a deep, intimate understanding of God Himself, a task that is accomplished only by prayerfully seeking Him in Scripture and responding with trusting obedience. Our goal and intent should be to enter His presence. We must fully comprehend that we are not independent; we belong to Him (v. 3). Once we realize and concentrate on who He is (good, merciful, and true) and concede that we are His, we can confidently trust Him to care for us. Our loving and faithful Heavenly Father maintains control of our destiny. With our thoughts consistently concentrated on these truths, we—like the Pilgrims—can abound in praise and thankfulness (vv. 4-5), even during the severest of challenges in marriage or life.

The Preciousness of Marriage

Read Hebrews 13:4

When we think of something as precious, our mind often imagines precious jewels, precious babies, or even precious memories. The dictionary defines "precious" as having great value. This could refer to something or someone that is highly esteemed. We do not ordinarily think of marriage as being precious, but God states that it is to be held in honor. The word "honor" means to esteem someone or something in a very high position, or to count it as extremely precious. The same root word used for honor in Hebrews 13:4 is translated as "precious" in 1 Peter 1:19 to describe the blood of Jesus. It is no accident that our Holy God is exalting the value of marriage to such a notably high level. Before the institution of the church, before the institution of human government, God designed marriage to be the foundation upon which all institutions rest and are dependent upon for survival.

Unfortunately, the preciousness of marriage has been forgotten in our culture. As a result, it has become a disappearing institution in America! The percentage of households that are home to a married couple has decreased from 78% in 1950 to only 48% in 2010.[77] In a radio broadcast, Dr. Al Mohler noted, "Americans are living longer, marrying later, exiting marriage more quickly, choosing to live together before marriage, after marriage, in-between marriage, and as an alternative to marriage."[78] God challenges couples as well as society in general to pause and consider their view of marriage. The stability of our families and the future of our nation depend upon the church re-capturing the preciousness of marriage. Do you make jokes and degrading comments about marriage to others? Do you view your marriage as a prison or as precious? We glorify God when we celebrate the preciousness of marriage.

A DIVINE DISPLAY

Read Hebrews 13:4 and Ephesians 5:32

In a Newsweek magazine article titled "Yes to Love, No to Marriage" a woman named Bonnie states, "I do not believe in a religion that says romantic, committed love is moral only if couples pledge joint allegiance to God. I don't need a white dress to feel pretty, and I have no desire to pretend I'm virginal. I don't need to have Jeff propose to me as if he's chosen me. I don't need a ring as a daily reminder to myself or others that I am loved. And I don't need Jeff to say publicly that he loves me, because he says it privately, not just in words but in daily actions."[79] Simply stated, she is saying, "I do not need marriage, and we can live together as we see fit." Unfortunately this attitude is gaining momentum in America. Why does God place such emphasis on the institution of marriage?

In today's reading, Paul helps us gain an understanding by stating that marriage is the ultimate earthly display of the covenant relationship between Jesus Christ and His church (Eph. 5:32). That is, Christian marriage is meant to be a divine picture of the heavenly relationship between Jesus Christ and His bride! No wonder God says we are to view marriage as precious (November 24). A couple who cohabit denigrates marriage and tramples its sacred meaning under their feet. When I view marriage as an earthly representation of a heavenly relationship, and live it out according to God's design, I glorify Him. When our children, our neighbors, and those we brush shoulders with see that our marriages are a daily celebration, we become a living example of the love between Jesus Christ and His bride, the church. Does your relationship with your spouse show your children, neighbors, and the world around you that you view marriage as precious?

NUMB

Read Ephesians 5:14, Isaiah 60:1, and Proverbs 4:18

I woke up early this morning with no feeling in my left arm, all because I had slept with it curled under my body. My arm felt lifeless! As I arose and started rubbing it and moving it around, it started to tingle. The numbness began to dissipate, and I regained the use of my arm.

In today's reading, Paul invites the one who is numb in the darkness of sin and unaware of their lost condition to awaken to the gospel of Jesus Christ (Eph. 5:14). The prophet Isaiah challenges listeners to arise and shine because of the light that the glory of God brings (Isa. 60:1). Just as I had lost the feeling in my arm and had to revive it, the lost person (unbeliever) is entreated to arise from the dead, to repent of sin, and allow the invigorating light of Christ to shine upon them. Solomon compares the conduct and lifestyle of a righteous person to the progression of daily sunlight that gets brighter and brighter from dawn to midday (Prov. 4:18).

Many marriage partners are numb because they are asleep in a dream world of doing things their way rather than God's way. They are often looking for a quick fix, through some psychological ploy or humanistic scheme that lists five steps to a successful marriage. However, for spouses to experience the deep, abiding satisfaction and joy that only God can give, the first step is a relationship with Him. Couples must awaken to the truth of their need to change their way of thinking and behaving, and trust in Jesus Christ as Lord and Savior. Only then will the deadness and numbness of a dreary, dry marriage begin to brighten and be revitalized with light and life in Christ! Are you asleep and deadened to your sin? In faith, cry out to the Lord, relying on His character and what He has done on the cross as payment for your sin. Surrender your will to His. He will rescue you from the darkness of your sin (Rom. 10:9–13). Do you know a couple who needs Christ? Pause and pray they will realize that without Him, their marriage is numb and cannot experience the deep satisfaction only God gives.

OUT OF PLUMB

Read Amos 7:1–9 and Ephesians 5:25-33

When I was young, I would often go with my dad to his job sites. Many times he would pull out a cord with a little weight on the end of it. He called this simple contraption a plumb line. He would drop the weight down the side of a wall as it was being constructed and use it as a guide to build the wall completely straight. When it was finished, you could look down along it and see no bulges or crooked places.

Israel was a wall God had built using His plumb line to ensure it was true and straight, without deviation from His holiness. In the vision He gave to Amos, God Himself was standing on the wall with a plumb line in hand. The line revealed where the wall had become crooked. Wherever the wall (Israel) was out of plumb, God would tear it down (execute judgment) so it could be rebuilt to His specifications.

God has also constructed the marriage relationship using a plumb line. His design instructs the husband to emulate Jesus Christ by being a servant leader to his wife (Eph. 5:25–33). He instructs the wife to submit to her husband's headship, be a loyal companion, and assist him in fulfilling God's calling upon his life. The marriage is sealed by a covenant in which both spouses promise to remain faithful to each other till death. If the relationship is in plumb according to God's plan, it will be a joyful celebration. Whenever a marriage experiences troubles, the couple should immediately stretch God's plumb line down the wall of their relationship and humbly allow Him to show them where it's out of alignment. Ignoring God's design will yield results similar to those described in Amos 7:9—pain, sorrow, and often desolation. Do you need to stretch God's plumb line down the wall of your marriage to determine where it needs to be adjusted?

FROZEN BRANCHES

Read 2 Corinthians 3:18

I awoke to a winter wonderland outside my home. Because of a steady, freezing rain last night, every branch and twig was covered with a thick layer of ice. I cautiously slipped and slid to my vehicle. The door, the handle, and the lock were covered with ice. After working my way into the car, I drove down my treacherously steep driveway to the street. I immediately slid sideways, crashing through the beautifully adorned low hanging white pine limbs, breaking brittle branches from the tree. Finally, I arrived at the main road and paused to gaze at the spectacular display of the sun glistening on the frozen branches. The glory of God was brilliantly displayed in His creative handiwork.

In today's reading, Paul speaks of the unobstructed view believers have of the glory of Jesus Christ. Not only can we see His glory, but like the sunbeams bouncing off the ice, we can reflect it. That is, the more we look upon Him, the more we become like Him, and His character radiates from our inner being.

The beauty of the icy trees did not appear instantaneously, but was the result of a layer by layer accumulation throughout the night. Similarly, a Christian is a work in progress. Studying the attributes of the Lord, meditating on the way He lived, and reading how His followers felt about Him gradually expands a believer's knowledge of Him. Each response of obedience and praise, thought by thought, action by action, builds His likeness in us, causing us to sparkle and shine a little brighter. When a husband and wife are both growing in their knowledge of Christ, the glistening effect is accentuated as the multiple facets of their two different lives display His likeness. Their home becomes more and more like heaven—a wonderland of praise. Is His glory increasing in your life? Is your home glistening?

THE GOLDEN RULE

Read Matthew 7:12

The rule of gold says, "He who has the gold rules." In this mind-set, the gold represents wealth, power, or position. If you want to rule, you must be either wealthy or in a position of great authority or influence. Unfortunately, this worldly thinking not only permeates our society in general, but also impacts many marriages. For example, husbands incorrectly view their provision and headship as a license to rule and dominate their wives. Wives who earn higher salaries than their husbands assume the right to control major financial decisions.

Jesus, however, interprets the Golden Rule very differently. His approach is the antithesis of the worldly view described above. Jesus teaches that whatever you want people to do to you, do the same for them (v. 12). If you want to be treated with kindness, you should show kindness. If you don't want to be ignored, don't ignore others. If you don't want to be made the brunt of someone else's joke, don't degrade others with hurtful humor. How revolutionary it would be if husbands and wives lived out their relationship according to Jesus' interpretation of the Golden Rule. Spouses would love each other as they desired to be loved. A wife would surprise her husband with a cup of coffee because she delights in kind acts. A husband would kiss his wife when she walks in the room because he enjoys it when she shows him affection. Living in this understanding of the Golden Rule would transform a couple's marriage.

Left to ourselves, we are incapable of living this way. We have an innate desire to exercise control to ensure that we get what we want. However, God empowers His children by His Spirit to daily die to self, to put on Christ, so that we will not be "self-focused," but "others-focused." We can then employ our will and determination to ensure we give our spouses what we consider pleasing and valuable. What would be pleasing to you today? Arrange to do it for your mate.

THROUGH GOD'S EYES

Read Luke 13:10–17

miracle had just taken place. A woman who had suffered pain and disfigurement for 18 years had been freed of her infirmity! Yet the only response given by the ruler of the synagogue as he observed the deliverance was criticism. As Jesus replied to the ruler's reaction, He not only declared the religious leader to be a hypocrite, but also pointed out something very significant. The one whom He had healed was a "daughter of Abraham" (v.16). Jesus affirmed the woman's value, and declared her to be a fellow heir of the blessings of Abraham. Even though she was a woman, she was an heir of the promise just as they were. They were viewing her incorrectly through the eyes of snobbery.

In the culture of her day, this woman was not only scorned because she was female, but she was likely laughed at, made fun of, scoffed, and ridiculed because of her illness. She probably felt worthless, without any hope of her miserable condition ever changing. When others walked by, they viewed her with disdain. How condescending! In today's passage, we see Jesus making an earnest point, not only to the religious rulers, but to each of us. We must be careful to always look at others through our Father's eyes. What do you see when you look at your husband or wife? Do you see someone who is a fellow heir of the grace of life (1 Pet. 3:7)? Do you see your mate as a precious image-bearer of God (Gen. 1:27)? Or do you see them through self-centered eyes of rejection, frustration, or self-righteousness? How you view others, especially your spouse, depends on whose eyes you are looking through.

Make a conscious effort to look at others today through the eyes of the Lord, and give special attention to the way you see your mate. Contempt will be transformed into compassion.

DECEMBER 1

FEASTING DURING
THE HOLY DAYS

Read Exodus 12:16 and Deuteronomy 12:5–7

We enjoyed celebrating the Thanksgiving holiday. Our boys came home from college, and they didn't do any homework. We didn't work in the yard or devote time to household chores. We started a jigsaw puzzle, played cards, and watched football games on TV. Everyone relaxed except when it came to preparing food. My family expected a feast of turkey, gravy, dressing, casseroles, cranberries, and pumpkin pies. It was a lot of work, but I found pleasure in cooking meals when I knew my husband and sons would enjoy them very much.

I was intrigued when I read the description of the holy days in the Bible, as seen in today's passages. During those times, the Israelites were instructed to cease from occupational labor. The only work allowed was preparation of food (Exod. 12:16). How closely we follow this tradition!

Eating was a major part of the holy days during Bible times. These days were even called feasts, including Feast of Weeks, Feast of Trumpets, and Feast of Tabernacles. They had sacred spiritual significance, and were often festive. The sacrifices were always respected and performed reverently. The sacrificial ceremony included a meal in which the family sat down together. Deuteronomy 12:7 describes the meal for a holy day. The family was to remember and discuss the specific blessings God had given them. They were to praise Him as part of their mealtime conversation, and speak of the spiritual significance of the day. When verse seven says that the household shall eat before the Lord, the Israelites viewed the occasion as literally having a meal with God, a sign of peace between Him and the family. As you plan your meal time for the Christmas holiday, talk together as husband and wife about how you can share it with the Lord by discussing His goodness. Declare His blessings. Worship Him as you eat. Peace will permeate your home.

SET ME AS A SEAL

Read Song of Solomon 8:5–7

When I am about to leave home on a trip for several days, Debbie will grasp my hand, and ask for a kiss and hug. We affirm our love to each other and I reluctantly leave. In today's reading, Solomon is preparing to leave for a trip (v. 5). Shulamite's arms are resting on his arms and her head is snuggled against his chest. She is drawn to him, and she longs for an affirmation of his love before he leaves.

Shulamite asked Solomon, who was king, to set her as a seal upon his heart, and as a seal upon his arm. A seal was a type of signet that left an impression denoting authority and ownership. Her desire was to be stamped or engraved upon his heart and arm, expressing ownership of her as Solomon's most prized possession.

Shulamite requested that Solomon engrave her upon his heart because his affections belonged to her. When her husband was away, she wanted him to remember the responsibility that accompanied his committed love for her. The names of the tribes of Israel were engraved in the twelve precious stones on the breast plate Aaron wore as high priest so he would be continually reminded to be concerned and to passionately pray for the specific needs of his people (Exod. 28:11). Knowing that her name is sealed upon Solomon's heart assures Shulamite of his constant affection and loyalty.

Next, Shulamite asks Solomon to set her as a seal upon his arm. Often a wife will hold her husband's arm to demonstrate her desire for security and protection, safety and comfort. The arm seal is a promise to always fulfill these responsibilities.

When a husband places his wife as a seal upon his heart and arm, he acknowledges that he belongs to her and he is committed—in thought and action—to lovingly care for her. The seal is an incredible bond that withstands the trials of separation.

STRONGER THAN DEATH

Read Song of Solomon 8:6

*I*n yesterday's devotion, Shulamite petitioned her husband to set her as a seal upon his heart and arm. To enforce this request, she makes a case for the power of her love which has constrained her to ask him for these seals.

She presents her case as a defense attorney defending a client by making the opening statement, "Love is stronger than death." No doubt, death is strong because one day, every person will face it. The familiar saying declares, "Nothing is certain except death and taxes." Physical death is unavoidable. It cannot be ignored. It is final and irreversible. Death ends a physical life and abandons those left behind. But love is stronger than that because it does not abandon life, but encourages and enhances it. True love fights and sacrifices for the well-being of loved ones. True love takes a stand for loved ones while death forsakes them. Love offers hope. Love is stronger than death.

Shulamite may have been pondering the fact that the couple will be separated for a period of time. Death is a separator—the most permanent, definitive separator of two individuals. But love is stronger than death because true love will abide in a lover's heart after the death of the loved one. Just because someone dies does not mean love for that person will end. Love withstands separation, even death. The greatest love, that of Jesus Christ, overcomes death. Without Him we are spiritually dead, but His love rescues us and leads us into life. We will never be separated from Him because His love is stronger than death.

Shulamite is telling her husband he can put the seal of ownership on his heart because her love for him is genuine and stronger than death. Nothing can keep her from loving him. If you are a Christian, you have Christ's "stronger than death" love available to give to your spouse. Allow Him to empower you so that nothing can keep you from loving your mate.

DIVINELY JEALOUS LOVE

Read Song of Solomon 8:6 and Exodus 34:14

*L*ike a defense attorney, Shulamite adds supporting evidence to her case that Solomon should seal her on his heart and arm. She first establishes he can have the confidence to seal her because her love is genuine and stronger than death (see December 3). Next, she interjects that her divinely jealous love proves her commitment. Just as the grave relentlessly holds a body, this godly jealousy will not release its lover. It never gives up or fails!

This is not to be confused with the distorted jealousy that is prevalent in our culture. In a negative sense, a jealous lover is someone who does not trust you, even if you are trustworthy. The motive of this person is to control and benefit self. If unchecked, the relationship can become abusive. Contrast this with God's loving jealousy that is referenced six different times in Scripture. In fact, Exodus 34:14 records that God's name is "Jealous." The reason for His jealousy is that He wants our hearts to remain pure and fixed on Christ—not distracted by or shared with another (2 Cor. 11:2, Exod. 20:1–6). He jealously protects His bride and will not allow anyone to steal her from His love (John 10:28). His love is an unyielding, unrelenting passion, demonstrating the same power the grave holds over its captive. This love insists on complete devotion—for our good and for His glory.

Dr. Martyn Lloyd-Jones states, "It is a characteristic of love always to demand certainty. Love not only gives, love also demands. Any hesitation, any doubt, any query in the love relationship leads to misery; love demands certainty."[80] Shulamite's divine jealousy proves the certainty of her love, which is another reason for Solomon to seal her on his heart.

Divinely jealous love gives each spouse security and protections from outside threats seeking to destroy it. It does not strive to control the object of its love, but provides unyielding devotion for the good of the one being loved. Can your marriage be sealed because of divinely jealous love?

FLAMING LOVE

Read Song of Solomon 8:6, Hebrews 12:29, and Revelation 3:14–18

everal years ago, we arranged for the local fire department to burn down a dilapidated old building near our home. As the building burned, the flames grew to such magnitude that no one could stand within fifty yards of the fire. The flames actually reached up and melted some of the insulation off of the nearby electric lines. The heat was so intense that leaves on trees twenty yards away turned brown and crumpled. Soon the ugly structure was gone, and only ashes remained!

In Song of Solomon 8:6, Shulamite describes the power of love using the analogy of hot coals with a blazing flame, burning within her soul for her lover. The phrase literally refers to "the fire-flame of Jehovah" (Heb. 12:29). This is the only reference to the name of God in the Song of Solomon. His love is like a raging fire that consumes imperfections and leaves a much purer specimen. This type of love has its source in God, for He is love. It consumes all that is ugly and replaces it with the beauty of holiness! Writing to the believers at Laodicea, Jesus describes their love to Him as lukewarm (Rev. 3:16). He urges them to buy gold tried in the fire that they will be rich and be clothed in white garments (Rev. 3:18). The Lord desires that the love of His bride be like gold refined in a fire, where extreme temperatures draw out and eliminate all impurities. This love is so powerful that it does not let up until everything in its path is devoured. Such committed love is the greatest force known to man. When manifested in marriage, this love creates a pure relationship untainted by distractions that blemish its beauty. Shulamite closes out her song by reminding the reader that the flaming love she shares with Solomon is sourced in none other than Jehovah God! Is your marriage set aflame in His love? When marriage is fueled by the flaming love of God, the result is a pure love.

LOVE THAT CANNOT BE QUENCHED

Read Song of Solomon 8:7

Niagara Falls is one of the greatest natural wonders in the world. For anyone who has seen it, it is an awesome, breathtaking experience. Each second, more than 600,000 gallons of water flow over the nearly half-mile-wide crest line, at approximately twenty miles per hour. The force generated by the water would demolish a house into splinters! The noise produced by the falling water is so incredible that it drowns out all other sounds. Observers are forced to direct their attention to its magnificence. Surrounding nature pales in comparison to the splashing display. As a result of harnessing this mighty force, no other natural phenomenon in the world produces more electric power.

In today's reading, Shulamite declares that the wonder of love cannot be displaced by the sounds or sight of waters as magnificent as Niagara Falls. The intensity of this love consumes, evaporates, and dispels all thundering streams or even floods that come against it. It is so powerful that it echoes alone within her heart, continually resounding in the recesses of her inner being. It seeks out and searches every empty crevice and hollow hole within her, replacing indifference, coldness, and death. Such is the power between two married people who allow God to permeate their souls with the burning fire of His love. It becomes a fire that cannot be quenched!

In the New Testament, Paul emphatically states that neither tribulations, distress, persecution, death, life, angels, rulers nor anything else can extinguish the love of God (Rom. 8:35–39). How comforting to know that His love is greater and will empower us to overcome any marital struggle or trial we face! Draw upon divine love to help you conquer whatever you are facing in your marriage or family. God's love cannot be quenched.

CAN'T BUY ME LOVE

**Read Song of Solomon 8:6-7, Revelation 22:17,
and Matthew 4:8–10**

A survey was conducted several years ago where the participants were asked, "What would you do for $10 million?" Twenty-five percent of those surveyed said they would abandon their families. Twenty-three percent said they would become a prostitute for a week, and 7 percent said they would kill a stranger. To many people, the allure of this world is greater than the love of even family or mate. In Song of Solomon, Shulamite concludes her defense of the power of love with one last argument. She states that all of a rich man's wealth would be inadequate to purchase the love she has for her husband, love sourced in Jehovah God! Her love cannot be bought at any price, and to suggest the possibility is an insult!

The Beatles were correct in their popular song titled, "Can't Buy Me Love." The song pled a case for someone who couldn't give a diamond ring or money to their lover because they had nothing to give but love. It's marvelous to know that in the melody of marriage, the love required to set it on fire is available as a gift from God. The flame of Jehovah's love is free to all who will come and receive it (Rev. 22:17). God's love cannot be purchased by any human effort or works, but is only received through faith in Jesus Christ as Lord and Savior (Rom. 6:23). In addition, no offer is great enough to persuade the Lord to abandon His bride, the church (Rom. 8:38-39). Satan offered fame, fortune, and power in an attempt to persuade Jesus to forsake the Father's purpose, but He refused (Matt. 4:8-10). A spouse who emulates this love relationship will despise and reject anyone who offers an enticement that would lead to abandonment or betrayal! Shulamite presented the case that Solomon could be confident she belonged to him since no one could offer anything that would entice her to forsake him. Her love was non-negotiable because its source was the steadfast love of God. Have you convinced your spouse that no one can buy your love? It is meant for your mate only.

ME, MYSELF, AND I

Read Proverbs 6:16–17, 1 Corinthians 4:6–7, and Philippians 2:3–10

One of the chief goals of the devil is to wreck marriages. Because it can be difficult to recognize and eliminate, he often strategically employs pride as the catalyst that ignites controversy. Promotion of self can take many disguised forms—defensiveness, "It's not fair how my spouse treats me," or justification, "I have my rights," or exaltation, "I know I am right about this." The focus of a proud person is totally on self, and how every event or circumstance affects that individual's rights or preferences. A proud person often speaks harsh words that are degrading to the spouse, in order to promote superiority of self. Andrew Murray states, "Pride—the loss of humility—is the root of every sin and evil."[81] The apostle Paul rhetorically declares we have no right to boast because we have received everything from God (1 Cor. 4:6–7). C.J. Mahaney defines pride as, "When sinful human beings aspire to the status and position of God and refuse to acknowledge their dependence upon Him."[82] Pride enthrones self and dethrones God. No wonder God states that He hates pride (Prov. 6:16–17).

How do we counterattack pride? The Bible urges us to esteem others better than ourselves (Phil. 2:3–4). That instruction is much easier said than done, but Paul details the counter moves when he instructs Christians to develop a mind-set centered on Christ and the cross (Phil 2:5–10). Martyn Lloyd-Jones states, "There is only one thing I know of that crushes me to the ground and humiliates me to the dust, and that is to look at the Son of God, and especially contemplate the cross. When I see that I am a sinner ... that nothing but the Son of God on the cross can save me, I'm humbled to the dust ... Nothing but the cross can give us a spirit of humility."[83] To effectively defend your marriage from Satan's most vicious attack, refocus from self to the cross.

HIM AND HIM ALONE

Read Philippians 2:5–10 and John 3:30

*J*esus is the ultimate example of humility. God the Son was abiding in Heaven, recognized there by all beings as equal to God, when He set aside His glory and reputation and took on the likeness of man (incarnation). He became a servant, and was obedient to a cruel death on the cross to atone for our sins (vv. 5–8). No wonder Thomas Aquinas stated, "If you are looking for an example of humility, look at the cross."[84] To have the mind of Christ is to set aside personal glory and reputation and to bear one another's burdens and difficult personality traits.

What would it be like to have a marriage where both partners exercised the mind of Christ in humility? Andrew Murray eloquently gives us an answer when he describes humility as, "Perfect quietness of heart. It is to have no trouble. It is never to be fretted or irritated or sore or disappointed. It is to be at rest when nobody praises me and when I am blamed or despised. It is to go in and shut the door and kneel to my Father in secret, and be at peace as in the deep sea of calmness when all around and above is trouble."[85] Can you imagine what your marriage would be like if you daily lived out this definition of humility? Look back over the definition for a moment. Reflect on it. There is perfect quietness, no fretting or irritation, no reaction to being falsely accused. In humility, a person forgets self and how life is unfair or difficult and concentrates instead on the righteousness and goodness of God. The humble spouse completely trusts the biblical teaching for husbands and wives, and finds gratification in obeying. This mindset fills the home with peace. Because this individual is focusing on the greatness and the sovereign control of the Lord, he or she can comfort and inspire a discouraged mate with truths about Him.

Restoring humility in our marriages requires both spouses to set aside self concerns in order to yield to the Lord's purposes. He must increase, and we must decrease (John 3:30). Reflect together, as husband and wife, on the humility of the perfect God-man, Jesus Christ. Let this mind be in you.

EXCHANGING LIKENESS

Read 1 Samuel 18:1–4 and Ephesians 4:22-24

After Jonathan and David make a covenant with each other, Jonathan, the legal heir to the throne of Israel, humbly strips himself of his robe, weapons, and belt and gives them to David (vv. 1–3). He places his royal clothing upon his friend to acknowledge that David is chosen by God to be king. David now outwardly bears the likeness of Jonathan's royalty. The robe, weapons, and belt symbolize to David that he would take on Jonathan's likeness, his strengths and weaknesses, and his enemies.[86] They took on covenant likeness.

Similarly, after a person comes into covenant with God through Jesus Christ, we see an exchange of likeness exemplified when this person is commanded to "put off" his former way of doing things—the old man—and "put on" Christ's way of doing things—the new man (Eph. 4:22–24). He is to put off pride and put on humility, put off harshness and put on kindness and goodness, put off impatience and put on longsuffering, put off selfishness and put on selflessness, put off un-forgiveness and put on forgiveness. Each of God's children is a new creation in Christ Jesus and is clothed in His robe of righteousness. Therefore, each one should begin to reflect Christ-likeness to the world.

In marriage when the husband and wife become "one flesh," they each bear the likeness of a new person. The groom should no longer portray a carefree single guy, but a responsible married man. The bride should not flirt with other guys, but express a devoted commitment to her husband. The couple should be proud to be married to each other. They are now to share like goals, dreams, and purposes in their marriage covenant. Thinking switches from "me" to "we," from "mine" to "our." The relationship is not competitive, but rather complementary. Have you exchanged "clothes"? Do you wear the likeness of a loving spouse who is committed to the relationship?

EXCHANGING STRENGTHS AND WEAKNESSES

Read Ecclesiastes 4:9–12 and 1 Samuel 18:1–4

The exchange of belts between David and Jonathan symbolizes partners exchanging their strengths and weaknesses (v. 4).[87] In a covenant relationship with Christ, one is able to replace all of his or her weakness and inabilities with His strengths and abilities. Similarly, entering a marriage covenant implies that you and your spouse take on each other's strengths and weaknesses.

The old saying that opposites attract is often true in marriage. We have found in our marriage that where one of us is weak the other is usually strong. We compensate for each other's weaknesses. This truth is also expounded by Solomon when he teaches that two are better than one. If one falls down, the other can lift him up, and when two lie down together they warm each other (vv. 9–11). When I am discouraged, I'm thankful for a wife who encourages me. When it's cold at night and the bed is freezing, Debbie is thankful that she can snuggle up to my warmer body. Because of my personality, I am a decision maker, and I naturally handle the routine financial decisions. Tedious record-keeping stresses me, so Debbie balances the checkbooks. When faced with the need for decisions concerning car maintenance and repair, I understand enough to make a confident choice where Debbie would nervously feel at the mercy of the advice of the mechanic. When the boys are hungry, she consistently provides tasty, nutritious meals when I would settle for easily prepared junk food. God has made us differently; that's why we need each other so much. We complement each other's strengths and weaknesses.

In marriage, the Lord intends for this principle to edify and strengthen both husband and wife. However, many couples allow their differences to become points of division rather than using them to mobilize their strengths. Recognizing strengths in physical abilities, personality, and special talents allows spouses to function as partners pulling in the same direction. Take a minute and discuss how you exchange your strengths and weaknesses.

EXCHANGING WEAPONS

Read 1 Samuel 18:1–4

*W*hen Jonathan transferred his weapons to David, he was committing to join forces with him against any enemy David had.[88] This was especially significant since David's primary enemy was none other than Jonathan's father, King Saul. Similarly, when a man and woman enter into the marriage covenant, they join as one force against any foe that would try to separate their union or harm them individually.

Andrea was devastated when she first discovered that her husband was addicted to pornography. She would wake up in the middle of the night and find Mark staring at vulgar sites on the Internet. When she investigated the "900 toll" charges on the phone bill, she found out Mark was contacting sex operators. She was horrified. Her first impulse was to attack his character, but she remembered her pastor teaching that her spouse was not her enemy. Andrea pulled herself together and acknowledged that the true adversary was Satan himself. She determined to stand against the enemy that was attacking her husband.

Her prayer life intensified and she took authority against the evil influences. She cried out for deliverance for Mark. Then she confronted him. She assured him that she was on his side and that she was battling for him. Mark admitted that he was struggling, but he just could not let go. Andrea investigated Christian agencies that minister to people with sexual addiction, and she insisted that her husband attend counseling. When Andrea first discovered Mark's addiction, she had the ammunition and motive to initiate major marital conflict. She chose instead to join forces with the Lord against her spouse's enemy. Pray together that God would give you discernment to recognize where you need to exchange weapons and join forces against the enemy that is attacking your marriage and family.

CONFUSING CIRCUMSTANCES

Read Luke 1:5–25 and Ephesians 3:20-21

Every couple is faced with challenging, unexplainable, heartbreaking circumstances. An honest, faithful, hardworking husband is laid off right before Christmas. A child suffers with cancer. Parents teach their children God's love and ways, but one of them chooses to rebel. In today's passage from Luke, we read about Zacharias and Elizabeth. They are godly, obedient, and faithful, but they are old and have no children (vv. 6–7). This is a heartbreaking disappointment for any couple who loves children, but in Bible times it is excruciating. In that culture, barrenness implies divine disfavor (v. 25). Anytime Elizabeth goes to the market and notices a mother pulling a cloak around a child or consoling a crying baby, she aches with a deep void. Each time a family brings a child to the temple for circumcision, Zacharias wonders why he has not been blessed with a child. When families with several children whisper to each other, Zacharias and Elizabeth immediately suspect that their personal lives are being scrutinized as to why God would withhold such an important blessing. But Zacharias and Elizabeth face their heartbreak together. This is not just Elizabeth's disappointment, but Zacharias shares her concern. Rather than give in to depression, they continue to serve God (vv. 8–9). The couple takes their challenge to the Lord. They persistently seek His help and His answer (v. 13).

Zacharias and Elizabeth's story is not a promise that God will answer prayer the way we plan, but it offers direction in confusing times. As a couple, we can share disappointment and heartache. Through obedience to God, we can choose to live godly, righteous lives. We can call upon Him concerning the matter, and we can continue to trust and serve Him. In His perfect timing, He will answer super-abundantly, above all we dare think or dream (Luke 5:13–15, Eph. 3:20–21). What confusing or discouraging challenges are you facing? Console one another with a hug and a renewed commitment to serve the Lord together. Confidently look to Him.

HIGHLY FAVORED

Read Luke 1:26–36 and Titus 2:11

*M*ary is mentioned fifty-one times in the New Testament. She is probably the best known woman in history, and hers is one of the most popular names given to little girls worldwide. Mary, however, never sought this acclaim. She was a common teenager from the obscure little town of Nazareth. The only other facts we know about her is that she was a virgin and she was engaged. She is never described as attractive, educated, or impressive. Yet, God sent one of His choice messengers to approach and address her as one favored by Him. The word "favor" literally means grace. Mary was selected by God, not because of her achievements or merit, but solely because of His goodness. Mary was the object of God's marvelous grace.

Can you imagine how she must have felt? Maybe she thought, "But Lord, why would You say this to me? I'm just an ordinary girl. God, what have I done that You would favor me above all the other teenage girls in town?" It's likely that thoughts of personal inadequacies may have crossed her mind. As she meditated on the angel Gabriel's words, perhaps she began to reflect upon the word "favor." Maybe at that moment she realized she had done nothing to merit grace, yet she still received it. Mary was receiving nothing that she earned, but rather what she didn't deserve, the grace of God. Titus 2:11 explains that God's grace makes salvation available to all people. He pursues sinners in order to forgive them and redeem them from their sins. Even as God chose Mary, He has chosen those who by faith have trusted Christ as their Lord and Savior. As dear children of God, each one of us is highly favored! This is the message of Christmas.

Celebrate the holiday season by telling your spouse the reasons you are grateful to be chosen by Jesus. Also, share with one another how you are highly favored to have been chosen as his or her mate.

BELIEVING THE BIZARRE

Read Luke 1:26–56

Sometimes God asks us to do something that seems bizarre to others. He may ask you to give missionaries the down payment you have been saving for your house. He may lead you to quit your professional, secure job in order to start an inner city mission. He may ask you to set aside all responsibilities for several days in order to withdraw and pray. Your family, your friends, even your spouse may not understand. How do you face the criticism?

God required Mary to do something bizarre. She was to carry a child as an unwed mother. She would be criticized and accused of adultery. Her family and her betrothed husband would not understand. Mary was able to bear the criticism because of three wise responses.

When the angel delivered the news regarding God's plan, Mary listened and then confirmed the message by asking questions (v. 34). She made sure she understood the message, and then surrendered to God's Word (v. 38). She also confirmed the message by responding to the news of Elizabeth's miraculous conception (vv. 36–37). She immediately visited Elizabeth. Her faith probably increased when she saw that what the angel revealed about her cousin was true. She could bear the criticism because she confirmed God's Word, and then surrendered to it.

In addition, Mary sought counsel from a godly person (vv. 39–41). Elizabeth did not criticize and discourage Mary, but inspired her to live with the majesty of God foremost in her thoughts (vv. 42–45). Mary could endure the disapproval of family and friends and even Joseph because she spent time with someone who walked intimately with God and could encourage her through the power of the Holy Spirit.

Mary set aside all distractions and praised the Lord from the depths of her heart (vv. 46–55). She strengthened herself in an environment of godly counsel and worship for three months. Focusing on the goodness and greatness of God dispels darkness and discouragement. When He calls us to a special assignment that our spouse or no one else understands, He will empower us to perform it when we look to Him.

THE MICROSCOPE

Read Luke 1:46–55

*I*n high school biology class, we cut a small portion of a plant stem, mounted it to a slide, and examined it under the microscope. What was a sliver of green became an amazing system of xylem and phloem tubes surrounded by individual cells. Higher magnification of an individual cell revealed a wall, chloroplasts, vacuoles, and a nucleus. Textbook descriptions of plants and cell functions suddenly deepened in meaning. The enhanced view helped us understand the amazing intricacies of how every part fit together, bringing purpose and life to the plant. Prior to magnification, we acknowledged what the textbook explained, but the facts were boring. Now, through personal experience, the information was verified and we could convey it in a more convincing, understandable way.

Today's passage reveals a similar dynamic. When Mary faced so many complicated changes that her life seemed to become a blur, she used magnification to enhance her view and increase her understanding. This prepared her to communicate more effectively when she later discussed the situation with Joseph. Mary magnified the Lord with all her heart and emotions (v. 46). She examined the details of His character. After reviewing specific instances of God's dealings in history, she noted His might, mercy, and goodness, and how they affected her world (vv. 51–55). Her spirit rejoiced when she considered the intricacies of how He fit into her life (vv. 47–49). Her faith and understanding increased as she confirmed the details of His character. She could now convey the truth of God's plans in a convincing, understandable way.

Likewise, when the various aspects of our married life are so crammed together that we only see a blur, we can view the Lord with a spiritual microscope by magnifying His character and works. This exercise will increase our understanding of how He is currently working, enabling us to rejoice and communicate more effectively. Is God directing you to an unexpected task or mission that you need to discuss with your spouse?

JOY TO THE WORLD

Read Luke 1:57–79

*H*ave you ever noticed that mothers love to discuss every aspect of the birth experiences of their children? They compare duration and intensity of labor, morning sickness, medications used, pain levels, due dates, and where their babies were born. On a broader scale, when someone endures a phenomenal ordeal, the news story includes great emotional detail. Journalists report specifics of the suffering, coping techniques, future plans, and family perspectives of the event.

Because of her age, Elizabeth's pregnancy and delivery were the highlights of her community. This birth was the fulfillment of Elizabeth's "impossible dream." Every lady who knew her was probably eager to compare baby stories. The average woman would delight in repeatedly sharing her childbirth story, but instead Scripture states that Elizabeth declared the mercy of the Lord (v. 58).

Nine months earlier, when the angel revealed the miraculous conception, Zacharias had entered the temple with complete vocal capabilities. When he exited, not a sound could issue from his mouth. He lived mute for nine months, communicating with facial expressions, body language, and paper. What an incredible experience, especially for a preacher! When his voice returned, he did not exclaim his relief that such a difficulty was over, but immediately praised God (v. 64). This couple was unusual. They were Spirit-filled. This was evidenced by the way they impacted their friends. Rather than marvel at her feats of childbirth and rather than impress crowds with the extraordinary frustrations of nine months of silence, Elizabeth and Zacharias chose to spread joy to the world (vv. 58, 66). Their stories directed attention away from their achievements to the greatness of God. A Spirit-filled couple eagerly responds to opportunities to spread joy to the world by diverting attention away from themselves, and instead exalting the works and magnificence of the Lord.

THE MIRACLE

Read Luke 1:20, 57–79

When I hear missionaries tell of prayers for the impossible that have been gloriously and miraculously answered, I am embarrassed at my lack of faith. I tend to ask for and expect the logical. I may pray for extraordinary requests, but many times I don't anticipate an answer. Zacharias was like this. For years, he and Elizabeth had prayed for a baby. He was a godly man who was obedient and faithful to God's work, but he did not believe the Lord would perform such a miracle. Zacharias didn't expect Him to answer his extraordinary prayer (v. 20). In time, however, God erased all doubt from his and Elizabeth's mind. Zacharias insisted they obey the Lord's message by naming their child John (v. 63). He declared his confidence in the Lord. His strengthened faith was evident in the prophecy and praise that he pronounced at John's birth. Zacharias announced the miracle that God had visited His people and sent the Messiah—the Redeemer—the Promised One (vv. 68–70).

As we read Zacharias' words today, he challenges us to have faith because God keeps His promises and will protect us (vv. 71–74). Believing this, we should continually, confidently, and enthusiastically serve Him in holiness and righteousness (vv. 74–75). Anything less demonstrates a lack of faith in the promises and miracles of God. Zacharias further proved that he expected the Lord to completely fulfill His promise by proclaiming John's purpose in life (vv. 76–79). Our God has not changed. Although we cannot predict and choose the specifics, we can still expect Him to be active in His supernatural power today. As a couple, enthusiastically expect and experience miracles from God in your life and marriage.

WHOSOEVER

Read John 3:16 and Luke 2:8–20

*L*ike many children, the first Bible verse I learned was John 3:16. In my simplistic mind, I pictured a grandfatherly man with a kind smile peering down on a globe filled with tiny people. I envisioned myself as one of those people. I understood that He loved all of us. As an adult, God enabled me to comprehend His love as intimate and individual. My relationship with Him had to be personal. I began to understand the conclusion of John 3:16, that "whosoever" believed in Him would not perish. The "whosoever" requires a personal response and an individual relationship. The Christmas story demonstrates this. The angel declared good news to all people of the world (Luke 2:10). However, the revelation of this truth was personal to the particular shepherds who were watching their sheep in the fields outside Bethlehem (v. 8). The message was confirmed to them personally when they found the baby lying in a manger (vv. 12, 16). The shepherds responded to the birth of Christ in the unique way that fit their situation. They went straight to the manger and worshipped Him. Their relationship was different from Mary's and Joseph's, different from Anna's and Simeon's, and different from the relationship each disciple would have with Jesus years later. The message applied to all men, but the response was personal and individual.

I rejoice that salvation is available to all people, but I delight in the personal aspect. God relates to me individually. He has special plans, just for me. As a Christian husband and wife, we have an intimacy in Christ that binds us together and strengthens us. When your relationship with Christ is unique and personal, you, like the shepherds, will glorify and praise Him for what He does in your life (v. 20). Make sure you have individually responded to the "whosoever" of John 3:16, so you can personally experience the life Jesus offers. As a Christmas praise, tell your spouse the special ways Jesus demonstrates He is personal to you.

DECEMBER 20

WHY AND WHY RIGHT NOW?

Read Psalm 77:1–15, Matthew 1:20-24, and Luke 1:35-55, 2:1–7

*A*close friend cried to me in anguish. She was overcome with unreasonable circumstances that could have easily been avoided if someone else had fulfilled their responsibilities. The problem was complicated by new, job-related policies that added an urgent time restraint. The challenge also opened piercing wounds from the past. The timing of the predicament heightened her anxiety level. The security of her entire future seemed to hinge on dealing with this problem. The obvious questions surfaced, "Why, and why right now?" To varying degrees, we've all experienced these frustrations.

In Psalm 77, Asaph laments a similar dilemma. The complaining overwhelms him (v. 3). As he meditates and searches his spirit, he feels abandoned, but he eventually draws a powerful conclusion. In the midst of anguish, he remembers the works, wonders, and words of God (v. 11). The reader experiences the calming effect just by meditating on the memories Asaph recites.

Similarly, Joseph and Mary could have drowned in their dilemma. Although God had chosen and honored them, the community probably rejected them because their story was too unbelievable. The emotional strain had to be frustrating. In addition, a foreign, despised government was levying a tax that required an inconvenient registration (Luke 2:1). The timing of the required travel added to the stress because Mary's baby was due (v. 6). When Joseph discovered there were no vacancies in the town of Bethlehem, where Mary needed to give birth, he could have complained and been overwhelmed with the questions, "Why and why right now?" (Ps. 77:7). Instead, when faced with uncertainty, the couple remembered God's works and wonders (Luke 1:46–55). They were strengthened by recalling His specific words to them (Luke 1:35–38, Matthew 1:20–24). They probably marveled when they reflected on Micah 5:2, prophecy that declared the Messiah would be born in the exact city where they were required to register. Recalling the Lord's work, wonders, and words is the answer to the questions, "Why and why right now?"

Are you facing uncertainties or frustrations that are stressful to your marriage? Follow the example of Mary and Joseph. Recall the Lord's words, works, and wonders.

A JUST AND MERCIFUL HUSBAND

Read Matthew 1:18–24 and Proverbs 11:12–13

The Bible describes Joseph as a just man (v. 19). He lives a life of righteousness and is concerned that God's ways be honored. Out of respect for the holiness of God, he cannot ignore the fact that his betrothed wife is pregnant. He does not cover it up or proceed as though nothing has happened. He is ready to face the truth. Denying it, no matter how painful, will harm the people we love. The way the truth is handled, however, makes all the difference. Proverbs 11:12–13 warns that people who belittle their neighbor lack sense, but whoever keeps a matter quiet is considered trustworthy. Joseph proves he is trustworthy when he refrains from publicly humiliating his wife-to-be.

I have observed a tendency in some husbands and wives to attempt to prove their superiority by poking fun and publicly humiliating their mate. For example, one spouse will gather an audience and tell stories that vividly relate ridiculous details of a mistake made by the other. The story may evoke explosive laughter or amazed disbelief from the listeners, but at the expense of the spouse's dignity. The countenance of the ridiculed mate reflects the pain of inadequacy and rejection. Sometimes husbands and wives reveal details of their private married lives in order to elicit sympathy or even respect for their long-suffering. In today's passage, we see that Joseph understands the principle of mercy. He is wise enough to deal with his predicament tenderly and privately. His long suffering allows the Holy Spirit liberty to open his heart to prove Mary's innocence. God uses Joseph's gentle nature and sensitivity to accomplish His mighty purposes. No matter how unbelievable the actions of one's mate, every husband or wife should be sensitive to the dignity of his or her spouse and to the promptings of the merciful Spirit of God.

BETWEEN A ROCK
AND A HARD PLACE

Read Matthew 1:18–25

*H*ave you ever heard people say they feel like they're "between a rock and a hard place?" This expression is often used to describe the anxiety someone experiences when facing a dilemma that requires an unpleasant or undesirable choice. Since Mary was pregnant, and she and Joseph had not consummated their marriage sexually, Joseph was "between a rock and a hard place." Should he divorce her privately, causing her no shame, or should he should report her situation publicly, and have her stoned as the law demanded?

Fortunately, God came to the rescue. He planted a dream in Joseph's mind in which an angel declared the reason for Mary's conception. The child she bore was not the result of her unfaithfulness to her wedding vows, but was conceived by the Holy Ghost. God was using Joseph's wife to fulfill the Old Testament prophesy that a virgin would conceive and deliver a son named Emmanuel (Isa. 7:14). What would Joseph do? Would he obey God's voice given through this supernatural dream, or would he ignore God and do as he pleased? Joseph chose to do as the angel had instructed him (v. 24). As a result of obeying God, he experienced the privilege of being the earthly father of a perfect Son who was the Savior of the world.

The next time you feel like you are "between a rock and a hard place" in your marriage, remember to look to God and listen for His direction. God gave Joseph guidance through a dream. He may choose to give us direction through His Word, prayer, circumstances, or perhaps even a dream. Once we affirm the direction of God, then we must obey as Joseph did. God is sovereign. He has a plan to glorify Himself and benefit us. Trust Him especially when He prompts you to give your spouse the benefit of the doubt. He can use difficult circumstances to strengthen and bless a marriage.

SURPLISE

Read Luke 2:8–18

few nights ago, our family was driving up the driveway to our house when we noticed a UPS package on the front porch. No one could remember ordering anything. We retrieved the package, and what a surprise we received when we opened it! It was a tower of bright Christmas boxes with different goodies in each one. Two days later, we were working in the office when we noticed a florist's delivery truck. I eagerly anticipated receiving a poinsettia. What a surprise when the delivery person handed us a large bag tied with red and green ribbon! It was packed with the cutest Christmas mugs I've ever seen, along with a matching wall hanging.

Christmas should be filled with surprises. The first Christmas certainly was. The shepherds were hoping for a peaceful, uneventful night. Instead, God delighted them with the surprise of their life. An angel personally appeared to them with a message for the entire world. Then, a glorious, angelic choir filled the sky with praises to God. The shepherds probably assumed that only priests or prophets would ever be honored with such a revelation. They could not, in their wildest imaginations, have planned such a magnificent display. I believe that God enjoyed every moment of this fantastic surprise. He was sharing the Christmas spirit by delighting in the joy of others.

The shepherds did not hoard their surprise. After confirming the angel's announcement, they eagerly shared the amazing news. Everyone who heard it was surprised, and filled with wonder (Luke 2:18).

Our doorbell just now rang again. This time the delivery person held a different surprise—a beautiful poinsettia! As you plan special delights that you and your family can pass along to others, take time to glory in the shepherds' surprise with your spouse. This will fill your marriage with Christmas spirit.

AROMA IN THE AIR

Read 2 Corinthians 2:1–17

Christmas is a time when our spirits are lifted not only through the exchange of gifts, but also by the wonderful aromas from scrumptious goodies being baked in the kitchen. The smell of sugar cookies, pumpkin pie, apple cake, gingerbread, brownies, and other holiday treats permeate the entire house. This aroma reaches out to every one of us and seems to say, "Taste me!" After sampling these goodies you can't help but tell others how delicious they are, and give hugs and kisses to the cook for her labor of love.

In today's passage, the apostle Paul reviews ministry difficulties with the church at Corinth (vv. 1–13). In verse fourteen, he transitions from the negative to the positive and offers thanks to God! Even though he is experiencing trying times, he can still triumph in Christ. He pictures this victory by using the imagery of a triumphant Roman processional. In the parade, sweet-smelling incense would be offered up to the Roman gods. When bystanders smelled the aroma in the air, they knew immediately that it represented thanksgiving for victory experienced in battle. Similarly, Paul implies that when difficulties and depressing times surface, believers can spread the sweet aroma of victory everywhere they go by embracing and, without compromise, speaking the truths of life in Christ. Everyone—whether believer or non-believer—is affected by the aroma of the Savior. It silently but powerfully compels the lost to acknowledge that life without Him is hopeless, leading to everlasting spiritual death. At the same time, it inspires believers to experience the Christian life more fully. In verse seventeen, Paul concludes that the aroma of Christ is powerful because unlike the message of peddlers who manipulatively trick customers into purchasing their wares, the message of His goodness is irresistibly commissioned by God.

Notice that the passage refers to the pleasing scent spread by a triumphal parade. Such a procession infers more than one person. What better Christmas fragrance could there be than the tantalizing aroma of Jesus Christ, radiating from a believing couple who, in sincerity, celebrate His birth together.

HE GIFTS OF CHRISTMAS

Read Matthew 2:2–15

The wise men (Magi) were astrologers who most likely traveled from Persia and were members of a prominent religion called Zoroastrianism. They were intelligent and cultured people, noted for their generosity. The Magi (priests) of Zoroaster built high towers from which they charted the courses of planets and stars. They believed that some events in the heavens were linked to events on earth. For example, the "greater" the person who was born, the brighter his heralding star. Using the extraordinary brilliance of Christ's star, the Holy Spirit of God was working within the Magi to create a hunger for truth which would only be satisfied in the person this star was silently, but boldly proclaiming! The Spirit used astronomy and the Word of God recorded by Daniel and other prophets to cause the wise men to expect and desire a coming Messiah. Believing that the promised King had been born, they brought gifts suitable for royalty—gold, frankincense, and myrrh (v. 2). The gifts were a true reflection of the character of the child who would receive them. The gold represented Christ's deity and purity. Frankincense symbolized the fragrance of His life. It was used in the holy offerings at the Jewish temple, and only released its scent in the heat of fire. The results of the fires of trials and adversities in Christ's life would be a pleasing aroma to God the Father. Since myrrh was used as an embalming fluid, it depicted Christ's sacrificial death. In addition, myrrh pictures the bitterness of repentance, leading to sweet forgiveness and divine acceptance. The gifts of gold, frankincense, and myrrh also provided the monetary needs required to sustain Mary, Joseph, and Jesus when they traveled to Egypt (v. 13).

As we celebrate Christmas we, too, should honor our King with gifts of gold, frankincense, and myrrh. We should first present the gift of a pure and holy life (gold), which can only be achieved by allowing Christ to live in and through us. We should have the fragrance of Christ emanating from our lives (frankincense), providing refreshment and joy to everyone around us. We are commanded to die daily (myrrh), to take up our cross and follow in His steps (1 Peter 2:21). When these three gifts are manifested in our household, we as a couple are empowered, like Joseph and Mary, to lead our family as God directs (v. 13-15). Worship the King with these gifts, and experience His sustaining strength in your family.

APPRECIATION

Read Philippians 4:14–20 and Proverbs 31:10

I often think about what motivates me day after day to keep preparing food for my family when the results of my efforts disappear so quickly. My mother always said she enjoyed cooking for people who liked to eat. My husband does enjoy eating, and he always specifically comments on our meals and thanks me for preparing them. When he expresses his gratitude, I am encouraged and motivated. His appreciation energizes me.

Today's passage conveys Paul's appreciation for specific acts of kindness the Philippian believers had done for him. He admires their good work and tells them they are valuable to him and to God. This heartfelt gratitude would motivate them to continue serving the Lord. In the same way, verbalizing gratefulness will encourage a spouse to serve joyfully.

Although Proverbs 31 has traditionally been taught as guidelines for wives who wish to manage their homes effectively, the original message was written to a man. It challenges husbands to understand the great value of a wife is who is willing to prepare meals, manage a home, and nurture a family. When a husband expresses understanding gratitude for specific actions, his wife feels her effort is worthwhile.

In the same way, a wife can appreciate the value of a hard-working mate. I can consider the ways my husband provides physically, emotionally, and spiritually, and take notice of all the details he handles. I can follow Paul's example by complimenting my spouse for specific deeds. I want my husband to know that I admire him. Paul not only considered the sacrifice of the givers and the personal benefits to him, but he was renewed by the thought of God receiving the gifts as an offering to Him (v. 18). Appreciation then becomes an act of worship (v. 20) in which you request blessings for your spouse (v. 19). Take the time to express specific verbal appreciation to your spouse today. May God be glorified, your mate be blessed, and you be strengthened.

WALKING IN THE DARK

Read Isaiah 50:10 and Job 1-2

Have you ever helplessly fumbled across your bedroom in the middle of the night trying to find your way to the bathroom? As you attempt to locate the light switch, you stump your toe and writhe in pain. It's very difficult to walk in the dark.

Interestingly, Isaiah describes someone who is walking in darkness. This person is experiencing a difficult period where there appears to be no light or way of escape. He or she may feel that the sun has set and there will never be another sunrise. This darkness could describe a time of financial reversal, a time of sickness, or even a marriage that has plummeted into a valley of hopelessness where them seems to be no solution.

It is important to note the character of the person who is walking in darkness. This discouraged individual is not someone who is suffering because of sin (Heb. 12:7-11), but rather someone who has a deep reverence for God. This person loves and obeys the Lord and is walking in intimate fellowship with Him, but the circumstances of life are overwhelmingly filled with despair. A good example in Scripture of this person is Job. He is described as God fearing (1:1), yet God allows Satan to kill his children, to destroy all of his possessions and take away his health (1:12-19). This did not happen because of sin in Job's life, but rather so that God would be glorified (2:3). It is not unusual for a Christian to experience these times of darkness (1 Peter 4:12).

Every marriage and family will experience times of darkness, but it doesn't necessarily mean that the difficulties are a result of sin. Our Heavenly Father works in the midst of darkness that He might be glorified and the God-fearing husband and wife might grow in intimacy with Him. Be reassured with these words, and encourage another person or couple you know that is walking in the dark.[89]

TRUST IN THE NAME OF THE LORD

Read Isaiah 50:10 and Job 2:9, 13:15

We saw in yesterday's devotion that the person or couple described in our text who is walking in darkness is not someone who is being punished because of sin, but rather one who deeply respects or fears God. Fortunately, in the heart of Isaiah 50:10, God reveals what individuals experiencing darkness should do.

First, God states that he or she should trust in His name. Often, when we cannot understand what is happening and cannot see our way out of the darkness, we ask God, "Why?" We want Him to give us an explanation for our difficulties. After God directed us to go into full-time ministry, we experienced some depressing financial times. When we questioned Him about why we were going through these difficulties, He gently answered that the Creator does not owe the creation an explanation. We are simply to trust Him! We were reminded of the statement we had often heard, "When we can't trace Him, we can still trust Him." Job concluded that though God allowed all of his darkness and he didn't comprehend why, he would still trust Him (13:15).

When Job's wife should have been an encouragement, she discouraged him instead by telling him to curse God and die (2:9). When we experience confusing or depressing challenges in marriage, it is essential that we face them united as a couple, encouraging one another by reminding each other of the different names of God. Each one represents an unchanging, dependable aspect of His character. For example, He is called El Roi—the God who sees, El Shaddai—the God Almighty, Yahweh Jireh—the God who provides, Yahweh Shalom—the God of peace, Yahweh Rapha—the God who heals. As a couple, take time to investigate the names of God in the Bible. Meditate on these names and be encouraged to unify and trust Him.

LEAN ON THE LORD

Read Isaiah 50:10-11

*G*od continues to expound what we should do when we experience darkness. He tells us to "rely" upon Him. The Hebrew word actually means to lean on. God is telling us that when the darkness overshadows us and we become weary, we are to trust or look to Him (see yesterday's devotion) and then lean on Him. The Lord wants us to understand that He is bigger than our health problems; He is bigger than our financial cares; He is bigger than our marriage problems. He is Almighty God. We can lean upon and take comfort in Him!

When God directed us into full-time ministry in 1983, we started an inner city outreach called Christian Cinema. Debbie and I were barely surviving financially, and we experienced some of the darkest struggles of our married life. Often, it appeared we would not have food to eat or money to pay our rent. At Christmas, when a dad wants to buy special gifts for his children and wife, I had no money. I remember feeling like a complete failure as a husband and father. It was during these times, however, that we leaned upon the Lord and saw Him miraculously provide. Time and time again, He answered our prayers and met our needs in unexpected ways! Looking back, that stressful season gave us some of the most precious memories of our married life. God proved He had not abandoned us, and we could lean upon Him.

In verse 11, God warns not to attempt to escape difficulties by lighting our own fire or doing things our way in our own strength. If we do, He says we will lie down in torment. During discouraging times we are to leave the solution with Him. If we conquer the darkness through our own efforts, we get the glory (credit and honor). Since God demands to be glorified in all circumstances, He says we are to leave it to Him. What dark times are you experiencing as a couple? Where do you need to look to the Lord, lean upon the Lord, and leave the situation with Him?

PRIVILEGES

Read Ephesians 1:3–14 and John 4:14

After marrying your spouse, you are able to enjoy privileges you never had prior to becoming one with him or her. You may now mutually own property. You have the privilege of unashamed physical intimacy. The insurance provided by your mate's job may cover you with benefits. You can file joint income taxes and include more deductions. Unfortunately, since each of us is a sinner married to a sinner, these benefits also come with some strings attached—personality quirks, previous debt, crazy in-laws, or propensities that could be harmful to the relationship. Christians are frequently referred to as the bride of Christ (Isa. 62:5). As His spouse, however, we experience no harmful side effects … only marvelous and blessed privileges.

In his letter to the Ephesians, Paul declares that Christians have been granted every spiritual blessing (v. 3). He proclaims these heavenly benefits by describing them in the longest sentence in the Bible (vv. 3–14). These blessings include: being chosen by God in salvation (v. 4a), being made holy (sanctification) to commune with Him in loving devotion (v. 4b), being adopted into the family of God as His dear child (v. 5a), being accepted by the Father in the beloved (v. 6), receiving redemption and forgiveness of sins (v. 7), and receiving His wisdom (v. 8). And if that isn't enough, we are guaranteed an inheritance as a joint heir of Jesus Christ (v. 11). He further adds that all of these blessings are sealed (secured) by the Holy Spirit (v.13). Wow! So, when you call yourself a Christian, you are claiming that you are a partaker in all of these grand privileges!

Understanding and embracing the scope of these divine gifts empowers a husband or wife to freely and unselfishly give to their mate from the overflow of Christ within them (John 4:14). Take time now to meditate on the benefits of these spiritual blessings. Let your heart overflow with gratitude to God. Reflect on the blessings you have experienced in your marriage. Let your heart overflow with gratitude to your spouse.

TAKE A BREAK

Read Mark 6:30-32

Over the past few months, our work load has been intense. We have been examining and editing devotions, writing scripts, and filming sessions for premarital training, speaking at conferences, preparing for a mission trip to Kenya, counseling couples, and filing tax reports for our fiscal year end. Although we began our workdays with devotions and a walk, our brains quickly became overloaded. We worked so intently that many times we glanced at the clock and realized we forgot to take a break for lunch. Much of the counseling and training took an emotional toll as we experienced deep concern for the lives we were directing. We invested so much energy and passion into our work that we felt like we were operating on an empty tank. We marvel that the grace of God empowered us to accomplish the tasks before us, but if we stopped to consider how much we had to pack into the next day, we could easily become depressed. This is typical of the current American lifestyle. Couples live in a frenzy to get all of their responsibilities completed. Much of what they are doing is vitally important, but if they are not careful, they will wear themselves down.

In today's passage, the disciples faced a similar dilemma. Jesus had instructed them to spread out into the local towns to minister healing and declare truth. They, like us, consistently worked long hours, pouring their hearts into their mission. They also experienced the added emotional strain of the murder of John the Baptist. When they reported the results of what they had done and taught, Jesus perceived they were approaching the point of burn-out. He instructed them to get away to a place with no distractions. They had given and given, and they desperately needed renewal.

Married couples need to heed the same advice. When you experience a period of intense pressure or workload, the two of you should separate from distractions and routine responsibilities and concentrate on refreshing yourselves. Find a babysitter for your children, take a few days off from work, and get away together. Leave the computer at home. Rest and relax. The renewal will energize you to be much more efficient and effective when you return. As you prepare to begin a new year, ask one another, "Is it time for a break?" If so, get it on the calendar now!

NOTES

JANUARY

1   Matthew Henry, *Matthew Henry's Commentary on the Whole Bible: Complete and Unabridged in One Volume* (Peabody, MA: Hendrickson Publishers, 1994), Matthew 18:15–20.

2   Jay Adams, *Marriage, Divorce, and Remarriage in the Bible* (Grand Rapids, MI: Zondervan, 1980), 12.

FEBRUARY

3   Janette Peel, *The Truth Behind Valentine's Day.* http://www.helium.com/items/779340-the-truth-behind-valentines-day. Accessed April 26, 2013.

4   *Leadership Now*, "Quotes on Character." http://www.leadershipnow.com/characterquotes.html. Accessed April 24, 2013.

5   Dr. Ed Wheat, *Love Life for Every Married Couple* (Grand Rapids, MI: Zondervan Publishing House, 1980), 82.

6   Ibid, 107.

MARCH

7   John Piper and Wayne Grudem, *Recovering Biblical Manhood & Womanhood* (Wheaton, IL: Crossway Books, 1991), 426.

8   D.M. Lloyd Jones, *Life in the Spirit* (Grand Rapids, MI: Baker House, 1974), 124–125.

9   Webster's Ninth New Collegiate Dictionary (Springfield, MA: Merriam Webster, 1990), 200.

10 "Divided Families, Single Parents." http://www.enotalone.com/parenting/4476.html. Accessed April 23, 2013.

11 Noah Webster, *American Dictionary of the English Language 1828* (San Francisco, CA: The Foundation for American Christian Education, 1983), Marriage.

12 Merriam-Webster Dictionary, Web-based online App on iphone 4, 2013

13 Sam Wood, *What is Marriage?* (Jamestown, TN: Family Fortress Ministries, 2004), 24.

14 D.M. Lloyd-Jones, *Life in the Spirit* (Grand Rapids, MI: Baker House, 1974), 153.

15 H Clay Trumbull, *The Blood Covenant* (Kirkwood, MO: Impact Books, Inc, 1975) 219–220.

16 A.W. Tozer, *The Purpose of Man* (Ventura, CA: Regal, 2009), 25–26, 32.

17 "How Many Children are in the Average Family," *Answers,* (accessed January 26, 2013). <http://wiki.answers.com/Q/How_many_children_are_in_the_average_American_family>

18 Haya El Nasser and Paul Overberg,"Census Reveals Plummeting US Birthrates," *USA Today*, June 24, 2011. http://usatoday30usatoday.com/news/nation/census/2011–06–03–fewer-children-census-suburbs_n.htm. Accessed January 26, 2013.

19 Dr. Ed Wheat, *Love Life for Every Married Couple* (Grand Rapids, MI: Zondervan Publishing House, 1980), 85.

APRIL

20 Milton Vincent, *A Gospel Primer* (Bemijdi, MN: Focus Publishing, 2008), 25.

21 John Bevere, *The Bait of Satan* (Lake Mary, Fl.: Creation House, 1994), 3.

22 Warren W. Wiersbe, *Wiersbe's Expository Outlines on the New Testament* (Wheaton, IL: Victor Books, 1992), 68.

23 Jay E. Adams, *From Forgiven to Forgiving* (Amityville, NY: Calvary Press, 1994), 12.

24 Andrew Murray, *The Holiest of All* (New Kinsington, PA: Whitaker House, 1996), 114.

25 Ibid, 125.

26 "15,000 to 18,000 Divorced Men Commit Suicide Every Year." Web-based Statistic. antimisandry.com http://antimisandry.com/marriage-divorce-children-choice-men/15-000-18-000-divorced-men-commit-suicide-every-year-17392.html#ixzz2Rovvxfnq. Accessed April 24, 2013.

MAY

27 Jaine Carter and James D. Carter. "Relationships: Communication Can Pay Off in Fewer Fights About Money," Holland news Service, www.detnews.com, July 15, 1997.

28 David Jeremiah, *Searching for Heaven on Earth* (Nashville: Thomas Nelson, 2004), 125-132.

29 Ben Patterson, *The Grand Essentials* (Waco, Texas: Word, 1987), 17.

30 Wayne Coleman, *Obedience the Key to Prosperity* (Mt. Juliet, TN: Cross Reference Books, 1985), 20.

31 Warren W. Wiersbe, *The Wiersbe Bible Commentary* (Ontario, CA: David C. Cook, 2007), 613.

32 John Murray, *Principles of Conduct* (Grand Rapids, MI: Eerdmans, 1957), 229.

33 Albert Martin, *The Fear of God Part 1*. http://ibrnb.com/articles1/?p=13. Accessed May 10.

34 Murray, *Principles of Conduct*, 233.

35 Jerry Bridges, *The Joy of Fearing God* (Colorado Springs, CO: Watermark Press, 1997), 18.

36   Arthur Pink, *The Attributes of God.* http://www.godrules.net/library/pink/43pink_f1.htm. Accessed April 25, 2013.

37   J.I. Packer, *Knowing God (*Downers Grove, Ill.: Inter Varsity, 1973), 76.

38   A.W. Tozer, Albert Martin, *Ingredients of the Fear of God.* http://ibrnb.com/articles1/?p=20. Accessed May 10, 2013.

39   Information about oxytocin and its affects were drawn from Wier's explanations. Terry Wier, *Holy Sex,* (New Kensington, PA: Whitaker House, 1999), 58–59.

40   Simple 50th Wedding Anniversary Statistics. http://answers.google.com/answers/threadview/id/223968.html. Accessed April 26, 2013.

41   Susan M. Hillier and Georgia M. Barrow, *Aging, the Individual, and Society* (Belmont, CA: Wadsworth, 2011), 183.

JUNE

42   Matthew Henry, *Matthew Henry's Commentary on the Whole Bible: Complete and Unabridged in One Volume* (Peabody, MA: Hendrickson, 1994).

43   Glenn Greenwood and Latayne C. Scott, *A Marriage Made in Heaven* (Dallas, TX: Word Publishing, 1990), 16-22.

44   John MacArthur, *Putting on the New Man, Part 2.* http://www.gty.org/resources/sermons/2148/putting-on-the-new-man-part-2. Accessed April 26, 2013.

45   Dan B. Allender and Tremper Longman III, *Intimate Allies* (Wheaton, ILL: Tyndale House Publishers, 1995), 217.

46   *"March 19, 2011 - Is There a Difference, The Look of Happiness."* www.evvabe.com/media/sermons2011/2011-03-19.doc. *Accessed April 26, 2013.*

47   CA.Gov Consumer Affairs, "A to Z Guide to Credit Cards." *http://www.dca.ca.gov/publications/a_z_creditcard.shtml.* Accessed April 26, 2013.

48   Depression, Understand it, Treat it, Beat it, "Medical Causes of Depression." http://www.clinical-depression.co.uk/dlp/depression-information/medical-causes-of-depression. Accessed April 26, 2013.

JULY

49   Albert Mehrabian, *Silent Messages,* qtd in Jan McLaughlin, "Don't Just Talk, Communicate!" *Jan M. McLaughlin, CSP,* http://yourcommunicationconnection.com/resources.html/. Accessed January 25, 2013.

50   Terry Wier, *Holy Sex* (New Kensington, PA: Whitaker House, 1999), 60-61.

51   Warren W. Wiersbe, *The Wiersbe Bible Commentary: The Complete New Testament in One Volume* (Colorado Springs, CO: David C. Cook, 2007), 743.

52 Gary Smalley, "It Doesn't Begin in the Bedroom." http://smalley.cc/it-doesnt-begin-in-the-bedroom. Accessed April 26, 2013.

53 The Flamingos, "I Only Have Eyes for You," *STLyrics*. http://stlyrics.com/lyrics/somethingsgottagive/ionlyhaveeyesforyou.html. Accessed January 25, 2013.

AUGUST

54 Wikipedia, https://en.wikipedia.org/wiki/Four_temperaments. Accessed May 25, 2013.

55 Oswald Chambers, *My Utmost for His Highest* (Grand Rapids, MI: Discovery House, 1992), April 19.

56 John Bevere, *The Bait of Satan* (Lake Mary, FL: Charisma House, 1994), 9.

57 Roy Hession, *The Calvary Road* (London: Christian Literature Crusade Publications, 1990), 109.

58 Roy Hession, *The Calvary Road* (Fort Washington, PA: CLC Publications, 1950), 31.

59 Ibid, 32.

SEPTEMBER

60 D. Martyn Lloyd Jones, *Spiritual Depression* (Grand Rapids, MI: Eerdmans Publishing, 1986), 103.

61 Thomas Chalmers, *The Expulsive Power of a New Affection*. http://www.monergism.com/Chalmers,%20Thomas%20-%20The%20Exlpulsive%20Power%20of%20a%20New%20Af.pdf. Accessed April 26, 2013.

62 John W. Sanderson, Jerry Bridges, *The Practice of Godliness* (Colorado Springs, CO: NavPress, 2008), Chapter 9.

63 Shaunti Feldhahn, *For Women Only* (Atlanta, GA: Multnomah Books, Veritas Enterprises, 2004), 15.

64 *The Amplified Bible, Expanded Edition* (USA: Zondervan Corporation and the Lockman Foundation, 1987), 1453.

65 Milton Vincent, *A Gospel Primer* (Bemidji, MN: Focus Publishing, 2008), 6.

66 Brother Lawrence, *The Practice of the Presence of God*. http://www.ccel.org/ccel/lawrence/practice.iii.i.html. Accessed April 26, 2013.

OCTOBER

67 Stephen F. Olford, *A Time for Truth* (Chattanooga, TN: AMG Publishers, 1999), 6.

68 Corrie ten Boom, *Each New Day* (Grand Rapids, MI: Fleming H. Revell, a division of Baker Book House, 1977), December 9.

NOVEMBER

69   Timothy Keller, *The Freedom of Self-Forgetfulness* (Chorley, England: 10 Publishing, 2012), 32.

70   Bob George, *Classic Christianity* (Eugene, OR: Harvest House Publishers, 1989), 103.

71   Uplift Program, *Depression Facts and Stats*. http://www.upliftprogram.com/depression_stats. html. Accessed January 28, 2013.

72   Abraham Lincoln Research Site. http://rogerjnorton.com/Lincoln84html. Accessed January 28.

73   Christian.com, *Charles Spurgeon on Depression*, accessed January< http://christian-quotes.ochristian.com/christian-quotes_ochristian. cgi?find=Christian-quotes-by-Charles+Spurgeon-on-Depression

74   Carl Meniger, *Have a Life Full of Joy*. http://www.montelione.com/Believe/lifeofjoy.html. Accessed April 26, 2013,.

75   Roy and Revel Hession, *We Would See Jesus* (Fort Washington, PA: CLC Publications, 1958), 61.

76   Marc Driscoll & Gerry Breshears, *Doctrine* (Wheaton, IL: Crossway, 2010), 178–179.

77   Sabrina Tavernise, "Married Couples Are No Longer a Majority, Census Finds," http://www. nytimes.com/2011/05/26/us/26marry.html?_r=0. Accessed April 26, 2013

78   What's Happening to Marriage? *StudyMode.com*. Retrieved May, 2008, from http://www. studymode.com/essays/What-s-Happening-Marriage-150608.html. Accessed June 10, 2013

79   *Newsweek* Magazine, "Yes to Love, No to Marriage," January 14, 2008 http://www.thedaily-beast.com/newsweek/2008/01/05/yes-to-love-no-to-marriage.html. Accessed June 8, 2013

DECEMBER

80   D. Martyn Lloyd-Jones, *Exposition of Chapter 8:5-17 Romans* (Carlisle, PA: The Banner of Truth Trust, 2011), 384.

81   Andrew Murray, *Humility* (Minneapolis, MN: Bethany House, 2001), 16.

82   CJ Mahaney, *Humility: True greatness* (Colorado Springs, Co: Multnomah Books, 2005), 30.

83   Ibid. 66

84   Andrew Murray, *Humility,* (Minneapolis, MN: Bethany House, 2001), 21.

85   Andrew Murray Quotes. http://www.goodreads.com/author/quotes/13326Andrew_Murray. Accessed January 28, 2013.

86   Kay Arthur, *Beloved A Daily Devotional* (Eugene, OR: Harvest House, 1994), June 1–June 30.

87   Ibid.

88   Ibid.

89   Thoughts for the devotions on darkness were inspired by a message preached by Rev. Ken
     Trivette (our pastor) at Temple Baptist Church, Chattanooga, TN in 1991.

Contact the authors:
info@familyfortress.org

For more marriage-building resources, please visit:
www.FamilyFortress.org
www.PreparingForPartnership.org